AMERICAN WELFARE

Reclaiming the Dream for All of U.S.

Tracy Evans

CORNERSTONE PRESS

Copyright © 2026 by Tracy Evans.

All rights reserved.

No portion of this book may be reproduced, stored in a retrieval system, or transmitted in any form or by any means—electronic, mechanical, photocopying, recording, or otherwise—without prior written permission of the publisher, except in the case of brief quotations embodied in critical articles or reviews, as permitted by U.S. copyright law.

Excerpts from published works are quoted and cited in accordance with U.S. fair use principles.

Published by Cornerstone Press
Arlington, Virginia

First edition: March 2026

Library of Congress Control Number: 2026904109

ISBN 979-8-9941526-0-7 (hardcover)
ISBN 979-8-9941526-1-4 (eBook)

For information about permissions, bulk purchases, or speaking engagements, please contact: Cornerstone Press at publisher@cornerstonepressllc.com

contents

Introduction 6

Author's Note 11

Section I 16

1. Welfare Wasn't A Bad Word 17

2. An American Illusion 40

3. The Blame Trap 70

4. The Fatalism Trap 97

Section Ii 122

5. Well-Being Is Constructed 123

6. The Dual Edge Of Systems 146

7. The Forces We Face 172

Section Iii 198

8. The Architecture Of U.S. 200

9. Belonging By Design 224

10. Democracy By Design 250

Epilogue 267

Technical Author's Note 268

Endnotes 270

Selective Bibliography 342

Appendices 348

Acknowledgments 356

For Tim and Sean—

my constant sources of love and joy

AND

To the human services workforce—

who embody what it means to

build well-being from the ground up

INTRODUCTION

When my son was in the eleventh grade, he came home with a project from his history class: "What is the American Dream to you?" I remember pausing—because I was in the early stages of research for this book, and that question resonated deeply. It is a question that should belong to all of us, not just as a homework assignment but as a shared civic reckoning. What does the American Dream mean today, and who gets to claim it?

This book is my response to that question.

For the past 25 years, I have worked in human services—the system of public and community supports that show up when life gets complicated. These services are foundational to our nation's well-being, yet they are widely misunderstood, undervalued, and too often maligned. Human services include the systems people turn to at key moments in their lives. They encompass child and family supports, housing and food assistance, behavioral health care, aging and disability services, and the local organizations that bring these services to life. Systems built to promote well-being have been distorted by stigma and stripped down by policy, leaving them fragile at the very moment we need them most. Yet beneath that fragility lies possibility: these systems remain the scaffolding of a stronger democracy if we can see them clearly and reimagine them together. In that sense, *welfare*—our collective well-being—is not a program but a measure of how soundly the structure holds for all of us.

At the heart of this dilemma is the word *welfare*. Originally meaning "the condition of faring well," the term once described collective well-being. Over time, it has been warped by stigma, racism, and misinformation until even those who work within the system avoid using it. Today, it too often signals dependency, waste, or failure. But that narrow story hides a larger truth: *welfare* has always been about how we care for one another, especially in times of need. It is not the enemy of democracy—it is its measure, both at the level of individual well-being and the health of the whole society.

We are living through a time when that truth is under siege. Political sound bites reduce people to stereotypes. Narratives of blame and fatalism—of believing nothing can change—harden into policy. Even compassion has become a source of controversy. Yet silence carries its own risk. If we avoid these stories, we leave them unchallenged. This book seeks to name these stories clearly, trace their origins, and offer a fuller, more truthful narrative that can take their place.

Old stories are resurfacing again: warnings against "dependency," broad cuts to the programs that keep families afloat, shutdowns that stall essential systems. These are not new crises but recurring tests of how sturdy our democratic scaffolding really is. This book begins from the recognition that we can stop mistaking repetition for inevitability, and start rebuilding the framework of care and possibility that democracy requires.

This book unfolds in three parts. First, it excavates the roots of America's welfare story: how ideas of deservingness and exclusion, from the Poor Laws to the "welfare queen," created cultural traps of blame and inevitability. Second, it brings systems into plain sight, showing how they can both harm through neglect and exclusion, and heal when redesigned for fairness and trust. Finally, it turns to the future, asking how we can design a democracy where well-being is recognized as shared infrastructure—as essential as roads or schools—and where the American Dream is not rationed but realized.

I come to this work as both a practitioner and a storyteller, shaped by decades inside the systems this book examines. My professional life has spanned roles as a litigator, a child advocate, a state human services director, a federal advisor, and the CEO of a national association representing public human services leaders. Along the way, I have seen both the quiet heroism of frontline workers and the deep misunderstandings that cloud public conversation. I also write from my own identity: as a white woman from a middle-class background, aware of both the privileges and limits that perspective brings. My commitment is to solidarity, not division, and to ensuring that our social systems do better for all of us.

We are at another inflection point in our history. Inequality is widening, democracy is strained, climate disruption and technological change are reshaping our future, and disinformation is deepening our mistrust of the government and each other. These challenges are real. But they are not destiny. Narratives are not fixed. Systems are not immovable. We can choose differently.

This book is not a policy manual or a partisan call to arms. It is an exploration of the stories that shape our public systems, how their design helps or harms us, and the possibilities they still hold. It is an invitation to ask two democratic questions: What kind of society do we want to be, and how do we live up to the ideals we have always claimed?

The answer begins with the stories we choose to tell ourselves. If we can rewrite the old stories of blame and inevitability, reclaim the meaning of welfare as well-being, and design systems for belonging rather than control, we can create a democracy that keeps its promises. That is the dream my son was asked to write about, and the one I believe we can still realize together.

AUTHOR'S NOTE

Reclaiming the Story Together

Throughout this book, I've chosen to use the word *we* when describing how public systems in the United States were built, how they have helped and how they have harmed, and how they might yet be reimagined by all of us.

This choice is intentional, and it's important to explain why.

In a country marked by deep division and growing distrust, the idea of *we* can feel complicated. For those who have been harmed, excluded, or unseen by public systems, it may not feel like a word that fully includes their experience. I want to acknowledge the reality that there is no single experience of America, and the wounds of injustice have not been evenly shared.

Yet I also mean *we* as an invitation. The *we* in this book is not fixed or uniform. It asks each of us to bring our own stories, perspectives, and questions into the conversation. Every reader holds a piece of this collective story, and it is through our shared telling—across different histories, communities, and vantage points—that new understanding and possibility emerge.

Using *we* is not an attempt to flatten difference or erase accountability. It does not excuse the harm that systems have caused, often disproportionately to Black, Indigenous, disabled, immigrant, LGBTQ+, and low-income communities. It is not meant to blame frontline workers who are too often stretched thin working in undervalued systems. And it is not a rhetorical shortcut to avoid hard truths.

Rather, I use *we* to ground this work in something I believe we desperately need: an orientation of shared humanity. A belief in mutual care. A commitment to what we can still build together.

This matters because the story we tell about *poverty* is also a story about *us*. Throughout this book, I use the word *poverty* in its broadest sense, not only as a measure of income, but also as the lived experience of hardship—the instability of living paycheck to paycheck, the chronic stress that wears on the body, the barriers to child care, health care, mental health services, education, and decent work, and the greater exposure to criminal justice involvement. These are conditions shaped as much by the systems around us as by our individual circumstances.

By the same token, when I write about *human services,* I mean the network of public and community institutions that surround daily life; the ones that support children and families, safeguard health and well-being, foster connection, respond in crisis, build resilience and help people navigate the hardest edges of our economy. These systems are often invisible until they are needed, yet they are essential to the promise of a society in which all people can live and flourish.

And there is another reason. *We* is a democratic word. Democracy itself depends on our collective authorship that every choice about well-being is also a choice about belonging. Who counts? Whose needs matter? How do we live up to our founding promise to promote the general welfare? To ask these questions in the language of *we* is to resist corrosive us-versus-them thinking and to affirm that systems do not exist apart from us. We shape them through policy, practice, silence, and participation. And we can shape them in our stories.

Too often, our shared story has been steered by traps: blame, which casts poverty as personal failure; and fatalism, which convinces us inequality is inevitable. Both have distorted our politics and narrowed our imagination. Using *we* is one way to resist these traps and to recover a fuller truth that the systems and stories we inherit are not fixed, and we can change them.

We is both invitation and responsibility. It is an imperfect, evolving pronoun, but it is a necessary one if we are to imagine a future in which prosperity and well-being are not rationed but realized for all of us.

This book is a story of reckoning and repair of what has been done and what can still be undone. And if we do that work with honesty and imagination, *we* can design a future that works for *all of U.S.* in a democracy in which our well-being is shared, our belonging is real, and we realize the American Dream together.

This *we* belongs to all of us who are willing to see, question, and build better systems.

We can tell of a past that was nothing but defeats and cruelties and injustices, or of a past that was some lovely golden age now irretrievably lost, or we can tell a more complicated and accurate story, one that has room for the best and worst, for atrocities and liberations, for grief and jubilation. A memory commensurate to the complexity of the past and the whole cast of participants, a memory that includes our power, produces that forward-directed energy called *hope*.[1]

—Rebecca Solnit

SECTION I

Excavating the Roots

CHAPTER 1

Welfare Wasn't a Bad Word

Until We Made It One

> The great force of history comes from the fact that we carry it within us, are unconsciously controlled by it in many ways, and history is literally present in all that we do.
>
> —James Baldwin
>
> The good we secure for ourselves is precarious and uncertain, is floating in mid-air, until it is secured for all of us and incorporated into our common life.
>
> —Jane Addams

In America, no word meant to signal care has been turned so sharply against its own people as "welfare." I learned early in my career that this single word could stop a conversation cold. In meetings with policymakers, hearings at the state capitol, or even in casual conversations in the community, the moment it was spoken, faces hardened and minds closed. It didn't seem to matter whether we were discussing food for children, health care for seniors, or job support for families, the word carried a weight far heavier than its true meaning: well-being. Few words in American life are so charged, pointed, and loaded with accusation. And few words have so profoundly distorted not just our view of social policy but also how we see each other.

As a leader in American human services, I felt the weight of language constantly. Words like *poverty, public benefits,* and especially welfare didn't spark dialogue; they shut it down before it even began. By the time I became CEO of the American Public Human Services Association in 2011, I knew policy alone wouldn't shift the public narrative. We had to be far more intentional about the words we used, because they shaped what people were willing to hear. So we began paying close attention to language: which words opened doors, and which ones closed them. Sitting squarely at the top of our "do not use" list was one word: *welfare*.

Looking back, I can see that this attention to language was more of a spark than a solution. It revealed just how powerful—and how dangerous—our shared words could be, and how easily they shape what feels possible in the public imagination. It also raised a question that would shape the next decade of my work: If a single word could distort reality so profoundly, what other stories were steering our understanding of welfare, and what would it take to rewrite them?

What I couldn't shake was the question beneath it all. How had a word that once meant well-being—enshrined in the Constitution's call to "promote the general Welfare"[1]—come to be so poisonous? For nearly seven decades, it was embedded in the name of the American Public Human Services Association, formerly the American Public Welfare Association. So why had we felt compelled to banish it from our internal vocabulary?[2] To answer that, we have to return to the beginning of America's welfare story. Only by unearthing how the meaning of the word became distorted can we begin to imagine how to reclaim it, and ourselves.

The Power of a Single Word: From Well-being to Weapon

The word "welfare" traces its roots to the Old English *wel faran*, meaning "the condition of doing well."[3] Initially, it described a state of good fortune; it was a term of prosperity, wholeness, and health. The Founders enshrined it in the Preamble of the Constitution alongside "Justice," "Tranquility," and "Liberty," capitalizing each to reflect their gravity, a common practice at the time.[4] These were not mere rhetorical flourishes; they were declarations of intent. Promoting the "general Welfare" referred to the well-being of people as a central aim of our new republic.

In this sense, welfare originally referred broadly to flourishing or prosperity, both at the individual and collective levels. Its usage encompassed a general state of well-being rather than any specific program or policy. This older meaning survives in phrases like *child welfare*, though even here the term carries some stigma. Over time, however, the public meaning of the word shifted dramatically, increasingly tied to government assistance programs and the political debates surrounding them.

Today, those early ideas of welfare—centered on shared well-being—are largely unfamiliar to most of us. In the United States, welfare has shifted from representing shared societal prosperity to becoming a topic of public ridicule and blame. Instead of symbolizing overall community health or civic responsibility, "welfare" suggests dependence, lack of effort, and fraud—a sharp turn that reflects not only semantic drift but also intentional political manipulation. For many Americans, the word no longer stands for the public good; it now reflects government failure and personal shortcomings.

This shift did not happen by accident; it reflected who had the power to define the story and whose voices were pushed to the margins.

Reductive Storytelling and the Rise of a Single Narrative

Author Chimamanda Ngozi Adichie warns in her popular TED Talk that our tendency to oversimplify human experiences into repetitive, single stories reduces people's agency and limits our understanding of the world.[5] A single story creates a significantly incomplete view of a person or group, often leading to stereotypes that make that one story the only story. As Adichie explains, power dynamics also reinforce this narrative—those in positions of power can tell, shape, and repeat a dominant storyline. At the same time, they can marginalize or even eliminate alternative perspectives. The dominant U.S. narrative about welfare presents a single story: reliance on public benefits makes people undeserving and to blame for their situation.

A potent mix of American history, policy, media, and politics shaped this narrative. Radicalized tropes like the "welfare queen" invoked by President Reagan and later intensified by President Clinton's pledge to "end welfare as we know it," sharpened it.[6] Terms like the "nanny state" used to describe the government, and dehumanizing labels such as "moocher" and "freeloader" for people who receive benefits, only increased the stigma.[7] Over time, these terms fostered a simplified story that shaped a common cultural attitude about who "ends up" on welfare and how society should respond.

I recognize that naming these myths carries a risk. Psychologists note that even when we try to debunk false or stigmatizing stories, repeating them can make them feel more familiar—and therefore more believable.[8] That is why it isn't enough to simply negate harmful narratives. To loosen their grip, we need to tell a fuller, truer story that reflects how people actually live, how systems actually function, and how our nation has long designed opportunity in unequal ways. Refusing to repeat harmful myths without offering a more accurate account leaves a vacuum; providing a truer narrative gives people something stronger to hold.

Dr. john a. powell's concepts of "othering" and " breaking" offer insight into the power of these kinds of reductive narratives.[9] "Othering" refers to the act of perceiving people not only as different but also as less deserving and lacking equal dignity. "Breaking" is the practice that leads to othering by denying "the full stories, complexities, and . . . humanity" of those we categorize as "other."[10] By reducing people to a single identity or mindset, we create distance between us. This is the story of welfare and antipoverty programs. In the American imagination, welfare became shorthand for the Other: someone who is not "us," who doesn't work hard, who drains resources rather than contributes to society. Not only have we marginalized people and groups with this single story, but we've also justified their exclusion altogether. This was not by accident but by design.

This singular narrative about welfare, rooted in othering and meant to marginalize, did more than shape public perception, it helped standardize our cultural expectations about who deserves support and how society should respond. Stories, especially when repeated and reinforced by those in power, don't just reflect harmful attitudes. They create them. Over time, they become part of the social fabric as norms—unspoken rules about what we believe most people do and what we think they should do.[11] Understanding how these norms and narratives connect is key to understanding why certain beliefs about poverty persist, even in the face of contradictory evidence.

Norms and Narratives: How Beliefs Take Root

Norms and narratives work together, often without us noticing. Norms shape what we think is typical and what we believe is expected.[12] Narratives supply the stories that make those expectations feel natural.[13] When a story is told often enough, it begins to set the boundaries of what seems normal, acceptable, or even possible. Once we can spot these patterns—how a repeated story becomes an unspoken rule—they become easier to interrupt. Naming the pattern loosens its grip.

Two Kinds of Norms
- **Descriptive:** what we think is *typical*.
- **Injunctive:** what we think is *expected*.

Both grow out of the stories we hear again and again.

When harmful stories like the "welfare queen" circulate for decades, they don't just stigmatize individuals, they set expectations. People begin to assume that *most* benefit recipients are gaming the system. And they start to believe that all of us should therefore be suspicious and stingy when offering help. The same thing happens with the "nanny state" stereotype because it feeds a broader belief that government support breeds dependency and fraud. Over time, these narratives harden into both descriptive norms ("people abuse the system") and injunctive norms ("we should be strict to keep them in line"). They stick because media, influencers, and political leaders repeat them until they sound like fact.

But norms are never neutral. In America, they are deeply shaped by race and class. As public conversation grew more hostile toward people receiving assistance—an evolution we explore in the chapters ahead—the imagined face of "welfare" changed. In the public's mind, it shifted from a white rural family to a Black single mother in the city.[14] That shift carried powerful consequences. It reshaped whom the nation saw as deserving of help and recast government itself from a shared public good to a suspect bureaucracy.

Those beliefs eventually seeped into policy and practice. This is the quiet power of narrative: it influences how we judge worthiness, how programs are designed, and how people are treated, often without conscious thought. And when stories and norms reinforce one another, they create a cycle that's hard to break. To change course, we have to interrogate not just the rules written into law but the stories underneath them—the stories we have told ourselves about who is worthy of help and who is not.

How did we get from "the condition of faring well" to a system that too often turns help into suspicion? To answer that, we need to return to the beginning.

Foundations of Deservingness: From England to Early America

Welfare has always been a mirror, reflecting back who we believe is worthy of help and who is not. To understand why that mirror still shows distorted images today, we must look at where the glass was first forged—in Western democracy, under the English Poor Laws of the 1600s.[15]

The English Poor Laws created one of the most enduring cultural archetypes in Western society: the "idle pauper." This figure embodied suspicion toward people in poverty, suggesting a moral deficiency with little room for empathy. The laws established a national system of relief that required local parishes to provide minimal aid—usually food, shelter, or work—to those deemed "deserving," while punishing those judged "idle" or "unwilling to work."[16] Overseers decided who merited help and who did not, often through subjective assessments of character.[17] For those labeled undeserving, punishment was built into the system, including workhouses, forced labor, or public shaming.[18]

These ideas did not stay in England. When settlers crossed the Atlantic, they brought the Poor Laws with them, not always as formal statutes but always as a ready-made worldview about poverty, responsibility, and social order. In the colonies, that worldview took root quickly. Local overseers—often church elders[19] or town officials—

decided who would receive help and under what conditions, applying the same moral tests that had governed aid in England. Early Poor Laws in the original thirteen states were a form of "reluctant public charity," strictly rationed to local residents deemed worthy of assistance.[20] Widows, orphans, and some people with disabilities might receive relief, but for many others, support came with strings attached: compulsory labor, indentured servitude, or even expulsion from the community. Even for those considered deserving, the system could be harsh. Children were frequently placed into indentured servitude, which was justified as training but, in practice, often indistinguishable from exploitation.[21]

In this system, society did not see poverty as a structural failure but as a personal flaw. That belief became a cultural reflex. It is an inheritance that still shapes policy today, visible in the strict verification rules, bureaucratic hurdles, and often unforgiving work requirements that continue to define who is seen as "deserving" of help. The blueprint of conditional, moralized aid proved remarkably durable.

A Patchwork of Minimal Help

By the nineteenth century, these colonial systems had hardened into structure. Our American approach to relief remained highly local, selective, and moralizing—*a patchwork of minimal help*. Local laws required individuals to prove residency before receiving assistance, and the support offered was deliberately meager, designed to prevent starvation but not upward movement. Many communities relied on poorhouses—institutions that confined and managed those who needed help—which reinforced the belief that poverty was a personal failing requiring discipline rather than support.[22] Responsibility for alleviating hardship continued to fall on local governments, charitable organizations, and neighbors, while the idea of a collective, systematic, and compassionate approach remained a radical concept.

Through this patchwork, lasting norms were reinforced that aid could be limited, officials could act as gatekeepers, and exclusion could be justified as civic duty. Put another way, the cultural belief that poverty was an individual flaw, not a structural one, became cemented in society. The concept of shared, federal responsibility for well-being would not emerge for centuries; when it did, it faced strong opposition, shaped by these early precedents.

The moral scaffolding of England's Poor Laws—sorting, suspicion, and scarcity—became the foundation of American welfare thinking. Even as new reform movements took root, they did so atop this uneasy inheritance of systems built to manage and distance poverty rather than prevent it. The traces of that logic are still visible today, depicted in the conditional design of modern welfare programs.

> ## Modern Reflections of Poor Law Logic
>
> The mirror of England's Poor Laws is still reflected in America's welfare policies. The central inheritance is not any single rule but rather a worldview that aid should be conditional, closely monitored, and reserved for those who can prove they deserve it.
>
> That logic shows up across many modern programs:
>
> - **Supplemental Nutrition Assistance Program (SNAP):** Strict eligibility rules, frequent paperwork and recertification, and limits that shape how families manage scarce resources.
> - **Temporary Assistance for Needy Families (TANF):** Time limits on assistance, behavioral and family-structure requirements and wide state discretion over who qualifies.
> - **Medicaid:** Complex eligibility rules, extensive documentation requirements, and ongoing income or work verfication.
> - **Housing assistance:** Long waiting lists, strict income cutoffs, and rigid rules tied to residence and duration.
>
> Each of these programs reflects a familiar pattern: conditional aid offered sparingly and with suspicion. This approach was forged in the seventeenth century and carried into modern systems through culture, law, and political storytelling.

The Poor Laws may seem distant, but their cultural legacy endures. What began as a moral division in seventeenth-century England became a social norm in America, backed by law and custom. Our foundational systems weren't designed for inclusion but for sorting and control, which is a logic that remains today. As we'll examine shortly, this was worsened by America's own history of slavery and Indigenous displacement, creating a blueprint for a welfare system that categorizes, patronizes, and excludes—a plan whose shadow we have not yet been able to shake.

From Fiction to Framework: The Pauper as Archetype

The logic of deservingness lived not only in laws and local rules but also in the cultural imagination. One of the most enduring creations of the seventeenth century was the "idle pauper," portrayed as lazy, immoral, and in need of firm correction. By the early 1800s, this archetype had become a staple of political speeches and popular storytelling, quietly teaching the public what to expect of people in need and how society ought to respond.

Charles Dickens's *Oliver Twist* helped crystallize this mindset. His novel was meant as an indictment of England's Poor Laws, yet its vivid scenes of workhouses, stern overseers, and starving children did something else: they normalized a paternalistic script that people experiencing poverty must perform their desperation to earn help. In one of the novel's most iconic scenes, young Oliver steps forward and asks for more food ("Please sir, can I have some more?").[23] Asking for help became a moral performance—one that reinforced the belief that compassion must be conditional. In this way, literature unintentionally reinforced politics.

This cultural framing mattered. It trained generations to see poverty not as a shared social condition but as a test of character, with clear lines between the "deserving" and the "undeserving." The archetype crossed the Atlantic with the same force as the Poor Laws themselves, shaping early American attitudes about assistance and making paternalism feel like common sense. And once that script was in place, it could be easily adapted—and eventually racialized—to justify exclusion and control.

It was into this narrative landscape, where poverty was imagined as a moral drama and helpers assumed the role of benevolent gatekeepers, that reformers like Jane Addams and Ellen Gates Starr stepped forward. Their work sought to replace distance with proximity, judgment with relationship, and paternalism with the radical idea that people flourish when we build lives *with* communities, not *for* them.

A Different Way Forward: The Settlement House Movement

By the late nineteenth century, the harsh realities of poorhouses and the visible suffering in America's rapidly industrializing cities made clear that we needed a different way forward.

The settlement house movement, led by reformers such as Addams and Starr, signified a major shift away from the Poor Law tradition of judgment and punishment. Instead of viewing poverty as the result of laziness or personal failure, Addams and her colleagues argued that it stemmed from social conditions—exploitative labor, unsafe housing, and the absence of civic infrastructure.[24] For the first time, reformers began to address poverty as a social design problem, not as a personal defect.

What made the movement innovative was not only its philosophy but its practice. Reformers chose to move into the very neighborhoods they hoped to improve.[25] At Hull House in Chicago, founded in 1889 in a densely populated district on the Near West Side, Addams and Starr lived alongside immigrant families, opening a community hub that provided education, childcare, arts, lectures, and opportunities for civic engagement.[26] Democracy, they believed, was not just about government structure but also about daily life. People needed "common ground in our human experiences," as Addams said, to make democracy truly real.[27]

Settlement houses modeled a new kind of public good—one rooted in shared experience and care for one an other. This was a markedly different story from the one of moral judgment we had inherited from the English Poor Laws. Rather than policing people or labeling them, the settlement house movement sought to improve social conditions and build community capacity by sowing the seeds for what public systems could become if they were designed around empathy, solidarity, and human potential.[28] The movement sparked the professionalization of social work and influenced early municipal reforms, laying groundwork for future public welfare departments and state-level human services systems.

Yet even this radical experiment had boundaries. The idea of "uplift" often came with the expectation of assimilation.[29] Even with the focus on community, cultural difference was seen less as a strength to be celebrated than as a barrier to be broken down. Reformers organized social club by ethnicity and nationality, often reinforcing the very divisions they sought to overcome. Moreover, most settlement houses reflected the racial and class hierarchies of their time. For example, Black families weren't served at Hull House in its early years, not by official policy, but through neighborhood segregation and social custom.[30]

In this way, the settlement house movement was both visionary and constrained. It challenged the punitive spirit of the Poor Laws but also reflected racial and cultural hierarchies of its era. In its best moments, it came closer to the spirit of the Constitution's promise to "promote the general Welfare" than anything that had preceded it, offering a glimpse of what welfare could mean if built around empathy, shared responsibility, and civic participation. Its promise was only partial, however, because the circle of belonging remained tightly drawn. It gestured toward a democratic idea—community as scaffolding for shared well-being—while still limiting where people could stand on that scaffolding.

> **Hull House and the Possibility of Proximity**
>
> Hull House embodied a radically different approach focused on community instead of control:
>
> - **1889 – Hull House Founded (Chicago):** Jane Addams and Ellen Gates Starr open Hull House in a working-class immigrant neighborhood, living alongside the families they served.
> - **Programs and Services:** Hull House offers child care, job training, arts and music, English classes, lectures, and public health initiatives. It became a hub for civic engagement and cultural exchange.
> - **Philosophy of Proximity:** Settlement leaders believed that poverty stemmed from social conditions. Reform, they argued, required living in relationship with communities, not policing them from above.
> - **Boundaries of Belonging:** Despite these innovations, most settlement houses didn't reach Black and Indigenous families and expected immigrants to assimilate into white, middle-class norms. The democratic experiment was genuine but incomplete.

The story of the settlement house movement reminds us that systems built on the name of progress can still replicate the hierarchies they hope to dismantle. This truth continues to shape America's uneven socio-economic infrastructure today.

To understand why the American welfare state has never lived up to its democratic ideals, we must take a deeper look at the boundaries around them. The sobering truth is that exclusion was not incidental; it was embedded in the very design of this nation's earliest systems.

Exclusion By Design: The System Was Working As Intended

What began as a moral hierarchy under the English Poor Laws hardened into a racial hierarchy under colonial rule. The early welfare practices drew sharp boundaries between those deemed "deserving" and those labeled "idle" or "immoral." These distinctions did more than categorize poverty; they reflected the deeper hierarchies built into the nation's identity. The legacy of slavery, displacement, and caste did not merely influence welfare, it determined who could benefit from it.

Reclaiming the true meaning of *welfare* requires honesty about what stood in the way of well-being for all. The scaffolding inherited from the Poor Laws—dividing people into the "deserving" and the "undeserving"—melded with the racial hierarchies of slavery and colonization. Together they produced a welfare order built not to lift everyone but to secure some lives while exploiting or erasing others.

The Promise Betrayed: How Caste Logic Shaped the Welfare Blueprint

Early colonial laws codified both economic exploitation and racial hierarchy. Enslaved Africans were denied all legal rights; Native peoples were displaced from their lands and stripped of sovereignty.

Meanwhile, white laborers—though often poor—were granted paths to property and citizenship.[31] In this design, exclusion wasn't a flaw but the main feature on which the system rested.

The Preamble to the Constitution promises to "promote the general Welfare," yet that promise was never intended for everyone. As Dr. Martin Luther King Jr. reminded us, "Black men and women, the creators of the wealth of the New World, were stripped of all human and civil rights. And this degradation was sanctioned and protected by institutions of government, all for one purpose: to produce commodities for sale at profit."[32] Likewise, historian David Treuer shows how the myth of Indigenous disappearance was a fiction devised to justify dispossession.[33] These were not byproducts of nation-building but the blueprint.

With both Black enslavement and Native removal, we built a national economy on extraction: of labor, of land, and of humanity itself.[34] Exclusion from prosperity was not a failure of execution but a deliberate design of early governance. Our legal systems reinforced racial hierarchy and justified inequality as the price of progress. This pattern of defining belonging through exclusion became the through-line of America's welfare story.

The wealth created by Black hands and on Native soil financed the very republic that denied them freedom. A caste logic then defined who could belong, who could prosper, and who would be written out of the nation's welfare story. As Isabel Wilkerson notes in *Caste*, it wasn't until 2022 that America has been an independent nation for as long as it practiced slavery—proof that our inequality is not distant history but our living inheritance.[35]

The caste system born of slavery and colonization organized our social order and became the blueprint for both public and private institutions, including those intended to support human welfare. The gap between our founding ideals and our exclusionary practices runs through every part of the nation's welfare architecture. To repair that design, we must also repair the words that built it.

The Americanization of welfare did not create a universal system of care. It produced a selective one, primarily serving white Americans through much of our history.[36] Even well-intentioned reformers could not escape the frame. Over time, poverty was punished through bureaucratic cruelty: eligibility rules, surveillance-heavy systems, and public stories steeped in suspicion. Those design choices shaped both who received help and how we thought about it.

The Stories We Teach, the Stories We Live

Most of us first encountered the word *welfare* through the stories we were taught—perhaps in a civics textbook describing the Constitution's promise to "promote the general welfare" or in everyday conversations that carried a different lesson altogether. For some, the word appeared in history books and political debates; for others, it was spoken in the hush of adult conversations or felt in the quiet calculation of whether a system meant to help might also shame. However we came to know it, the experience left its mark.

Across generations, Americans have absorbed conflicting messages about what *welfare* means—one taught as a civic ideal, the other lived as a social risk. Needing help came to carry dangers of exposure, judgment, or punishment. Over time, media portrayals and political rhetoric fused those personal experiences into a collective stigma. *Welfare* became a symbol of failure rather than shared responsibility. Even within the human services field, professionals learned to avoid the term altogether, as if protecting the mission of well-being required hiding the word itself.

In truth, the meaning of *welfare* in the U.S. has long been shaped less by its constitutional promise than by a powerful cultural story that casts suspicion on those who need support.

Reclaiming The Language of Welfare: Words Carry Design

Language can be reclaimed, and so can design. The welfare state we inherited was not built for all of us, but it can be rebuilt by all of us. That work begins with telling the full story of how racial exclusion and moral sorting shaped our welfare beliefs, and with recognizing truth-telling as the first act of repair.

The stories we inherit shape what we believe and, therefore, what we build. Once we recognize how exclusion was embedded in our earliest systems, we can see how it endures in our words. Language signals who belongs and who does not. The same vocabulary that once justified control can be reclaimed to express care and shared responsibility. Rebuilding a more truthful welfare story begins by reclaiming the language itself.

Historian Timothy Snyder reminds us that reclaiming democracy begins with reclaiming words like *freedom*.[37] We might add *welfare*.

Language can obscure reality or illuminate it. Returning welfare to its original meaning—our collective well-being—reminds us that care for one another is the measure of who we are as a people.

For generations, welfare was deliberately separated from connection, drawing a line between "us" and "them," between the deserving and the undeserving. But the word itself tells a different story. Welfare once meant a shared state of prosperity and security. To promote the "general welfare" was to recognize that individual well-being and national strength are inseparable.

Over time, that understanding was eroded by politics, racism, and fear. The language of well-being narrowed into the language of suspicion. To change policy, we must first change that story—returning welfare to its original meaning and rebuilding systems that support both individual and community well-being.

American welfare reflects who we believe deserves help, whom we invest in, and whom we let struggle. The chapters that follow trace how public stories hardened around blame and shame, solidifying a cultural mindset that treats poverty as personal failure and public support as threat. But those stories can change—and so can what we choose to see.

A Century Later, the Call Remains: From Compassion to Collective Repair

Jane Addams and her peers once urged the nation to confront poverty* as a shared responsibility rather than a moral defect. Their movement signaled that another way was possible, even as it remained constrained by the limits of its time. Today, we are called again to reimagine what it means to promote the general welfare. The promise remains unmet, but we now see more clearly why.

We have sharper tools, deeper data, and greater insight into how race, class, gender, ability, age, geography, and power shape opportunity and belonging. We can see how the stories we tell shape what we build, what we ignore, and what we dismantle. Understanding history alone does not free us, but it gives us the tools to choose differently.

This book is part of that choice. It invites us to examine the stories we have inherited and the systems they produced—and to ask: *What if we wrote a different one? What if welfare again meant well-being? What if human flourishing stood at the center of our democracy?* And, what's the cost if we don't?

---

*Throughout this book, I use the word poverty in its broadest sense—far beyond the federal thresholds—to include the instability, chronic stress, and structural barriers that shape people's everyday lives. For readers who want a brief guide to how poverty is defined and measured in the United States, I've included a short overview in Appendix A.

CHAPTER 2

An American Illusion

How We Rationed the Dream

What happens to a dream deferred? Does it dry up like a raisin in the sun?

—Langston Hughes

When James Truslow Adams first used the term *the American Dream* in his 1931 book, he painted a bold picture of a country in which life would be more rewarding and prosperous for everyone, no matter their social class or background.[1] This dream of opportunity became a defining part of our national identity, linked with ideas of liberty, hard work, and democracy. But Adams also warned about the nation's growing focus on materialism and the risk of confusing prosperity with greatness.[2] Even though Adams couldn't have predicted that his phrase would take hold as it has, he understood its duality: that the American Dream could inspire and exclude at the same time.

Fast forward to the 1950s postwar America and a new era of supposed prosperity. Yet for many, the dream remained elusive. Langston Hughes asked the haunting question: "What happens to a dream deferred?"[3] More than a decade later, Dr. Martin Luther King Jr. stood on the steps of the Lincoln Memorial calling that dream a promissory note America had yet to honor. James Baldwin cut deeper still, warning that the dream itself would collapse if America failed to reckon with its foundation in Black exploitation.[4] And, today, Reverend Dr. William Barber II reminds us that the American Dream is not a finished reality but an idea "that has never yet been," a vision both meaningful and unrealized.[5] Together, these voices reveal that the American Dream is neither achieved nor lost but remains unfinished and contested, still waiting to be claimed in truth.

The Myth and the Mirror: What the American Dream Conceals

In Chapter 1, welfare emerges as a mirror reflecting who America has believed is worthy of help. The American Dream holds up a different mirror—one that reflects who we believe deserves opportunity. Together, these mirrors tell stories of belonging and boundaries, revealing a nation still deciding whose well-being counts.

I saw this reflected in my own home with my son's high school assignment asking *What is the American Dream to you?* His class debated whether the dream was still real or already broken. In the end, they chose to believe in it, but with caveats. As my son said, "It's something we must aspire to." His words held both hope and honesty that the dream isn't gone, but it isn't whole either. It waits for us to decide whether we'll leave the dream distorted or make it a true reflection of what it can be.

That simple classroom moment captured the paradox of the American Dream itself: a story powerful enough to inspire belief even as its reflection remains uneven.

The American Dream as Meta-Narrative

The American Dream is more than a phrase; it is what sociologists call a *meta-narrative,* or a story so deeply embedded in our culture that it shapes how we see ourselves, how we see our nation, and how the world sees us.[6] It tells us that anyone, regardless of background, can rise through hard work and determination. That belief has motivated countless acts of resilience and innovation. Yet it has also masked the structural boundaries that ration opportunity by race, class, gender, and geography. The American Dream, in this way, is both a promise of belonging for all and a boundary of who we allow inside the circle.

Other nations have crafted different meta-narratives around what it means to live well. In Finland, the concept of *sisu* — perseverance joined with communal responsibility—anchors a social compact in which education, child care, and health care are treated as rights, not rewards.[7] New Zealand's Wellbeing Budget explicitly measures national success by levels of mental health, connection, and equity rather than gross domestic product.[8] Scotland's National Performance Framework sets a shared vision of fairness, kindness, and sustainability as benchmarks for government action.[9] These examples show that American individualism is not inevitable but a choice. We can choose stories that measure progress by collective flourishing as easily as we do by personal gain.

The Stories We Tell Ourselves

The American Dream is not only an aspiration; it is a story we repeat about who we are. Rooted in individualistic thinking, it frames success as personal merit rather than as the product of shared structures and collective investment. That framing has been so deeply woven into our national ethos that we rarely pause to question it, or even notice when its promise is rationed or deferred for some of us.

Like all cultural stories, the American Dream carries both promise and peril. The FrameWorks Institute describes these as *cultural mindsets* — deeply held and often unconscious assumptions about how the world works. They do not shape *what* we think but *how* we think.[10] Mindsets can expand our imagination or narrow it; they can invite us to embrace new possibilities or cause us to automatically reject them. The American Dream can inspire hope and agency while also masking exclusion and fueling blame.

Every nation tells itself a story, but it can change that story, too. In France, the revolutionary cry of *liberté, égalité, fraternité* still shapes civic life, even as far-right movements try to weaponize it.[11] In South Africa, the "Rainbow Nation" ideal of post-apartheid unity continues to inspire, even as persistent inequality tests its promise.[12] In the United States, the American Dream reflects our ideals and conceals our exclusions. National stories are never neutral. We can bend them in any direction, including toward unbounded belonging.

Each generation has been taught a version of the American Dream that centers on hard work and self-reliance while downplaying the role of shared infrastructure such as public schools, health systems, and accessible social services that make upward mobility possible. That selective storytelling has allowed the nation to obscure the collective scaffolding that made mobility possible for some.

Over time, the American Dream has shifted from a shared aspiration to a measuring stick that often reveals inequality more than opportunity. Instead of inspiring collective effort, it is too often weaponized against those who struggle, implying that if the dream is out of reach, the fault lies with the individual. This distortion hides the deeper truth that millions of Americans labor under barriers that foreclose opportunity, and that no amount of determination alone can overcome them.

For those left out, the American Dream is an empty promise. To make it real, we must be willing to examine the roots of inequality and exclusion, and commit to telling a fuller version of our national story. Only then can the dream stop being a myth rationed to a few and instead be realized for all of us.

Radical Promises Cut Short

Three times over the past 160 years, the United States has faced a moment when the gap between the American ideal and American reality could no longer be ignored. Each time, the federal government took unprecedented steps to expand opportunity, protect well-being, and make the promise of the American Dream more real. And each time, backlash cut the promise short. Reconstruction, the New Deal, and the War on Poverty were not identical, but they share the same arc. That arc still shapes how we think about poverty, government, and belonging today. Each cycle reveals how stories of deservingness and hierarchy repeatedly overpowered stories of solidarity, and how the American Dream has been both advanced and restricted by the narratives we tell about who it belongs to.

Reconstruction (1865–1877): The Dream That Might Have Been a Democracy

For a few brief years after the Civil War, the United States stood at the threshold of a multiracial democracy. Newly freed Black citizens voted, held office, and founded schools, cooperatives, and businesses. The Freedmen's Bureau embodied the radical idea that the government bore responsibility for securing economic and social rights for those it had formerly enslaved. For a moment, the nation experimented with an expansive definition of general welfare—one that linked freedom to material well-being.

Frederick Douglass emerged as the moral compass of this new democracy. A statesman as much as an abolitionist, he pressed the nation to see freedom not as the end of bondage but as the beginning of shared responsibility. Douglass warned that rights without resources would leave freedom hollow—a truth that would echo through every following struggle for inclusion.

Between 1865 and 1877, the Thirteenth, Fourteenth, and Fifteenth Amendments abolished slavery, defined citizenship, and extended voting rights to Black men, respectively. The Freedmen's Bureau, the nation's first large-scale social welfare agency, provided food, medical care, legal aid, and schooling to millions of formerly enslaved people.[13] Though underfunded and short-lived, it offered the first glimpse of what a federal commitment to well-being and belonging might achieve.[14]

This progress, however, met swift and violent resistance. Southern legislatures enacted Black Codes to restrict freedom; the Supreme Court narrowed federal authority;[15] and white supremacist groups used terror as political strategy.[16] By 1872 the Freedmen's Bureau was defunded; by 1877 federal troops had withdrawn from Southern states.[17] The collapse of federal enforcement reopened the door to the hierarchies Reconstruction had tried to end.

During Reconstruction, opponents of racial and economic inclusion turned to a new weapon: *socialism*. As historian Heather Cox Richardson observes, white supremacist Southerners repurposed a once-neutral term for utopian community into a political slur against federal intervention.[18] Any effort to extend rights or security was branded "socialism," a rhetorical maneuver meant to halt shared progress by casting it as alien and dangerous. The tactic outlived the era, resurfacing against the New Deal, the War on Poverty, and again today whenever collective investment threatens old hierarchies.

Frederick Douglass warned in 1876 that emancipation without land or legal protection would be a hollow promise.[19] He was right. The pledge of "forty acres and a mule" evaporated; land was stripped through seizures, predatory contracts, and punitive taxes.[20] Sharecropping, debt peonage, and the brutal convict-leasing system trapped families in generational poverty that often differed from slavery only in name.[21] Those who managed to build wealth faced mob violence, arson, and forced sale of their property.[22] The lesson was stark: progress cannot rest on law alone. It requires durable institutions and a cultural story that legitimizes them.

In the South, that vacuum hardened into Jim Crow: a social, political, and economic order built to reassert white dominance and restrict Black advancement. More than a set of segregation laws, Jim Crow became a total social code that regulated opportunity, dictated behavior, and normalized exclusion for generations. Across the country, new theories of "scientific" racism and eugenics lent this system an aura of legitimacy, recasting inequality as biology rather than injustice and once again turning hierarchy into supposed fact.[23]

Organized Memory and the Lost Cause

In the decades that followed Reconstruction, a new story hardened into place. The Lost Cause myth romanticized the antebellum South and reframed the Civil War as a noble struggle for "states' rights."[24] This was not private nostalgia; it was manufactured memory, deliberately constructed to overwrite the truth of enslavement and Reconstruction. Groups like the United Daughters of the Confederacy coordinated textbook campaigns, financed monuments, and shaped school curriculum to ensure that future generations inherited a sanitized version of Southern history.[25] Popular culture joined in: *The Birth of a Nation*, one of the most widely viewed films of its time, depicted the Ku Klux Klan as heroic protectors.

Through these coordinated efforts, racial violence was recast as virtuous, and white supremacy reestablished itself not only through law but through story. "The Lost Cause" became part of the invisible architecture of American life, scaffolding hierarchy into institutions, policy, and public imagination, embedding it as simply "the way things are."

Two Stories of Reconstruction

Reconstruction left two competing stories in its wake: one of radical promise and one of deliberate retreat.

The Promise

- Constitutional amendments abolished slavery, granted citizenship, and extended voting rights to Black men.
- The Freedmen's Bureau provided food, medical care, legal aid, and more, while building schools and hospitals (social welfare infrastructure).
- A glimpse of a more inclusive America in which well-being and belonging were extended beyond the few.

The Retreat

- Black Codes and Supreme Court rulings eroded protections and civil rights.
- White supremacist violence undermined federal enforcement and political will.
- The Freedmen's Bureau and other supports were dismantled, collapsing the first national system of relief and leaving states and localities to fill the gap unevenly.
- Cultural narratives like the Lost Cause recast Reconstruction as failure, embedding the idea that prosperity signaled worth and poverty reflected personal fault.

The Legacy

- Reconstruction demonstrated the potential of federally supported investments in inclusion and well-being.
- Its collapse entrenched racialized notions of deservingness and left enduring gaps in infrastructure.
- Both the progress achieved and the unfinished work remain part of our nation's welfare story.

Reconstruction showed what was possible when the nation invested in inclusion, and what was lost when it retreated. Larger than the collapse of any single program, the loss left behind a blueprint of exclusion that reappears whenever the nation edges toward broader belonging. Until we confront that inheritance not as the failure of one era but as the product of repeated choices, we risk reliving the same pattern of moments of progress met by organized resistance and retreat.

If Reconstruction's promise of land, education, and citizenship had endured, the United States might have become a true multiracial democracy whose prosperity was measured by inclusion rather than exclusion.

By 1929, when the Great Depression sent millions into breadlines, even those once insulated from hardship could no longer deny how fragile the American Dream had become. Once again, the nation faced a choice: move toward collective action or retreat into exclusion. That choice would define the New Deal.

The New Deal (1933-1939): Promise and Boundaries

Once again, two defining stories unfolded side by side in the New Deal: one of bold investment in human well-being, and one of deliberate exclusion that narrowed that investment's reach. The New Deal showed how far collective action could take us—and how quickly cultural boundaries could pull us back.

The Great Depression hit hard, making suffering impossible to ignore. By 1933, one in four U.S. workers—about 12.8 million people—

were unemployed, and millions more were losing their homes.[26] Breadlines snaked around city blocks. Hunger and eviction became visible everywhere, crossing class lines and fraying social stability. For the first time, the myth of self-reliance cracked under the weight of shared hardship.

Pressure mounted on the federal government to act. President Franklin D. Roosevelt responded with what he called "bold, persistent experimentation," launching the most sweeping expansion of public responsibility in U.S. history.[27] Over the next six years, the New Deal transformed the nation's relationship with the federal government. Social Security, unemployment insurance, public works programs, and banking protections became cornerstones of a new social contract that tied national recovery to collective well-being. One of the first laws of the period, the Federal Emergency Relief Act (FERA), allocated funds to states to provide direct cash aid for food and basic needs. This is a model we would echo nearly ninety years later during the COVID-19 pandemic.[28] The Social Security Act of 1935 marked a watershed moment: the first formal acknowledgment that government bore responsibility for economic security through all stages of life. Old-age pensions, unemployment benefits, and aid for families facing economic hardship redefined the purpose of public welfare.[29]

Frances Perkins, Roosevelt's secretary of Labor—and the first woman to serve in a U.S. presidential Cabinet—was the quiet architect behind many of these reforms. A Hull House alumna, she carried the settlement house conviction that democracy depends on the well-being of ordinary people. Perkins fought for labor protections and Social Security through years of political hostility, reminding colleagues that "the people are what matter to government."[30] Her persistence—often described as "patient tenacity with a conscience"—helped translate the language of compassion into lasting policy.[31]

These initiatives laid the foundation for the modern welfare state by establishing the principle that government has a responsibility to safeguard the economic security of its people, particularly in times of crisis. For the first time, millions of Americans experienced the federal government not only as a regulator or tax collector, but also as a direct provider of stability and relief.

First Lady Eleanor Roosevelt helped Americans see these changes as personal and moral, not abstract. Through her syndicated "My Day" column, she chronicled her visits to job programs, children's homes, and institutions for people with disabilities, giving the New Deal a human face.[32] She wrote about families without heat, workers locked out of jobs, and children without proper nutrition. She met with state and local leaders charged with implementing programs, insisting that policy was only as strong as its human reach. Decades later, I came across photos of her alongside the inaugural leaders of the national association I would one day lead—a reminder that the human services field was born from this same moment of imagination. Her advocacy made the New Deal feel like the work of a compassionate democracy.

Unlike today, most Americans in the 1930s viewed poverty as a systemic failure, not a personal flaw. Across party lines, government intervention was seen as legitimate and necessary.[33] It was a striking reversal from the English Poor Law logic that had minimized care and blamed hardship on character.

The New Deal proved that large-scale federal action could stabilize families, create jobs, and build infrastructure that "promote the welfare of the people."[34] It laid the groundwork for later gains during the War on Poverty and inspired future programs such as Head Start, Medicare, and Medicaid, which contributed to reductions in economic inequality in the decades that followed.

Yet the New Deal's inclusivity also had sharp boundaries. To secure Southern votes in Congress, Roosevelt agreed to exclude domestic and agricultural workers from Social Security, unemployment insurance, and wage protections—jobs held largely by Black and Brown[35] workers. These were not oversights but deliberate design choices to preserve the racial hierarchy of the South.[36]

Housing policy followed the same pattern. The Federal Housing Administration, in concert with the Home Owners' Loan Corporation, created "redlined" maps that blocked Black families from homeownership and thus generational wealth. Majority-Black neighborhoods were marked "hazardous" and denied mortgage insurance—scars that still mar the American landscape.[37] These weren't just lines on paper; they were part of the blueprint of inequality for decades to come.

From the outset, federal policymakers distrusted how ordinary people would use direct assistance, which shaped the system's paternalistic design. State and local leaders often favored cash aid, but federal officials doubted recipients' judgment and steered funds toward in-kind benefits and work programs instead.[38] That mistrust created a pattern we still repeat: conflating oversight with accountability and control with care. It foreshadowed the same debates that echo today over whether we trust people with money or insist on controlling how they meet their needs. This question returns in Chapter 9, where we take a closer look at the promise of guaranteed income.

For a brief time, the New Deal allowed Americans to live inside a story of shared responsibility for recovery. But its compromises revived the suspicion and stigma of the old Poor Laws and left intact the inequities of post-Reconstruction America. In doing so, it embedded structural racism into the modern welfare system and reinforced the idea that some groups stood outside the circle of concern. These were not accidental omissions but once again declarations of who counted as "American enough" to receive help.

The genius and the cruelty of the New Deal were bound together. It created a new social contract, but one bounded by the culture that produced it. Domestic workers and farmworkers were excluded by design, while Black communities were systematically shut out through redlining and other forms of silent consensus. Individualism did the rest. By framing public support as something to be earned, exclusion could masquerade as fairness.

Even at its most generous, the New Deal framed poverty as a temporary crisis, not as a structural failure. In this way, the same narrative that expanded the promise of government also narrowed it, teaching us to see benefits not as universal rights but as conditional rewards. That selective lens bridged the rationed dream of the New Deal to the enduring myth of meritocracy, which we explore in the next chapter.

Two Stories of the New Deal

The New Deal left behind two parallel stories: bold federal action and deliberate exclusion. Together, they reveal how progress and hierarchy were built into the same design.

The Promise
- Sweeping federal programs created jobs, regulated banks, and built infrastructure that lifted millions out of despair.
- Social Security established a new floor of economic security for older Americans.
- Bold public investment expanded the federal government's role in promoting collective well-being.

The Retreat
- Domestic and agricultural workers—disproportionately Black and Brown—were excluded from Social Security and labor protections.
- Redlining and discriminatory housing policies locked Black families out of wealth-building opportunities.
- The federal system of relief became fragmented because supports were framed as selective rewards, rather than universal rights, narrowing belonging.

The Legacy
- Core pillars of social policy and infrastructure reinforced racial and gender hierarchies in the welfare state.
- Government support came to be seen as temporary and conditional, not as a permanent tool for economic justice.
- A familiar pattern emerged: bold federal action followed by selective inclusion.

In the end, the New Deal told a story of national renewal that left millions outside the definition of "nation," yet it also revealed what becomes possible when a democracy treats well-being as shared infrastructure. Had those protections extended equally, without exclusions by race, gender, or geography, America might have built a more stable and equitable prosperity capable of weathering today's storms. Instead, the unrealized promise of the New Deal lingered in the background, waiting for another opening. That opening would arrive two decades later, but so would the fears that had once blocked it.

After the New Deal, two decades of post-war prosperity lifted many while deepening racial inequities. The GI Bill, suburban development, and industrial expansion built wealth for white families but largely shut out communities of color.[39] Even as the economy boomed, injustice remained visible to anyone willing to see it. The nation's conscience was jolted awake by what played out on television screens and front pages—the lynching of Emmett Till, the Birmingham church bombing that killed four girls, and the marches and sit-ins met with fire hoses and dogs.[40]

The Civil Rights Movement reframed inequality as a design problem. It exposed how systems, not individual shortcomings, determined whose opportunities expanded and whose were constrained. In doing so, it built the ethical and political foundation for the War on Poverty.[41]

The War on Poverty (1964-1973): Ambition Undermined

By the 1960s, the United States once again stood at a crossroads. Postwar prosperity had lifted millions into the middle class, yet poverty persisted in plain sight, as Michael Harrington revealed in *The Other America*.[42] The Civil Rights Movement made that contradiction impossible to ignore: How could a nation celebrate abundance while denying opportunity to so many of its people? Like Reconstruction and the New Deal before it, the War on Poverty invited the country to decide who was included in "us."

President Lyndon B. Johnson answered the moment with a sweeping vision. In his 1964 State of the Union address, he declared an "unconditional War on Poverty," insisting that the nation had both the means and the duty to confront deprivation directly.[43] Building on New Deal lessons—but with a sharper focus on civil rights and community participation—Johnson cast the effort as more than a campaign to ease hardship. By invoking the language of war, he signaled an ambition to end poverty altogether and framed the work as a collective obligation to finish what our democracy had begun more than once but never fulfilled.

A single photograph came to define the moment: Johnson on the porch of Tom Fletcher, an unemployed miner in Inez, Kentucky. Its appearance in *Time* magazine made it iconic—a visual shorthand for rural white poverty.[44] While Appalachia's suffering was real, the image narrowed the nation's gaze, masking the urban Black poverty that civil rights leaders were risking their lives to expose.

Within two years, the Johnson administration passed landmark legislation that still underpins our human services infrastructure.[45] The

Economic Opportunity Act created new pathways to jobs, and built in civic participation through the establishment of the federally funded Community Action Agencies and Volunteers in Service to America. The Food Stamp Act made nutrition assistance permanent. The Social Security Amendments of 1965 established Medicare and Medicaid. Major education and housing bills followed.[46] Together, these actions tackled poverty at its roots: education, employment, health, and community capacity.[47] Between 1964 and 1973, poverty rates fell from around 19 percent to 11 percent, evidence that federal investment could change lives at scale.[48]

This historic wave unfolded alongside the Civil Rights and Voting Rights Acts. Unlike the New Deal, the War on Poverty included explicit antidiscrimination language borrowed from the Civil Rights Act to bar exclusion "on the ground of race, color, or national origin."[49] It was an imperfect but intentional attempt to weave inclusion into the fabric of federal aid. While enforcement lagged, making it illegal to exclude or segregate program participants marked a historic step forward.

Perhaps its most radical innovation was "maximum feasible participation," the principle that people with lived experience should help govern programs that affected them.[50] Community Action Agencies embodied this idea, especially in Black and Brown communities, where residents designed and staffed services reflecting their realities. For many, this was the first time federal policy recognized their agency and voice.[51]

Sargent Shriver, the first director of the Office of Economic Opportunity, became the architect and conscience of the War on Poverty. He understood that poverty could not be solved from

Washington alone, and that communities needed both resources and agency. Shriver's insistence on "maximum feasible participation" was radical for its time: it put lived experience at the table as a source of expertise, not a problem to manage. His blend of optimism and pragmatism gave the movement its heartbeat, even as political headwinds mounted.[52]

Like Reconstruction and the New Deal before it, the War on Poverty provoked organized backlash. In the South, local officials saw federal funds that bypassed their control as a threat. Some accused Community Action Agencies of "stirring unrest."[53] Nationally, critics revived old tropes of fiscal recklessness and moral decay. The same hierarchies that had undone earlier reforms reemerged under new language—"taxpayer fairness," "dependency," and "big government."[54]

Two Stories of the War on Poverty

The War on Poverty left two parallel stories: bold federal investment that expanded opportunity and the backlash that narrowed its reach. Together, they show how progress and resistance have always been intertwined in America's pursuit of national well-being.

The Promise
- President Johnson declared the nation had both the resources and the duty to eliminate poverty.
- Landmark programs—Medicare, Medicaid, Head Start, and food assistance—extended health care, nutrition, and early education to millions.
- Community Action Agencies empowered local voices, especially in Black and Brown communities, to shape services that reflected their realities.

The Retreat
- Backlash framed antipoverty efforts as government overreach, overshadowing tangible successes.
- Backlash laid the groundwork for the introduction of the "welfare queen" stereotype that would further racialize poverty and turn public support into suspicion.
- The federal system of community-based relief was undermined as political compromises and cultural narratives narrowed its reach and legitimacy.

The Legacy
- The War on Poverty demonstrated what federal investment in people could achieve: reductions in child poverty, hunger, and barriers to opportunity.
- It left a divided story: real gains alongside narratives of dependency and failure.
- Many core programs started then remain foundational today, but public narratives delegitimizing them constrain further progress.

The "war" metaphor itself carried limits: wars imply enemies, victories, and endings. Poverty is none of these; it is a product of how we design systems and assign worth. When quick victory proved impossible, critics claimed the "war" was lost, and racialized stereotypes rushed in to fill the void.[55]

Even supporters grew frustrated. Dr. Martin Luther King Jr. praised Johnson's call as a "bold assertion of compassion" but warned it had been so underfunded that it could not win even a "skirmish."[56] From the outset, Johnson had pressed Shriver to keep the War on Poverty lean, ensuring funds remained for the Vietnam War and other priorities. This "unconditional war" was fought with conditional resources.[57]

The early framing had promised possibility and respect, "opening to everyone the opportunity to live in decency and dignity."[58] But the frame quickly narrowed. The widely circulated 1965 Moynihan Report, though acknowledging structural racism, shifted attention to the "deterioration of the Black family" as the cause of poverty.[59] Its release alongside the Watts uprisings in Los Angeles gave opponents a convenient narrative that poverty stemmed from cultural deficiency rather than systemic injustice.

> **The Devasting Effect of the Moynihan Report**
>
> No single moment illustrates the tension between policy and perception during the War on Poverty more than the release of *The Negro Family: The Case for National Action*, better known as the Moynihan Report. Written in 1965 by Daniel Patrick Moynihan, then assistant secretary of Labor, the report aimed to spark a national conversation about the economic and social conditions facing Black families in urban America. But its framing—blaming poverty on "the deterioration of the Black family"—had devastating consequences.
>
> Moynihan argued that a "tangle of pathology," particularly the rise of single-mother households, was the central barrier to Black progress.[60] Although he acknowledged systemic racism, the report ultimately shifted focus from exclusion to deficiency, placing blame on family structure. The result was a powerful reframing of poverty—not as the product of economic inequality, but as a symptom of cultural failure.
>
> Politicians and media amplified this racialized narrative, fueling stereotypes of Black dependency and female-headed households. In the decades that followed, it provided the foundation for "welfare reform" that sought less to address inequality than to police behavior.
>
> The Moynihan Report became a case study in how research frames can reshape national myths as powerfully as policy.

The War on Poverty was a turning point in social policy, and like its predecessors, it left unfinished business. The "war" metaphor, together with political compromise and rising backlash, narrowed its reach and distorted its legacy.

By the 1970s, the War on Poverty was recast as a cautionary tale of "government overreach." In the 1980s, President Ronald Reagan famously declared that poverty had "won," severing the moral link between antipoverty policy and civil rights and laying the groundwork for the racialized "dependency" narrative that still echoes today.[61]

Many of the War on Poverty programs—Medicare, Medicaid, Head Start, and SNAP—remain foundational today. Yet the larger vision of eradicating poverty faded, replaced by incrementalism, means-testing, and rhetoric of personal responsibility.

The War on Poverty was not a failure. It lowered poverty rates and expanded opportunity, but was constrained by the very structures it sought to transform. As resources dwindled and racialized stories hardened, its legacy grew muddled. Poverty was never intractable, it was narratively constrained.

Once again, the arc was familiar: a period of hope and investment met by organized resistance and retreat. Had the War on Poverty been fully funded and its narrative protected from racialized backlash, the United States might have built a nation defined by prevention and possibility instead of punishment and scarcity.

Its story reminds us that poverty policy is never just about programs; it is also about the stories we tell. Until we reclaim the narrative and see poverty not as individual failure but as the result of our collective policy choices, we will keep circling the same missed opportunities.

From Policy to Belief

The efforts discussed in this chapter show what becomes possible when government treats people's well-being as a national priority and how fragile that progress becomes when the story sustaining it goes undefended. When narrative falters, progress erodes not only in budgets and laws but in the nation's civic center: in what we come to see as normal, acceptable, or inevitable.

Across eras, policy design reflected not just resources but who society imagined inside the circle of belonging. Again and again, we've lived the same cycle: bold interventions followed by backlash; structural solutions weakened by cultural resistance. Each retreat reshaped public norms about fairness and responsibility until exclusion felt like common sense.

Understanding this pattern matters because the beliefs embedded in those policies never disappeared. They still guide how we think about poverty, government, and one another. When narrow stories dominate long enough, they harden into social norms that excuse inequity and make empathy seem naïve.

If policy is the visible structure of society, narrative is its blueprint. And America's blueprint has long been drawn around rugged individualism—the conviction that success is solely earned, and that needing help reflects personal failure. That story has shaped both our politics and our public ethics: what we call strength, what we call weakness, and who we imagine as fully American.

This mindset, rooted in our founding mythology, has outlasted every program and political era. Until we confront it and replace it with a story grounded in interdependence and shared power, we will keep repeating the same cycle.

What Could Have Been, What Still Can Be

Reconstruction, the New Deal, and the War on Poverty were more than policy eras; they were inflection points, moments when the nation glimpsed a more inclusive future. In each case, the federal government took unprecedented steps to confront hardship and expand opportunity. And in each case, those efforts were ultimately constrained not only by political resistance but by the deeper stories about who belonged. Those stories outlasted the programs themselves, shaping our instincts about parents seeking child care, workers asking for fair pay, and neighbors trying to get by.

These eras revealed both the promise and the fragility of our social contract. We proved we can build systems that strengthen well-being and expand democracy. But when those systems were built on foundations of exclusion by race, gender, class, or geography, they left millions outside the circle of concern. And when exclusion became the prevailing story, retreat came to feel like restoration—a return to an imagined past rather than a loss of shared possibility.

Across generations, America's social policy has been driven by an underlying sorting mechanism: Who is inside our concern? Who is expected to prove themselves? Who is allowed full claim to the American Dream?

The unfinished business of each era reveals a deeper truth: our faltering welfare system is not only a matter of program design. It is a matter of narrative and the social norms that grow from it. Every policy rests on assumptions about what people need and what obligations we hold to one another. Until we challenge those assumptions, the pattern repeats: crisis sparks investment, stability returns, and progress is rolled back, dismissed as overreach or repackaged as "personal responsibility."

This cycle is not accidental. It is rooted in cultural stories that have calcified into reflexes--ideas that prize independence over interdependence, cast government as suspect, and define hardship as personal failure rather than systemic exclusion. These narratives guide what we fund, what we punish, and what we overlook.

To chart a different future, we must go deeper. We need to examine the stories that define our sense of possibility and the norms they cement. We must rethink how narratives like the American Dream, meritocracy, and the "self-made man" became so entrenched that they still shape what we believe about welfare, poverty, and the role of government itself.

In the chapters ahead, we'll trace how these stories took root, how the bootstrap mentality became our default lens, and how it reshaped not just our views on poverty but our understanding of fairness, freedom, and democracy. Before we can change the system, we must reckon with and rewrite the stories that hold it in place.

Over four centuries, the rules that built our welfare system have changed in form but not in logic. This chart traces how ideas about "deservingness" have traveled from the Poor Laws to the present, reshaping policy, language, and public norms along the way.

How the Rules Traveled: From Charity to Conditionality

- **English Poor Laws (1601)—The Deserving Poor**

England's first national welfare law divided the "worthy" from the "idle," linking aid to moral behavior and work.
This hierarchy became the blueprint for America's first public-assistance rules.

- **Colonial and Early America—Independence as Virtue**

Early colonies imported the Poor Laws' logic and celebrated self-reliance as proof of godliness and civic virtue.
Help was local, temporary, and conditional—charity for others, responsibility for oneself.

- **The Settlement House Movement (1890s–1920s)—Poverty Has Causes**

Reformers like Jane Addams reframed poverty as a social condition, not a personal defect, advocating education, housing, and labor protections.
For a moment, the story shifted from judgment to justice—but only within limited circles of reform.

- **The New Deal (1930s)—Security Through Shared Responsibility**

The Great Depression shattered the myth of self-reliance and produced Social Security, jobs programs, and a new social contract.
Racial exclusions and gendered norms preserved the old boundaries of who was deemed "deserving."

- **The War on Poverty (1960s)—Participation and Prevention**

Federal action broadened again through Medicare, Medicaid, Head Start, and Community Action.
For the first time, people with lived experience were invited to shape solutions—but backlash quickly redrew the lines.

- **Welfare Reform (1990s–Present)—Work First, Prove Worth**

The 1996 Personal Responsibility and Work Opportunity Reconciliation Act recast aid as temporary and behavior-based.
Deservingness became policy again: help only for those who could "earn" it under strict conditions.

CHAPTER 3

The Blame Trap

How We Let Shame Take Root

> The cultural tradition of blaming the victim serves primarily to obscure the causes of social problems.
> —William Ryan

> It is a cruel jest to say to a bootless man that he ought to lift himself by his own bootstraps.
> —Martin Luther King, Jr.

I've lost count of how many times a conversation about my work has stopped cold after someone asks what I do and I explain that I work in human services helping communities design systems that support families in need. The response is often a polite nod, a quick change of subject, or a faint look of pity. The conversation folds into the silence that so often surrounds this work. I've learned not to take it personally. The discomfort isn't about me; it's about what the word *need* triggers in us.

Blame has become one of the most powerful lenses through which America views poverty. Instead of examining systems that ration opportunity, we are trained to focus suspicion on individuals. The story goes like this: If someone is struggling, it must be their fault; if someone receives help, it must mean they failed to take care of themselves. Over time, these ideas harden into a cultural reflex felt not only in our policies but also in our posture, tone, and the silences we keep. They obscure the real causes of hardship while reinforcing shame.

This chapter traces how that reflex took root in the decades after the War on Poverty, when structural explanations gave way to tropes of dependency and failure. Political rhetoric and media imagery turned poverty into a morality play—Nixon's "silent majority," Reagan's "welfare queen," Clinton's vow to "end welfare as we know it." Blame became the connective tissue between perception and policy, with shame at its emotional core.

Psychology and sociology help explain why. Once a story attaches to identity, it moves from opinion to instinct. It becomes something we feel. Narratives of shame then feed a loop: hardship sparks suspicion; suspicion drives punitive policy; punitive policy deepens the very inequalities it claims to solve. The result is more than bad policy. It is also a social reflex so familiar we mistake it for common sense.

The Five-Decade Drift: How Blame and Shame Took Root

The War on Poverty marked the last time in modern U.S. history that poverty was framed as a shared national challenge. But almost as soon as its programs took root, the story shifted. By the late 1960s, public discourse turned away from structural inequality and toward the supposed character of people experiencing poverty. What had briefly been understood as a collective failure of systems was recast—once again—as evidence of individual failure.

In the decades that followed, an expanding fixation on "personal responsibility" reframed the debate from tackling systemic barriers to interrogating individual behavior. The cultural current of blame moved quietly from newsreels and speeches into everyday judgment, changing not only what we believed about poverty but how we reacted to those who lived it.

This was no organic evolution; it was a deliberate narrative campaign to stigmatize and stall public investment. Media images, political soundbites, and policy choices fostered the assumption that poverty stems from poor effort and bad decisions. We absorbed those messages until they felt intuitive—even natural—so that shame now travels alongside need. What began as rhetoric calcified into automatic judgment.

But it wasn't always this way. During the New Deal and the years following World War II, most Americans saw poverty as a shared concern. Government programs received broad, if imperfect, support.[1] People understood that political and economic forces contributed to hardship and believed public institutions had a duty to respond. That consensus began to fracture in the late 1960s.

The 1968 Poor People's Campaign demanded economic justice alongside voting rights and desegregation.[2] Meanwhile, protests rose across the country, fueled by police violence and systemic neglect. Then came the assassination of Martin Luther King Jr. Images of unrest filled the nightly news, and the national mood shifted against protest and the idea that government had a responsibility to confront equality.

For many white Americans watching on television, fear replaced empathy. Footage of burning buildings and police confrontations activated long-standing racial anxieties, making protest appear as chaos rather than as planned demand for justice. Political leaders quickly tapped into that fear, recasting unrest as proof that social programs had gone too far. The overlap of the Civil Rights Movement and Johnson's War on Poverty blurred two distinct struggles into a single story of disorder.[3]

With that emotional reframing, addressing poverty stopped being a shared responsibility and became a marker of who was inside or outside the nation's concern.

The 1965 Moynihan Report reinforced this narrative, recasting systemic exclusion as family breakdown and blaming Black single mothers for conditions rooted in racism and disinvestment.[4] This was more than policy analysis; it was a story about human worth. By locating poverty in family structure rather than in systems of exclusion, the report cast Black families as the problem, obscuring the political and economic forces that had produced hardship across multiple generations.

Visual portrayals amplified the message. Early War on Poverty rhetoric leaned on images of white rural hardship to build support. By the late 1960s, the images had changed. In 1964, only 27 percent of photos accompanying poverty stories in major news magazines featured Black subjects; by 1967, it had climbed to 72 percent.[5] Photographs work as emotional shorthand by telling us who to picture when we hear the word *poor*, and over time those pictures become policy.

By 1968, Richard Nixon was building his campaign on this terrain. Invoking the "silent majority," he signaled to white, working-class voters that they had been ignored in favor of "special interests."[6] Poverty programs were recast not as compassionate investments but as failed experiments. Nixon's emphasis on "law and order" and "forgotten Americans" repackaged old narratives in new political language.[7] These phrases were racially coded, but they resonated broadly because they affirmed a powerful belief: that those who are secure have earned it, and those who are not have failed.

The shift from viewing poverty as structural inequality to treating it as personal pathology had moved into high gear. And soon, Ronald Reagan would carry it further.

An Important Side Note: Nixon's Failed Reform

As discussed further in Chapter 9, President Nixon's Family Assistance Plan (FAP) attempted a sweeping overhaul of welfare—a guaranteed minimum income for all families with children. It aimed to set a national floor, create work incentives, and stabilize households.[8]

The FAP failed to pass in Congress, defeated by an unusual coalition:

- Conservatives denounced it as an expansion of government that would grow welfare rolls.
- Liberals argued its benefits were too low to lift families out of poverty.
- Mothers on public assistance rejected its punitive work rules, especially because it was without child care or meaningful job training.[9]

Its collapse left a vacuum, and in that vacuum, narrative triumphed over design. Political energy swung from universal security toward conditional aid, paving the way for a rhetoric-driven attack on welfare that still shapes policy today.

Reagan didn't just critique welfare policy; he branded it. In the mid-1970s, he began telling a story about a so-called welfare queen, a woman who supposedly lived in luxury by cheating government programs.[10] The image was vivid, memorable, and deeply misleading—and that was the point. The real woman behind the anecdotes, Linda Taylor, lived a far more complex and troubled life, but her circumstances mattered less than the symbol she became.[11] Reagan turned her into a shorthand for a broken system, giving America one of the most potent and damaging stereotypes in modern politics.

Reagan's genius was emotional, not economic; he made suspicion feel righteous and austerity sound fair. His message was clear: welfare was a crutch, government the enabler, and people experiencing poverty—especially people of color—suspect. Throughout his campaigns and presidency, he invoked the idea that welfare discouraged work, promoted dependence, and fueled social decline.[12] His administration pursued deep cuts to family economic supports such as cash assistance, Medicaid, and food stamps.[13] The result was a sharp narrative turn: government was cast as bloated and inefficient, exploited by those unwilling to help themselves.[14]

These stories did more than justify cuts; they retaught Americans how to feel about people in need. Compassion became naiveté, and oversight became virtue. Reagan's rhetoric became a blueprint for reshaping how Americans perceived poverty and it worked. By the 1990s, the debate was no longer about whether welfare should be reformed, but how drastically. By the time President Bill Clinton declared his intent to "end welfare as we know it," Reagan's framing had become political orthodoxy.[15] The story had traveled so far that even those who once defended public investment now spoke its language.

The 1996 Personal Responsibility and Work Opportunity Reconciliation Act (PRWORA) didn't just reform welfare; it rewrote its terms.[16] Assistance was now conditional: work requirements, time limits, and behavioral checks presumed that people needed boundaries and discipline.[17] The law ended entitlement to cash assistance, replacing it with a block grant that gave states wide discretion to restrict access even further.[18] In the years since, new rules—from limiting what counts as work in the Deficit Reduction Act of 2005 to recent Medicaid and SNAP restrictions in the "One Big Beautiful Bill"—have only deepened this punitive trend.[19]

Policy reflects perception, and by the time of welfare reform perception had been shaped by decades of stories blaming individuals for their circumstances. Instead of asking, "What systems are failing and why?" we increasingly asked, "Why don't people try harder?" The narrative of personal responsibility had taken hold across party lines. Poverty wasn't seen as a systemic hardship to be addressed but a personal obstacle to be overcome.

By the 2000s, a new mantra dominated social policy: "waste, fraud, and abuse." These words became synonymous with public benefits. Never mind that most errors were administrative, not deceitful.[20] The perception of widespread cheating justified stricter controls, deeper suspicion, and weaker support. Programs meant to help became programs designed to test. Government's role shifted from promoting welfare to policing it. And in the background, the same story played on repeat: If you're struggling, it must be your fault.

For those living within these systems, the effect is deeply personal, perpetuated by constant stress and humiliation. As writer Linda Tirado notes in *Hand to Mouth*, "Poverty is bleak and cuts off your long-term brain."[21] That line captures how structural scarcity gets misread as personal failure, and how that misreading seeps into self-belief.

That is the narrative loop we are caught in today—frames that presume fraud and dependency, embed suspicion directly into policy, and normalize conditionality for meeting basic human needs. And it is not just politics at work; it is also psychology, sociology, and culture. Social psychologists explain how our need to believe in a "just world" fuels victim-blaming. Sociologists trace how racialized tropes and family stereotypes seep into policy design and public opinion. Cognitive scientists show how mental shortcuts keep these stories alive long after the evidence proves them false. Together, these insights reveal why the myths of blame and meritocracy feel so natural, and why they are so hard to unlearn.

The tragedy is not only that these myths persist but also that they change us. They dull empathy, train us to confuse worth with wealth, and make solidarity feel like a mistake.

The Meritocracy Myth

The last half-century has trained us to blame people in poverty for their own woes. The logic that makes this seem fair is the shared belief in meritocracy. At the heart of our national identity is the story that anyone can succeed if they work hard enough. This belief functions like a social contract: America doesn't promise equal outcomes, but it claims to guarantee equal opportunity. Study hard. Work harder. Persevere no matter what, and you'll rise. And if you don't? That's on you.

Here the story becomes a moral equation:

Your Effort = Your Worth.

Yet in practice, it often works in reverse:

Your Worth = Your Effort.

As law professor Daniel Markovits writes in *The Meritocracy Trap*, "True to its Latin etymology, meritocracy glorifies only earned advantage."[22] Meritocracy works like a camera lens. It determines what comes into focus and what falls out of the frame. In welfare policy, it keeps attention fixed on who qualifies for help, how long they can receive it, and what behaviors they must perform to keep it. Meanwhile, it blurs the broader landscape—systemic barriers like racism, gender hierarchy, generational poverty, and economic exclusion. Psychologists call this the *fundamental attribution error*: our tendency to overemphasize individual traits and underplay context.[23]

Even in programs designed to fight poverty, this assumption lingers. Interventions often focus on "fixing" the individual through job training, financial literacy, or parenting classes. While often helpful, they carry a hidden bias that the problem resides in the person, not in the system. The unspoken message is that success is proof of virtue, and poverty a symptom of your character.

Our belief in meritocracy turns inequality into moral math. If success is earned, then failure must be earned too. It becomes a trap: succeed, and you've proved your worth; struggle, and you've confirmed your flaw. That belief doesn't stay in policy debates; it seeps into the psyche.

People like to believe poverty is a character defect because it makes them feel safe. When the story is that simple, shame feels inevitable.

We learn that story early. We read *The Little Engine That Could*,[24] watch movies where the underdog wins, and hear sayings like "when the going gets tough, the tough get going." Popular culture celebrates the "self-made man" who triumphs through grit. These stories are so deeply ingrained that we rarely stop to ask what they teach us about one another—or what they leave out.

> **Sayings that Shape
> the American Story of Merit and Adversity**
>
> From everyday clichés to coded language, American culture is saturated with sayings that reinforce the belief that success or failure rests on individual effort. We repeat them without much thought, but they carry powerful assumptions about class, race, and worth.
>
> **Celebrating Grit and Self-Reliance**
> - "Pull yourself up by your bootstraps."
> - "What doesn't kill you makes you stronger."
> - "Sink or swim."
> - "When life gives you lemons, make lemonade."
> - "From rags to riches."
>
> **Casting Failure as Inherited or Inevitable**
> - "The apple doesn't fall far from the tree."
> - "He's a bad apple."
>
> **Marking Class and Racial Boundaries**
> - "From the wrong side of the tracks."
> - "Born with a silver spoon in their mouth."
>
> **Moralizing Poverty and Struggle**
> - "God helps those who help themselves."
> - "Idle hands are the devil's workshop."
> - "Earn your keep."
>
> Together, these sayings form a cultural shorthand. Hardship is cast as either a test of character or an inevitable fate. In both cases, structural barriers disappear from the story. By naturalizing success and failure as personal destiny, we reinforce a racialized and class-bound version of meritocracy—an American story told and retold until it feels like common sense.

We don't just hear these sayings. We absorb them. They become mental shortcuts, shaping what feels true before we have time to think. Over time, that instinct moves from our heads into our habits, such as the pause before we ask for help, and the lowered voice when we admit we need it. Simple phrases become the scaffolding of a larger story that normalizes inequality.

The myth of meritocracy endures in part because our culture gives struggle a moral charge. Even our everyday language turns hardship into judgment. A single word can cast a verdict, shrinking complex realities into simple labels: Moocher. Freeloader. Taker. These aren't just insults but rules of belonging. They teach us where the lines are drawn and how far we can go before we risk being shunned. This is the invisible burden of the bootstrap myth. It convinces us we must "make it" alone, isolates us when we can't, and punishes vulnerability instead of addressing the conditions that created it.

These pejorative labels have deep roots. As early as the mid-nineteenth century, *moocher* signaled moral weakness in someone who relied on others.[25] During the Great Depression, newspapers popularized *freeloader* as relief programs expanded, warning that some would exploit aid rather than "earn their keep."[26] By the late twentieth century, those older insults resurfaced in sharper, racially coded forms—the "welfare queen" and the "deadbeat dad." In the 2010s, political commentators revived the trope through talk of a "nation of takers," suggesting dependency at the expense of initiative.[27]

These words reveal more than slang; they trace how blame became convention. Each label helped normalize the idea that people experiencing generational poverty are unworthy of support and trained the rest of us to keep our distance. Judgment became a social expectation, a kind of civic politeness that hides exclusion behind familiar phrases. In this way, language itself became an extension of the meritocracy myth, using words to measure human worth and stigmatize those who struggle.

Beneath the sting of these terms lies a deeper creed: that we are each on our own. This belief—the mantra of rugged individualism—has shaped both our policies and our posture toward one another.

The Quiet Pull of Individualism

At the heart of these cultural stories lies a powerful focus on individualism: a value so deeply embedded in the American psyche that we rarely notice how it shapes our instincts. Individualism champions independence, self-reliance, and personal responsibility. Aspirational as these ideals can be, they also divide the world into rigid categories: *makers* versus *takers*, those who succeed by grit versus those blamed for their supposed shortcomings. We see this influence in our public benefit programs as well, which have long been framed around helping individuals "stand on their own" (often described as self-sufficiency)[28] rather than acknowledging how much we all rely on collective foundations to flourish.

This lens reinforces an *us-versus-them* reflex at every turn. It trains us to ask whether someone has *earned* help instead of whether our systems have been organized to promote well-being for all. We may not intend to stigmatize our neighbors, but the cultural pull of individualism makes it almost automatic. It whispers through small talk, in the awkward pause when someone admits they're struggling, in the instinct to turn away rather than toward.

How Stigma Keeps the Story Alive

Stigma keeps this reflex alive. Labels like *dependent, lazy,* or *undeserving* are rhetorical shortcuts that define who belongs and who does not. People in poverty bear the heaviest weight, but we all pay a price. Stigma erodes trust in the organizations working to alleviate hardship (a theme explored in the next chapter) and traps us inside a narrative that hides both the reality of poverty and the possibility of something different.

Over time, stigma becomes an invisible form of discipline, narrowing the boundaries of our compassion. It tells us that poverty is a private problem to be solved alone, not a shared responsibility. We learn to treat distance as virtue and detachment as strength. Individualism and stigma work hand in hand to redraw the line between "us" and "them," often without our awareness. As social psychologist Crystal Hoyt reminds us, the best chance to fight poverty comes when "stigma and antipathy toward those in poverty diminishes."[29] To reach that point, we must confront what drives us to make these automatic judgments.

Suspicion of the Common Good

Right now, the loop sustains itself. Meritocracy and individualism set the stage, stigma reinforces it, and together they make *us-versus-them* thinking feel natural, and even inevitable. Each time we absorb or repeat the story that people facing hardship are to blame for their own circumstances, we strengthen the loop, making it harder to imagine explanations rooted in history, policy, or design. The result is a culture fluent in sympathy but unpracticed in solidarity. The loop distorts how we see others and how we see ourselves, shrinking our sense of "we" and narrowing our vision of what's possible.

If the bootstrap story tells Americans that needing help is personal failure, another narrative goes further: it makes the help itself suspect. As economist Robert Reich notes, "socialism" has long been wielded as a political bogeyman. It is summoned whenever collective progress gains traction.[30] The charge is rarely about economics; it is about narrative power. Calling public benefits "socialist" functions as the "welfare queen" trope: it stirs suspicion, signals illegitimacy, and frames the common good as a threat to freedom. The word does its work beneath awareness. It makes solidarity sound dangerous and shared investment feel like loss.

This move is part of the larger blame loop: hardship sparks suspicion, suspicion is inflamed by words like *dependency* or *socialism*, and punitive policies follow. Those policies reinforce the very myths they claim to fix.

As we saw in Chapter 1, the word "socialism" was first weaponized during Reconstruction to tear at the load-bearing beams of collective progress. By the late twentieth century, it had become a routine demolition too, an easy way to erode trust in the very structures meant to hold communities up. In Chapter 9, we'll return to this theme and consider how we might reinforce the scaffolding of democracy with stronger materials—belonging, shared security, and mutual investment—so it can bear the weight of old fears without collapsing.

Victim-Blaming and the Just World Hypothesis

These tropes do more than stereotype individuals; they train us to see poverty in flattened terms, as if complex systems could be reduced to single stories. Once poverty is caricatured, fault becomes easy to assign. Social psychologist William Ryan named the pattern plainly: *blaming the victim.*[31]

What Daniel Patrick Moynihan framed as family pathology in his report was, in truth, systemic exclusion. But by shifting the blame, he'd handed the country a cultural script that would shape welfare debates for decades: if outcomes differ, character must be the cause. Behind this script lies one of our most persistent psychological defenses—the belief that people deserve what they get and get what they deserve. Social psychologist Melvin Lerner called it the *just world hypothesis.*[32] We all want to believe the world is fair and orderly. When we witness suffering, it unsettles that belief. To ease the discomfort, we rationalize: good things happen to good people and bad things happen to bad people.

This mental maneuver offers a comforting illusion of control. If poverty results from bad choices, then we don't have to face the possibility that it could happen to us or that the systems we rely on are flawed. The defense often surfaces as everyday judgment, especially toward people we don't know. If someone is unhoused, it must be because they don't want to work. If someone receives food assistance, it must be because they can't manage money. In this way, poverty becomes something that happens to "those people," while the forces that shape it disappear from view.

U.S. policies enforce this logic. Job training programs, a staple since the War on Poverty, presume a lack of skill rather than a lack of opportunity.[33] Parenting classes assume personal deficits rather than structural barriers families face. While such supports may help some, they carry a deeper bias: the fault lies in the individual, not the environment. Even compassion gets filtered through suspicion, as if empathy must be earned-echoes of our Poor Laws' inheritance.

When we cling to the belief that the world is fair, we explain inequality by blaming those at the bottom of the economic ladder. It soothes us to think the system works, even when it's working only for some. And some of the most enduring American stories have reinforced this bias, turning cultural myths into common sense and injustice into normalcy.

Justifying Policy Change Through Moral Panic

No story did more to cement the idea that poverty is a choice than the tale of the *welfare queen*. As we have seen, Reagan's version was exaggerated, racially coded, and strategically told to audiences already primed to believe it. The power of the story was in its symbolism: it conjured a single figure who embodied the public's deepest suspicions about welfare. Rare abuses became the headline, and anecdote hardened into proof. By activating this cultural archetype and fusing it with racial resentment, Reagan mobilized a powerful coalition against the very idea of collective care.[34]

Sociologists call this a *moral panic*: a collective overreaction to a perceived threat, repeated until it justifies sweeping policy change.[35] The welfare queen was never about one woman in Chicago; it was about priming us to see poverty as personal fraud and moral failure. The story endured not because it was true but because it tapped into deep cultural biases about race, gender, and work. The result was a climate of suspicion with policies that punished need and a politics that rewarded outrage.

We can recognize moral panics by how quickly they turn a story into "proof." The Red Scare, the "crack baby" epidemic, and recurring waves of alarm about immigration each show how a charged narrative can outrun evidence until policy treats suspicion as common sense. The pattern repeats: when insecurity rises, we reach for simple villains. At different moments, it has been "big government," "criminals," or "takers"—a rotating cast that keeps attention off design choices and power.

A Myth That Divided—and Weakened—Everyone

The irony is that these narratives did more than harm the people they unfairly caricatured; they impacted millions of families across race and region. By narrowing public compassion, the welfare queen trope made it easier to dismantle programs for everyone. In reality, most people who relied on food stamps, unemployment insurance, or Medicaid in the 1980s (as well as today) were white with, many living in rural or reindustrialized communities.[36] Yet the racialized story of fraud and dependency was so powerful that it masked this truth.

As Heather McGhee reminds us, this is the essence of the *zero-sum lie*—the belief that progress for some must come at the expense of others. In reality, we all lose when public systems are hollowed out.[37] Reverend William Barber II says it plainly: Poverty is not Black or white, urban or rural; it is systemic, and it thrives when we fail to see our shared stake in ending it.[38]

Yet another subtle harm lies in how privilege hides its own dependence. Many white Americans—and others with economic advantage—do not see their help after a job loss, informal child care networks, or inherited financial cushions as *assistance* at all. The same cultural story that shames public support normalizes private or generational support as virtue. That blindness fractures solidarity twice over: it allows those who benefit from invisible safety nets to believe they are entirely self-made, and it distances many white families facing poverty from seeing their own struggles as connected to others.

And fear fills the gap. Decades of political rhetoric taught white Americans to fear not only racial difference but the very idea of shared responsibility. When fear animates the story, collective investment looks like loss—of status, security, or control—and the people struggling beside us become rivals rather than partners.

The welfare queen myth was never about "them." It was about keeping "us" from seeing ourselves as one. It distracted the nation from solidarity and weakened support for millions of families.

The strategy proved so effective that it became a template. Once the public was primed to view poverty through a racialized lens, leaders could recycle the same playbook with new targets, most recently immigrants.

Today, we see similar dynamics in how immigration is framed. Politicians and media outlets deploy words like *invasion* or *flood*—language designed to trigger fear and urgency. Just as the "welfare queen" turned a complex social issue into a caricature of deceit and dependency, the immigration panic casts families seeking refuge or work as existential threats to national security and economic stability. Individual crimes by undocumented immigrants are spotlighted as if they represent an entire group. Rare abuses again become the norm.

The story is familiar: Immigrants are portrayed not as individual people navigating impossible choices but as dangerous crowds who drain our resources, including public benefits. That framing then justifies punitive policies and harsh enforcement that ignore data and erase immigrants' vast contributions to the nation's economy and culture.[39]

Both the "welfare queen" and the immigration "invasion" reveal how moral panics work. They distill complexity into a single villain, invite outrage and fear, and provide moral cover for control. They are not stories told to understand reality; they are stories told to retain power.

The Hidden Harm of Tropes

The welfare queen label may be the most infamous attack ever attached to public assistance, but it is far from the only one. American discourse has long trafficked in shorthand that wounds—*deadbeat dad, at-risk youth, broken family.* Each compresses complex lives into caricature and, in doing so, dictates how policies are written and whom they reach.

The **"deadbeat dad."** This trope gained traction in the 1980s and 1990s as policymakers doubled down on child support enforcement, portraying noncustodial fathers as willfully absent or irresponsible.[40] Yet the roots run deeper. Early welfare policy was built around mothers, not fathers. Mothers' pensions in the early twentieth century were designed for women raising children after their husbands died, and subsequent laws like Aid to Dependent Children carried a similar design.[41] From the start, fathers were cast as breadwinners, not caregivers, and their needs were invisible to policy.

As divorce and non-marital birth rates increased, that script held. Policymakers focused more on monitoring fathers' financial contributions than on supporting their caregiving role. By the late twentieth century, child support enforcement had become one of the most punitive features of welfare, prioritizing money collection over parental connection. Although today's approaches are more inclusive, the legacy of those mother-centered policies lingers.[42]

I saw that legacy firsthand in 2012, sitting with a fatherhood group at a California county office. The dads met weekly to talk about parenting, jobs, and navigating child support. They wanted to be present for their children yet felt unseen by the very systems meant to help families thrive. They spoke of love and commitment—and of the exhaustion that comes with being stereotyped as villains. What struck me most was a refrain I heard again and again: they had to learn to see themselves as caregivers, not only as wage earners. That shift changed how they moved through the world and fueled their advocacy for policies that included fathers.

Their stories reveal how tropes don't just exclude people from programs but also erode self-worth. As Matthew Desmond writes, "You may begin to believe, in the quieter moments, the lies told about you."[43] Joe Jones, founder of the Center for Urban Families in Baltimore, Maryland, sees it daily: "So many people come through our front doors with a look in their eyes that tells you in an instant they feel defeated . . . when they desperately want to do the right thing."[44]

The **"at-risk youth."** First popularized in the 1960s and 1970s, the term was meant to identify children vulnerable of dropping out of school or of delinquency.[45] But the label quickly hardened into identity.[46] Being called *at risk* lowers expectations, justifies harsher discipline, and narrows opportunity. It is often paired with *broken families*. As Professor Ruha Benjamin reminds us, "What we are called usually says a lot about what we are not called. To be labeled as gifted is to be deemed not at risk."[47] The focus on risk diverts attention from underfunded schools, disinvested neighborhoods, and systemic racism. It places the burden on young people instead of on the systems around them.

The **"nanny state."** Used as political rhetoric to dismiss regulations and public benefits, the phrase casts government as overprotective and infantilizing, treating adults as incapable of choice.[48] Like the terms welfare queen and deadbeat dad, it moralizes assistance, portraying collective investment as coddling and dependency. The metaphor belittles both public service and those who rely on it, feeding cynicism about government's role in shared well-being.

The **"breakdown of the family."** By the late twentieth century, this phrase became political shorthand for poverty itself, casting social and economic inequality as individual failure. Leaders like Reagan frequently used the image of the "broken home" to suggest not only that public programs had weakened self-reliance but also that "the breakdown of the family . . . has reached crisis proportions."[49] It also reinforced a narrow ideal of the "right" kind of family, implicitly judging single parents, divorced mothers, blended families, and anyone else outside a traditional two-parent household. This narrative blurred cause and effect. It blamed government for dependency while ignoring how wage stagnation, redlining, and disinvestment in communities had destabilized families in the first place. By framing hardship as a symptom of personal decline, the rhetoric of family breakdown deflected responsibility from policy design to private virtue; in doing so, it pitted the public against the very institutions meant to help people.

These tropes carry real consequences. When fathers are assumed to be absent, programs fail to support their presence. When youth are labeled as at-risk, their resilience is ignored. When families are described as broken, we blame parents and overlook how systems themselves have fractured opportunity. When government is dismissed as a nanny, we stop investing in people altogether. In every case, stigma substitutes for structure and blame crowds out design.

What tropes do in public discourse, heuristics do in the mind. Both flatten human complexity into shortcuts, shaping how we perceive others before we even realize it. They are the architecture of bias made visible, the cultural software that keeps inequality running in the background.

Narratives That Flatten and Separate

The most powerful cultural narratives are often the quietest. They speak in a whisper just beneath our mental awareness, shaping who we see as deserving of empathy and who must first prove their worth. Scholar john a. powell calls these "flattened stories." They strip away complexity, reduce people to symbols, and obscure the systems that shape their lives.[50] They guide our judgments before our thoughts ever catch up.

Social scientists call these shortcuts *heuristics:* mental patterns that help us organize information and make split-second assessments.[51] Our brains rely on them to navigate the world, filling gaps with what we already know—or think we know. They become our rules of thumb, efficient but biased. We gravitate toward stories that confirm the cultural frames we've inherited and the experiences we share.

These shortcuts help explain why, when many Americans picture someone on public assistance, they imagine a Black single mother, even though the largest group of recipients is white. Once that mental image takes hold, confirmation bias does the rest; we notice what fits the picture and ignore what doesn't.[52] When confronted with conflicting facts, we feel *cognitive dissonance*—the unease of contradiction—and often explain it away rather than revise the story.[53]

Psychologists Mahzarin Banaji and Anthony Greenwald call these hidden habits *mindbugs*.[54] Mindbugs are the mental glitches that cause even people committed to fairness to act in ways that sustain inequity. They aren't individual flaws so much as cultural software; these are stories written into our neural code. Naming them matters because it reveals that bias isn't just about personal prejudice but also about the residue of systems we've all lived inside. Heuristics, like narratives themselves, are not inherently harmful; they are the shortcuts that make human life possible in a world of constant information. The problem arises when they run unchecked—when we don't recognize the limits of our own mental scripts and they can be triggered and exploited to divide us, turning shared uncertainty into fear or blame. And like any software, these systems can be rewritten--once we recognize the code.

This is why shifting cultural mindsets is both difficult and essential. We don't just need new policies; we need new stories that become new mental defaults. We need stories that highlight resilience and potential, not caricature and blame. When we flatten people, we lose sight of their full humanity. And when systems adopt those same flattened stories, they fail too by replicating the distortions they were built to solve.

These flattened narratives redefine how we see poverty itself by reducing complex systems to simple labels and making it easier to assign fault. And that is how stories that divide and separate flow seamlessly into stories that blame, completing the loop that has shaped our national imagination for generations.

A Loop Reinforced by Blame

Over the past fifty years, we have absorbed a national story that treats poverty not as a shared failure but as a personal one. Politics, media, and psychology have all amplified it. The image of the "undeserving poor" was repeated so often it calcified into common sense.

Cultural myths like the bootstrap mentality supplied the guiding logic. America's faith in meritocracy became what sociologists call a *hegemonic narrative*—a story that explains inequality as the natural order of things.[55] If everyone supposedly has the same chance to succeed, then anyone who doesn't must have made bad choices. Poverty becomes proof of failure. Policy follows the storyline: aid turns into surveillance, support into suspicion. Stigmatizing programs reinforce stigmatizing stories, and the loop tightens.

The damage extends far beyond perception. People experiencing poverty carry the weight of that stigma. They absorb the shame and internalize the message that they—not the systems that exclude them—are the problem. That is the human cost of flattened narratives. Shallow stories erase the texture of real lives. Without context, compassion collapses; and when compassion collapses, so does policy.

We've been living inside this loop for decades, often without noticing. Each new crisis, whether personal or national, is treated as evidence that people bring extended hardship on themselves. That judgment comforts us with the illusion of fairness and licenses yet another round of punitive policy. The result is a cultural machine we keep cranking: crisis in, blame out, justification supplied, harsher rules delivered. It operates at every level—within families, within systems, within the nation itself—and keeps turning because it feels familiar.

But recognizing this pattern is the first step toward weakening it. Breaking the loop may not mean ending it entirely; history suggests that progress rarely moves in straight lines. It bends through struggle, learning, and renewal. The goal is not perfection but momentum: to fail forward, shorten each cycle of backlash, and widen the circle of belonging with each turn of the loop.

But blame is only one loop that we're caught in. The second is equally corrosive: the belief that poverty is inevitable. If the first mindset paints people as culpable, the second paints poverty itself as destiny. Entire neighborhoods, towns, and regions have been cast as permanently broken, as places where hardship is mistaken for fate instead of recognized as the result of disinvestment and neglect.

This fatalism is where we turn next. Chapter 4 explores how the story of inevitability—poverty as a permanent condition, often bound to place—deepens the loop and dulls our collective imagination. Breaking that pattern requires better policy design, a renewed belief that change is possible, and recognition that possibility itself is a public good.

CHAPTER 4

The Fatalism Trap

Why We Believe Poverty is Inevitable

The greatest threat to progress is not opposition—it's resignation.
—Adapted from community organizer wisdom

Fatalism is the projection of our ignorance of the causes of human suffering.
—Paulo Freire

We have been taught to mistake resignation for realism, but these voices remind us that fatalism is not truth. It is a story we can choose to unlearn.

If blame narrows our compassion, fatalism narrows our imagination. For decades, we have absorbed the message that poverty is not only widespread but *inescapable*—a stubborn fact that no policy or program can change. That belief breeds resignation; if hardship is permanent, then government efforts are wasted, and communities are destined to decline. Fatalism turns possibility into futility and resignation into common sense. But resignation is not inevitable. It is learned. And if we can learn it, we can unlearn it.

For nearly sixty years, we have been told two contradictory stories: poverty is both a personal failure and a permanent reality. Together they form a powerful trap: if poverty is inescapable, then government efforts to fight it are doomed from the start. And if government can't do anything about it, then poverty must be inevitable. This cycle—part cultural myth, part political tactic—has convinced generations of Americans that hardship is unsolvable and public investment a waste of effort.

This mindset has real consequences. Fatalism becomes a quiet policymaker. It justifies inaction, shrinks line items, and gives cover to cuts that would never pass if we believed change were possible. When resignation hardens into consensus, progress stalls. Fatalism convinces us not only that poverty is inevitable but that trying to end it is naïve.

Chapter 3 revealed how poverty has been framed as personal failure. This chapter turns to the second loop: the idea that poverty is unchangeable. When we see hardship as a fixed condition instead of a challenge to be addressed, resignation replaces determination. The story shifts from "they brought it on themselves" to "nothing can be done about it."

Here's where the trap tightens. Fatalism doesn't just follow blame, it reinforces it. As hardship is framed as permanent, distance grows. Poverty feels farther away, happening to other people, in other places. Government, too, begins to feel like "them," not a reflection of shared responsibility, but an external force that never quite works. In that space, it becomes easier to believe that poverty is both people's fault and a fixed condition. Blame and fatalism feed each other, narrowing what we believe is possible.

This sense of fatalism doesn't arise in a vacuum. It grows through repetition, through every headline declaring crisis inevitable, every budget framed as triage, and every conversation ending with "it is what it is." It is reinforced by how we talk about where poverty exists. Geography often serves as a proxy for judgment, shaping how we perceive entire communities before we even consider the people who live there.

Place as a Proxy for Stigma

When we think about people living in generational poverty, we don't think in abstract terms. We picture specific places. Certain regions have become shorthand for deficiency, carrying images and narratives that obscure their history and the policy choices that shaped them.

These associations are not imagined; they show up clearly in the data. "Persistent-poverty" counties—where poverty has remained above 20 percent for more than three decades—reveal sharp racial and geographic patterns. Black Americans, who comprise about 13 percent of the U.S. population, represent more than half of those living in these distressed communities. White Americans, by contrast, make up a much smaller share of persistent-poverty areas relative to their population. Regions like Appalachia, the Mississippi Delta, the rural South, the southern border, and parts of the Midwest carry the imprint of these disparities.

Regions Turned Into Stereotypes

American poverty has been mapped onto place for decades.

- **The inner-city** has served as coded language for poverty, crime, and decay in Black and Brown communities, flattening the legacy of redlining, disinvestment, and mass incarceration into stereotypes of dysfunction.[2]
- **The rural South** has been caricatured as backward and racially divided, obscuring both the history of extraction that impoverished the region and its deep traditions of resilience and mutual aid.[3]
- **Appalachia** has been portrayed as hopelessly dependent, defined by decline and, more recently, by opioid use, but rarely depicted as the site of labor movements or innovation that it is.[4]
- **Native communities** have been painted as desolate or "forgotten," their histories erased even as policies of land theft and broken treaties created the very conditions now labeled inevitable.[5]

These are not neutral descriptions of geography; they are cultural signals priming us to associate poverty with specific places and people. They trap whole communities in a story that says poverty isn't a problem to solve but a destiny that cannot be escaped.

As Kathryn Edin, H. Luke Shaefer, and Timothy J. Nelson write in *The Injustice of Place*, the places with the deepest poverty in America are also those with the most brutal histories—of slavery, of land theft from Native people, of Jim Crow, of labor exploitation.[6] Place itself has become a marker of exclusion, telling us who belongs and who does not.

Place carries the weight of history, but in popular discourse it is stripped of that context.

Images That Cemented These Stories

Photography and media coverage have reinforced these geographic stereotypes. During the 1960s War on Poverty, widely circulated images of Appalachian children wearing worn clothing and living in dilapidated homes reinforced the idea of a dependent, impoverished region.[7] Around the same time, nightly news broadcasts showed "inner-city" neighborhoods with stark images of burned buildings, police clashes, and decline.[8] The impoverished rural South became the butt of political cartoons and jokes.[9] Tribal lands were largely ignored except in moments of crisis.[10] These images left lasting impressions of incomplete stories, portraying poverty as the natural state of a place rather than the product of disinvestment and exclusion.

That pattern continues today. The public language we use—especially when entire cities are described as "dangerous dystopias"—is not only inaccurate but harmful.[11] Such narratives recycle old stereotypes in modern form, crowding out space for stories of progress, creativity, and resilience.

When Public Offices Become Symbols

Stigm also clings to the spaces where people encounter government systems. The welfare office itself became a cultural symbol of dysfunction, with long lines, worn buildings, plexiglass barriers, and security checks that signal futility over investment and suspicion over trust. Media, political rhetoric, and everyday jokes reinforce this narrow image, flattening complex realities. These depictions obscure the chronic underfunding and understaffing of public benefit offices, the skill and commitment of public servants, and the relief these programs provide to families. Instead, the office is reduced to a symbol of failure, a shorthand for "broken government" and "undeserving recipients."

These depictions stigmatize those who walk through the doors and reinforce a larger cultural shift of viewing government as "them" rather than "us." When that shift takes hold, fatalism grows. If "they" can't fix things, perhaps nothing can be fixed. Yet even as this image persists in the public imagination, it no longer tells the full story. Across the country, public agencies are redesigning service spaces as welcoming centers of support, often co-located with schools, libraries, and health clinics. These transformations, which we'll discuss in Chapter 8, show that when we change the environment, we can also change the story.

How Place Teaches Fatalism

This is how stigma operates on a geographic level. It allows us to distance ourselves from poverty by labeling it as belonging to "those neighborhoods" or "that part of the country." When poverty is seen as endemic to a place, it stops being a shared national problem and becomes a local pathology. By reducing structural neglect to geographic destiny, the story of inevitability is reinforced: poverty is not only someone's fault but also their fate.

These geographic shortcuts teach fatalism and prime us to see hardship as fixed in place, locked in history, and therefore beyond repair. That is the essence of fatalism: We stop treating poverty as a challenge to solve and start accepting it as a permanent fact of life.

That's why Dr. King's warning still cuts through with such urgency: "We are confronted with the fierce urgency of now. "[12] King spoke those words in 1967, but they remain vital today. Resignation is just another form of complacency, a surrender that keeps us from acting on what we already know is possible. To confront fatalism, we must reclaim our sense of agency and our collective resolve to meet injustice with action.

Fatalism doesn't just live in policy debates or media coverage. It seeps into our daily lives, shaping how we talk about hardship and what we believe is possible.

The Fatalism Trap: When Problems Feel Too Big to Solve

My mother often said, "It is what it is."[13] She usually meant it as reassurance when something bad had happened; it was her way of telling us not to worry about what we couldn't change. She wanted us to move on. Her instinct came from love, but it also reflected a common cultural reflex: to accept hardship stoically rather than ask what might be possible.

Many of us respond to poverty in the same way. When asked about the hardships it causes, Americans often say, "It's sad—but it is what it is. What can you do?" This shrug is not a lack of compassion. It is the product of living in a culture that emphasizes problems without context and rarely highlights what's working or where progress is being made.

The media amplifies this resignation. News stories fixate on dysfunction rather than success. Pundits speculate about causes before crises are even understood. Social media floods us with grief, fear, and outrage in what technologist Tristan Harris calls a "race to the bottom of the brainstem"—content engineered to hijack our most basic emotions.[14] We live inside a daily storm of "the sky is falling" coverage, a modern-day *Chicken Little* chorus.

Our brains are primed to absorb it. Negativity bias means we instinctively register threats more quickly and remember them more vividly than signs of progress.[15] That instinct once kept us alive, but in today's environment of constant information and disinformation, it backfires. It collides with another human tendency: we can only worry about so much at once. Flooded with messages about problems that seem unsolvable, we grow numb. Resignation becomes our default, not because we don't care, but because caring feels futile.

The Finite Pool of Worry

These crisis-focused stories don't exist in isolation; they tap directly into the way our minds ration attention. When we are already overwhelmed, we have less mental space to think about structural fixes. Poverty and inequality become vague, distant, easy to ignore as problems too big to solve. In that fog, the story of government failure feels natural, even inevitable.

Psychologists call this the *finite pool of worry*—the idea that we can only manage a limited number of concerns at once.[16] When worries about our own safety, jobs, or families take center stage, broader social problems fade into the background. The circle of concern shrinks.

False narratives exploit that limitation. When public attention is flooded with fear-based stories about immigrants, crime, or cultural decline, it leaves less space for focusing on real, solvable problems like affordable housing or child care. The emotional bandwidth consumed by division is bandwidth lost for progress.[17]

We've all felt it. We've all turned off the news not because we didn't care about the latest shooting, storm, or epidemic, but because we needed to protect our own emotional health. In those moments, we slip quietly into fatalism. Not out of malice, but out of exhaustion. That is what it feels like to reach the edge of your worry pool.

The danger comes when that edge becomes permanent. When fatigue hardens into belief, and belief shapes budgets. If every large-scale problem—poverty, inequality, injustice—feels inescapable, our expectations collapse. We begin to see policy as pointless. We lower our sights. We may even stop trying. And when that happens, fatalism becomes self-fulfilling.

When Systems Are Seen as Broken Beyond Repair

If believing that poverty is unavoidable breeds helplessness, then believing that our systems are beyond repair deepens the despair. For many Americans, it isn't just that poverty feels hard to solve; it's that the very institutions meant to help are seen as part of the problem. Across the political spectrum, we hear a familiar refrain: our public systems aren't working. Yet that apparent consensus masks very different diagnoses and leads to the same dead end.

On the political right, the dominant story emphasizes inefficiency and overreach: programs are cast as bloated, poorly managed, and wasteful. On the political left, critiques center on underinvestment and inequity: programs are seen as under-resourced, exclusionary, and unable to meet the scale of need.

Here's the challenge: both perspectives hold elements of truth, and both—when untethered from a shared commitment to repair—can lead to the same conclusion: that government itself can't be trusted.

"The system is broken" has become one of the most common phrases in American public life. Sometimes it serves as a call for reform, but increasingly it's used to justify inaction. Labeling social systems as permanently broken strengthens fatalism. It convinces us that poverty is inescapable, and that even imagining alternatives is naïve. When we think systems can't be fixed, we stop trying. We disengage. We give in to cynicism.

Stanford psychologist Jamil Zaki explains this shift in his book *Hope for Cynics*. Americans have long been skeptics, he notes, but are increasingly turning into cynics.[18] The difference matters. *Skepticism* asks questions and seeks information; *cynicism* suppresses curiosity and resists new ideas. Cynicism doesn't just corrode hope. It also corrodes trust, especially in government.

The numbers tell the story. According to the Pew Research Center, only about one in five Americans today say they trust Washington to do what is right "just about always" or "most of the time."[19] In the mid-twentieth century, that number was closer to three in four.[20] This collapse in trust feeds fatalism: If the government is seen as incapable or corrupt, then big challenges like poverty can't be solved. Resignation replaces resolve.

Long-standing tropes about government and its workers have only fueled this distrust. One of the most damaging is the old saying, "good enough for government work."[21]

> ### Good Enough for Government Work
> #### Once Meant Excellence
>
> The phrase most likely emerged during World War II, when "government work" referred to high-quality projects built for the war effort. Meeting rigorous standards for accuracy, safety, and durability, something *good enough for government work* once meant *the best*—built to endure.
>
> Over time, the meaning flipped. By the late twentieth century, the phrase had become sarcastic shorthand for mediocrity, suggesting that government work was done with minimal effort or low standards.[22] Long-standing stereotypes about public workers as lazy or ineffective reinforced this negative turn. This evolution captures a broader cultural shift from viewing government as capable and essential to dismissing it as inefficient and disposable.

The history of that phrase reminds us how easily cultural narratives can recast strength as weakness and how those stories, once entrenched, reshape public perception of government.

When we focus only on deficits—inefficiencies, gaps, failures—we diminish the capability of our institutions. When words like *ineffective*, *wasteful,* and *bureaucratic* dominate our descriptions of public agencies, we overlook the creativity, compassion, and quiet successes happening within them every day. This deficit lens harms not only the public but also public servants themselves, making it harder for those in government to see themselves as agents of change.

Throughout my career, I've spoken with staff at every level of human service agencies who internalize these negative narratives. When they hear, repeatedly, that their work doesn't matter—or worse, that it causes harm—it takes a toll. Morale suffers, innovation slows, and disillusionment spreads. Institutional internalized oppression spreads when the people inside systems start to believe the worst about the work they are doing.[23] And it is a direct result of the stories all of us have been told.

These patterns are not just abstract theories; they show up in the lived experience of the human services workforce itself. Chronic stress, diminished morale, and internalized narratives of ineffectiveness compound the very challenges staff are trying to solve. As Deborah Winograd and Beth Cohen argue in *Workaches: The Neuroscience Guide to Surviving and Thriving at Work*, the toll of these dynamics registers in both the brain and the body, shaping whether workers merely endure or are able to thrive within public systems.[24]

In conversations I've had with public sector leaders, many say one of their top priorities is helping their teams believe in their own effectiveness again. That shift begins with narrative—by reminding civil servants that their work matters, that government can do good, and that the public deserves systems designed to deliver on that promise.

Restoring trust, both inside and outside of government, is not naïve; it is essential. It is how we move from resignation to responsibility, and reclaim our capacity to design systems that deliver impact, belonging, and possibility.

Nostalgia as Reinforcement

Fatalistic thinking isn't sustained only by stories of government failure or the limits of human attention. It is also reinforced by nostalgia. Across the political spectrum, we are often invited to imagine an earlier time when things were simpler, safer, or more unified—an era when government supposedly functioned smoothly and communities cared for one another without friction. These stories tap into a very human longing for stability. But they also flatten history. They gloss over the exclusions, conflicts, and inequities that shaped earlier periods while implying that today's challenges are uniquely insurmountable.

We hear versions of this everywhere, from calls to "restore" what was lost to familiar laments that "things just aren't what they used to be." The trouble is that the past that is being invoked is selective. The midcentury prosperity so often idealized, for example, was built on racially exclusive housing policies, gendered labor norms, and a narrow definition of who counted as a full participant in civic life. Even the beloved image of small-town neighborliness overlooks the segregation and silencing that structured many communities.[25] When we romanticize that version of America, we mistake a partial story for a complete one. In doing so, we limit our sense of what's possible now.

Historians such as Jason Stanley and Timothy Snyder warn that this kind of nostalgia can be politically perilous.[26] It narrows our imagination by presenting the past as the best we could ever hope for. The present begins to feel like a decline, and the future a dead end. Nostalgia doesn't just comfort us. It convinces us that poverty, inequality, and division are permanent features of our national landscape. It replaces possibility with resignation.

When nostalgia blends with fatalism, it can erode trust in public institutions by suggesting that they once worked but don't any longer. It conditions us to expect less from government or to look for simple, sweeping promises of restoration instead of collective, democratic solutions. What begins as a sentimental story about "the good old days" becomes another layer of the inevitability trap.

The danger is clear: When we stop believing government can solve big problems, we begin to doubt democracy itself. We lose sight of the fact that public systems—however imperfect—are the shared scaffolding that allows us to weather change together.

But nostalgia can also be redirected. The yearning it reflects for community, reliability, and care is not misplaced. It is a clue to what we truly want from our democracy. What many of us miss is the sense of mutual responsibility that flourishes when public institutions are strong, fair, and trusted. As we explore in Chapters 6 and 7, our public systems can be redesigned not only to work better but also to work more equitably. Doing so requires us to challenge the defeatism that says they are beyond repair and to reclaim our collective capacity to build something stronger.

Using Scale to Fuel Futility

Even when we know individuals don't cause systemic poverty, many of us still cling to a persistent belief: the problem is simply too big. The numbers feel overwhelming. The need seems endless. And the story we absorb is simple: *this is just how the world is.*

We often hear about poverty through statistics: 37 million people living below the federal poverty line, 15 million in deep poverty, one in eight children growing up in it.[27] Advocates expand the view further, noting the millions living paycheck to paycheck, one setback away from crisis.[28] The numbers are staggering—a third of the country financially insecure. And even as I write them, I feel the pull of the trap I'm describing. Data meant to inspire collective action can just as easily numb us, making poverty seem inevitable or someone else's problem. When the story emphasizes only scale, the numbers become a reason not to act.

It's no surprise our first reaction is often to shut down. Psychologist Paul Slovic calls this *psychic numbing*—our compassion decreases as the number of people affected increases.[29] Our brains aren't wired to hold mass suffering. A single story can move us; a sea of zeroes can paralyze us. Faced with magnitude, we self-protect. We tune out.

We see this dynamic every day in headlines and political speeches. We are overwhelmed by percentages stripped of context, hope, or progress. Government mismanagement becomes the lead frame. Without examples of change, the numbers turn into a drumbeat of despair.

But numbers can tell a different story. PolicyLink, for instance, reframes the issue by highlighting not just those below the poverty line but the more than *100 million Americans* facing economic insecurity—crossing race, geography, and political lines.[30] That shift turns a statistic into a coalition. Reverend William Barber II makes a similar point in *White Poverty*, reminding us that hardship touches millions of white families as well as Black, Brown, and Indigenous communities.[31]

"Human stories can get lost in zeroes," writes Jacob Harold, former CEO of GuideStar.[32] Yet, as he also notes, "math is a way to honor the things that matter."[33] The challenge lies in how we tell the story—whether numbers become evidence of futility or roadmaps for what's possible. When used well, data can reveal patterns, track progress, and drive change.

Too often, the facts get buried. Instead of registering progress, we register paralysis. We dismiss solutions even when there is evidence they work. Consider the 2021 expansion of the Child Tax Credit, which temporarily increased benefits for families with children and delivered monthly payments.[34] The result? Child poverty in the United States was cut nearly in half within six months.[35]

This wasn't theory. It was action. It showed, in real time, that large-scale progress is possible when policy aligns with human need. Yet the moment passed quickly when Congress didn't renew the policy.[36] The reasons were complex and contested, but they had little to do with whether the policy worked. The larger loss was narrative. Even a clear success was recast as unsustainable, reinforcing the belief that big progress can't last. That is the fatalism trap: even when something works, we doubt its staying power.

But it doesn't have to be this way. When we stop seeing poverty as inevitable, we start seeing it as intolerable. Numbers, framed as stories of progress and possibility, can cut through resignation. They remind us that we are not passive onlookers to decline: we are the authors of its reversal.

The Zero-Sum Game Narrows Our Imagination

Fatalism also feeds on the widespread belief that prosperity is a zero-sum game. If resources are finite, then helping "them" must come at the expense of "us." This reasoning turns every policy debate into a contest between groups and narrows our imagination of what's possible.

As Heather McGhee shows in *The Sum of Us*, this mindset has skewed American policy for decades by pitting communities against one another while hiding the truth that shared investments in schools, infrastructure, and public health actually strengthen us all.[37] Zero-sum logic doesn't solve poverty; it normalizes it as the cost of someone else's comfort.

Together, zero-sum thinking and fatalism shut down our capacity to see shared solutions. Yet history proves otherwise. The United States has repeatedly shown that collective action can solve big problems.

Social Security is a clear example.[38] Before its creation in 1935, poverty among older Americans was widespread and severe. Many who could no longer work survived only through family, charity, or poorhouses. Within a generation, Social Security cut elderly poverty dramatically, offering a reliable income that allowed millions to retire with dignity. Today, Social Security remains the most effective antipoverty tool in modern history; without it, about 22 million Americans would fall below the poverty line.[39]

Medicare offers another powerful example. When it was created in 1965, nearly half of Americans age sixty-five and over lacked health coverage. Within a few years that percentage fell sharply; by 2012, just 2 percent remained uninsured.[40] Today, Medicare is one of the nation's most trusted programs. It has extended life expectancy and financial security for older adults.

Yet despite their reach and impact, programs like Social Security and Medicare are rarely included in our dominant welfare story. They are rebranded as "social insurance" or "health care," as though they were exceptions rather than core pillars of our public well-being infrastructure. This selective storytelling matters. By spotlighting government failures while treating its successes as invisible, we reinforce the myth of inevitability and overlook the evidence that disproves it.

> ## Proof and Possibility:
> ### Evidence That Defies—and Reveals—Fatalism
>
> Across U.S. history, major public programs have shown that poverty and insecurity are *not* inevitable. When we invest collectively, progress is measurable and swift.
>
> **Social Security (1935–today)**
>
> - **Before:** Widespread and severe poverty among older Americans.
> - **After:** Poverty rates for seniors dropped dramatically within one generation.
> - **Today:** Lifts more than 22 million Americans above the poverty line, including over 16 million adults age 65 or older.
>
> **Medicare (1965–today)**
>
> - **Before:** Nearly half of people over age 65 lacked health insurance.
> - **After:** Coverage expanded rapidly; by 2012 only 2% were uninsured.
> - **Impact:** Increased life expectancy and financial security for older adults.
>
> **Child Tax Credit Expansion (2021)**
>
> - **Action:** Monthly cash payments to families with children.
> - **Result:** Cut child poverty nearly in half within six months.
> - **Aftermath:** Allowed to expire after one year, showing how fatalism can erase progress even when results are undeniable.
>
> **The takeaway:** When we choose bold, collective solutions, significant progress is possible. The real barrier isn't capacity or cost; it's the stories we tell about what government can and cannot do.

Zero-sum thinking collapses in the face of these examples. From Social Security to Medicare to the Child Tax Credit, the record shows that when we commit to collective solutions, poverty can be reduced quickly and dramatically. Government can expand opportunity and strengthen the social and economic fabric for everyone. But too often, we hear the opposite story, and in repeating it, we mistake habit for truth.

Metaphors That Unintentionally Reinforce Fatalism

As we saw with the War on Poverty, metaphors don't just describe problems, they define what we believe can be solved. They act as mental blueprints, shaping our sense of possibility before a single policy is written. Too often, even our most well-intentioned metaphors work against us, reinforcing hopelessness instead of imagination.

Take one of the most familiar metaphors in antipoverty work: "breaking the cycle of poverty."[41] On the surface, it highlights how hardship can pass from one generation to the next through barriers like underfunded schools, limited jobs, or intergenerational trauma. But the metaphor of a cycle carries an unintended message: that poverty is as a perpetual motion machine—endless, mechanical, unbreakable. It often doesn't spark solutions; it breeds futility. Worse, it shifts the focus back to the individual: What did you do—or fail to do—to escape?

Another common metaphor is "trapped in poverty."[42] It's meant to evoke urgency and empathy, but it implies passivity and helplessness. Traps immobilize. They often require rescue from the outside. To be "trapped" is to wait for someone else to act.

Both metaphors strip away agency. They suggest people in poverty are static rather than striving, waiting to be rescued instead of navigating impossible choices every day. They create distance instead of solidarity and obscure the external forces that constrain options.

Even seemingly technical language like "the poverty line" reinforces fatalism.[43] Lines are fixed; they divide. This framing oversimplifies a continuum of insecurity, in which millions hover just above eligibility thresholds yet still struggle to afford rent, food, or health care.[44] It turns the poverty into a binary condition rather than a spectrum shaped by housing, health, caregiving, and community support.

Perhaps the most enduring metaphor is "the war on poverty." As discussed in Chapter 2, the language of war was meant to motivate urgency, but it set impossible expectations. Wars have enemies, victories, and clear endings. Poverty does not. This framing conditioned Americans to expect rapid triumph from long-term work and to equate ongoing effort with failure. Worse, war metaphors divide the field into *allies* and *enemies*. When progress is slow and budgets rise, the public doesn't blame the metaphor; they blame the people doing the work. This is the fatalism embedded in our language; even metaphors of urgency and care can backfire, becoming frames for futility and blame.

Metaphors aren't just words; they are conceptual containers. They shape how we process information, the emotions we attach to it, and the limits we place on it. If we want people to believe poverty can be solved, we must use metaphors that widen the lens.

What if, instead of *cycles*, we talked about *forging new pathways* so policy and community move forward together? What if, instead of *traps*, we focused on *lifting burdens that weigh parents down*?[45] What if, instead of *waging war on poverty*, we concentrated on *building what communities need to thrive*?

In chapter 5, we'll explore metaphors tested by cognitive scientists that can shift thinking in this direction. But first, we need to confront an even deeper fatalistic mindset: the belief that government itself is beyond repair.

When Government Becomes "Them"

In recent decades, a subtle but powerful shift in our thinking about government has taken hold. It is no longer widely seen as *us*—a reflection of our collective will—but as *them*—an external, inefficient, even hostile force.

This shift didn't happen overnight. It was built over decades through political rhetoric, media caricatures, and public frustration—some justified, much manipulated.[46] By the 1980s, even the language of family decline was used to indict public programs, turning social concern into a failing of government itself. Phrases like *big government, welfare bureaucracy*, and *entitlement state* became shorthand for dysfunction and waste. The work of civil servants, often invisible and thankless, was reduced to punch lines. Public institutions, once recognized as essential infrastructure for a functioning democracy, became the target of cynical jokes.

And here's the danger: When government is seen as *them*—as something apart from the people—it stops being a tool of democracy and becomes a target of discontent. Research from the FrameWorks Institute shows that many Americans now view government not as an extension of our collective will, but as an opponent to our interests.[47] We've been conditioned to be both skeptical and suspicious of government. In this framing, agencies are no longer tools of democracy—they are faceless *others*. We forget that they are staffed by people working every day to solve urgent and complex problems.

This detachment has real consequences. It lowers public trust. It discourages civic engagement. It erodes our ability to see government as part of our community. And it reinforces fatalism. If the very institutions meant to serve people face are seen as broken or illegitimate, then poverty looks unsolvable by definition.

When we lose the ability to see government as a partner in human well-being, we forfeit one of our most potent tools for collective care. When government is cast as *other,* poverty as inevitability is confirmed because no one believes our shared tools can be used for change.

The through line is clear. Whether through corrosive metaphors or corrosive distrust, fatalistic thinking hides the functioning of public systems. It conditions us to see these systems as broken symbols rather than as living structures that shape daily life. Reclaiming possibility begins with seeing government again, not as an abstraction or stereotype, but as an essential *part of us.*

From Fatalism to Possibility

Fatalism tells us that poverty is permanent, systems are broken beyond repair, and our best option is resignation. But like blame, fatalism is not destiny. It is a story taught, repeated, and absorbed until it feels like truth. If resignation can be learned, it can also be unlearned. And when we refuse inevitability, we create space for imagination. In that space, possibility returns. We begin to see poverty not as an unchangeable fact of life, but as a challenge we have the power and the responsibility to confront together.

Blame tells us poverty is a choice; fatalism insists it is permanent. Together, these narratives form closed loops that have held American thinking for more than half a century: if hardship is both someone's fault and beyond repair, then nothing needs to change.

Fatalism Across Eras

- **19th Century:** Moral and religious fatalism that poverty is divine will or personal fate.
- **Mid-20th Century:** Political fatalism that government is ineffective or overreaching.
- **21st Century:** Civic fatigue, or the belief that collective change is too hard or too late.

Each version narrows our sense of agency.

Fatalism is not new; it has surfaced in every era when progress slowed or hope seemed naïve. What feels distinct about today's version is its scope—a civic fatigue that tells us big change is no longer possible. Yet history itself refutes that story and reminds us hope can be relearned. It invites us to imagine what comes next.

What happens when we reject fatalism? What if, instead of resignation, we chose resolve? Imagine a nation where poverty is not treated as destiny but as design—something we created, and therefore something we can dismantle and rebuild into a system that works for all of us.

Breaking the loop requires more than new policies. It requires new ways of seeing. It requires us.

SECTION II

Systems in Plain Sight

Neither the life of an individual nor the history of a society can be understood without understanding both.

—C. Wright Mills

Section I explored the stories we carry. Section II turns to the structures that surround us. To move beyond individualism and fatalism, we must understand how systems actually work, not as abstractions, but through the daily realities they create for individuals, families, and communities.

These systems are often invisible until they fail. Yet they are always at work, shaping choices, opportunities, and futures through design or neglect.

If fatalism tells us nothing can change, visibility is the antidote. When we make systems tangible and see how they shape daily life, we replace despair with possibility. By bringing hidden systems into view, we reclaim the power to make them work for all of us.

Chapter 5 opens with a foundational shift for this section: learning to see systems clearly. Visibility is what allows us to direct effort where it matters and begin rebuilding the scaffolding that supports us all.

CHAPTER 5

Well-Being Is Constructed

What Surrounds Us: Shapes Us

> Most of us cherish the notion of free choice, but our choices are constrained by the conditions in which we are born, grow, live, work and age.
>
> —Michael Marmot

In the United States, we've been taught that well-being is something earned through hard work and personal discipline. If you succeed, you must have deserved it. If you struggle, it must be because you didn't try hard enough. This belief runs so deep in our culture that it barely feels like a belief at all—it feels like truth.

But what if well-being doesn't work that way?

What if it isn't just the product of grit or good choices, but something more collective—something built, maintained, and shaped by the systems that surround us? When I was leading the American Public Human Services Association, this insight came up again and again in our conversations with frontline workers, leaders, and communities. We eventually captured it in a line that still guides how I think about this work: *We build well-being from the ground up.* Human services exist to shape the conditions that allow people to live, work, and thrive; they are the quiet architecture of daily life. What surrounds us shapes us and social systems are the foundation.

This chapter widens the lens on well-being. Section I examined how cultural narratives shape what we believe about welfare and poverty. Now the book turns to how systems shape what people actually experience. Together, these beliefs and structures form the terrain that determines whether any of us can live a full, healthy life—or not.

The starting point is simple but profound. Human well-being is constructed; it doesn't happen automatically. It doesn't spring from good intentions. And it can't be willed into being. It is created brick by brick, policy by policy, relationship by relationship through the social systems that form the foundation of our lives. As systems theorist Donella Meadows reminds us, systems are "interconnected sets of elements that generate their own patterns of behavior over time."[1] When we begin to see systems this way, they come into view everywhere: in the schools we attend, the jobs we hold, the health we enjoy, and the communities we call home.

A Mindset Shift In Plain Sight

Most of us rarely think about systems until they break; but when they do, they snap them into view.

When COVID-19 struck, the health care system was not the only system suddenly visible.[2] Millions of us encountered human services in ways we had not imagined. Parents relied on expanded tax credits to make ends meet. Families turned to rental assistance to avoid eviction.

Broadband subsidies kept classrooms open online. For the first time, many households received Pandemic EBT cards—electronic benefit transfers traditionally associated with food benefits—to replace school meals lost during closures. That small piece of plastic made a public system suddenly visible and personal. What had once been seen as "for others" became shared resources, revealing how interdependent well-being really is. For a fleeting moment, the scaffolding of well-being was visible to everyone, not just to those who had accessed it before.

This was not unlike the breadlines of the Great Depression. Photographs in national magazines showed rows of men in coats and hats, shoulders hunched against the cold, waiting silently for a bowl of soup. For many Americans, that was the first time poverty appeared not as a distant misfortune but as a visible public emergency. The sheer scale of need made it impossible to maintain the illusion that hardship stemmed only from personal failure. Poverty was revealed as the product of faltering economic systems, not individual shortcomings.

Similarly, the images of cars stretched for miles outside food banks during COVID-19, echoing the breadlines of the 1930s, made visible what had long been denied: hardship was not a matter of individual weakness, but of systems not always working for people.

The Great Recession offered another window into visibility. Mortgage markets collapsed, jobs evaporated, and foreclosures swept across suburbs once thought secure. For many, the first sign was the sight of empty homes, with mail piling up, lawns untended, foreclosure notices taped to the door. Families who had never interacted with unemployment insurance, food assistance, or housing supports now found themselves navigating these systems for the first time. Just as with the Great Depression and the pandemic, what had seemed stable suddenly looked fragile. Well-being was revealed as less secure and more dependent on shared scaffolding than many of us had believed.

The racial justice movement that surged in 2020, after the murders of George Floyd and Breonna Taylor, offered yet another kind of visibility. Millions of people across race, class, and geography saw that policing and justice systems were not neutral backdrops but active forces shaping life and opportunity. For some, it was a first direct encounter with the idea that racism is not simply about personal prejudice, but about social structures.

As with the pandemic, the Great Recession, and the Great Depression, this movement pulled hidden systems into the light—this time around race and justice—forcing us to confront what had long been denied. It also raised a deeper question: *once we see systems clearly, will we choose to change them?*

Moments of crisis illuminate hidden scaffolding and reveal how fragile our supports can be. The challenge is not whether systems become visible in crisis, but whether we can learn to see and strengthen them in plain sight, all the time.

> **When Systems Become Visible**
>
> Think of the systems that shape our lives as scaffolding around a building. From a distance, it may look strong and stable. But when stress tests it, the weak points show.
>
> - **COVID-19 shutdowns** severely shook the economic and social sides of the scaffolding, revealing how thinly reinforced our supports for food, housing, childcare, and income security had become.
> - **The 2020 racial justice movement** exposed fractures on the justice side, showing that protections meant to guarantee safety and fairness were unevenly applied and, for many, actively harmful.
>
> Both crises pulled hidden structures into view. They reminded us that our well-being—and our democracy—rest on scaffolding we all need. And we can repair, strengthen, and redesign that scaffolding.

The pandemic and the racial justice protests were not separate stories but parallel awakenings. COVID-19 exposed how precarious our economic and social scaffolding had become, when millions discovered overnight that paychecks, food access, and housing security all rested on fragile supports. The renewed racial justice movement revealed a similar truth about justice: the safety, fairness, and equal protection were not stable guarantees but conditional—unevenly distributed and too often withheld.

Both moments forced us to confront that the structures we take for granted are not natural or inevitable. They are designed, maintained, and therefore capable of being redesigned. When scaffolding holds, people thrive. When it cracks, people fall. When it fails entire communities, the collapse becomes impossible to ignore.

These national awakenings were mirrored in my own leadership journey. As head of the American Public Human Services Association, I watched public systems rise to the occasion through true partnership with communities, showing both how interconnected our systems are and what they can become when they work together. At every level—federal, state, county, and local—human services professionals moved mountains to meet unprecedented needs. They adapted programs to deliver services safely and partnered with community organizations to ensure children and families had access to meals, health care, and education during the shutdown.[4] That experience reinforced for me what crises always reveal: systems are not abstract. They are living structures. And when we put our collective will behind them, they can adapt and serve.

For a time, the American story shifted. In those shared moments of heartache and hope, needing help was no longer a personal failing, but a shared reality. Yet these shifts in perception are fragile.

Rev. William Barber II likened COVID-19 to a medical contrast dye, illuminating the hidden poverty and inequality embedded deep in American life.[5] The pandemic revealed both the essential role of our systems and their weak points. We saw the lifesaving power of human services and the devastating consequences of decades of underinvestment. Human service leaders recognized the pattern: in earlier crises, the seams had also shown, as during the Great Recession, when cash-assistance programs couldn't meet the surge in demand.[6]

The lesson is clear: making systems visible is not enough. Seeing systems clearly means confronting where they fail, and recognizing the urgency of reimagining them. That is the challenge, and the possibility, we turn to in the next chapter. Because if we can see systems, we can change them.

Cognitive Dissonance and the Possibility of Change

Psychologists describe cognitive dissonance as the discomfort we feel when lived experience collides with deeply held beliefs.[7] Often, we minimize or rationalize the conflict to protect our prior beliefs. But sometimes that discomfort opens a door. It creates space to see—and, at times, believe—differently.

For many Americans, directly encountering systems they once thought of as "for others" creates exactly this kind of dissonance. Standing in a food bank line. Applying for unemployment insurance. Receiving a Child Tax Credit check. Each action feels out of sync with the story that self-reliance alone secures well-being. In that moment of tension, we can began to see these systems in a new light, not as symbols of failure, but as collective scaffolding that makes well-being possible.

When this dissonance leads to recognition rather than denial, it can be transformative. That shift from denial to recognition opens the door to wider questions: *what are the systems that shape our experiences, and why are these systems so hard to see?* Experiencing social systems firsthand punctures the myths of individualism, separation, and inevitability. It reminds us that we are not isolated strivers, but interdependent people whose well-being rests on shared foundations.

Once we experience a social system firsthand, the myth of separation begins to crumble. What once seemed like purely personal achievement or market-driven success—keeping a job, raising a family, building a business—reveals itself as part of a shared structure, sustained by public investment, collective risk-pooling, and the often-invisible labor of care that makes markets possible in the first place. Seeing that interplay clearly is part of seeing systems at all.

What Are Social Systems—And Why Don't We See Them?

We live within systems every day, though we rarely name them as such, even when we rely on them constantly.

Consider health care. It is one of the most recognizable systems, a vast network of services, policies, and institutions designed to prevent illness, provide treatment, and promote public health. It includes hospitals, clinics, insurers, regulators, and countless professionals. It involves the daily interactions of patients, providers, and government agencies, all working—sometimes smoothly, sometimes not—to keep people healthy. And yet, we tend to notice the system most when it breaks: when a family member falls ill and needs care, when insurance denies coverage, and when services become impossible to navigate.

But our social systems extend far beyond health. They shape the neighborhoods we grow up in, the schools we attend, the jobs we can access, and the care we receive as we age. They guide who gets second chances, who gets locked out, and who gets the benefit of the doubt.

So why don't we see them?

Because we've been trained not to. Our dominant narrative of individualism tells us that people succeed or fail based on personal effort, and that outside influences don't matter. That belief narrows our vision. It zooms in on individual choices and zooms out from the conditions that shape those choices. When we lose sight of conditions, we lose sight of the systems that create them.

That invisibility is uneven. Many of the systems that sustain people with privilege—professional networks, alumni ties, financial institutions, cultural expectations—are coded as neutral, simply "the way things are." Their scaffolding feels natural and legitimate. But when people without that same access receive support, it is often labeled as dependency or welfare. Hierarchy hides itself by normalizing the systems that advantage some while stigmatizing the systems that help others. Still, for most of us, systems only come into view when something breaks.

The Blended Nature of Systems

There is another reason systems remain hard to see: they rarely exist as purely "public" or purely "private." Every scaffolding of care—from child care to health care to housing to education—is built from both public and private beams. Most of us move between them without noticing.

Families with means often access human services through private markets—daycare centers, counseling, home health care—while others rely on public programs or community organizations funded by the same tax dollars. In truth, the distinction is more porous than we imagine: public systems subsidize private ones, and private systems depend on public infrastructure. When either side falters, the entire structure shakes.[8]

We tend to notice these systems only in short bursts, most often when something fails. The bus doesn't come. The water line bursts. The tax refund is delayed. The hospital miscodes our insurance. In those moments, the weakness in the scaffolding shows. But once our problem is fixed, our attention slips and the system fades from view again.

Let's be clear. Systems don't stop operating when we stop seeing them. They are always at work, shaping opportunities and outcomes. The real question is whether we are willing to recognize them as real and as changeable.

World War II rationing provides a vivid example. Families across America were issued ration books for sugar, meat, gasoline, and even shoes.[9] Suddenly, the distribution of resources was no longer invisible market activity but a national system everyone could see. Rationing transformed daily life and reinforced the idea that government could—and should—manage shared well-being in a time of crisis. It was not framed as shame or stigma, but as fairness and contribution. Everyone was asked to play a role in constructing the nation's resilience.

These wartime measures also reveal a challenge: systems should not become visible only during moments of crisis. The ration books disappeared after the war, but the underlying need for ongoing, fair distribution remained. Truly seeing systems requires zooming out, not just noticing them when we need them ourselves or when they fail. We need to recognize social systems as the ongoing infrastructure that supports us all. Unlike a physical ration book or an EBT card, systems often fade into the background, but they do not disappear. They continue shaping lives and opportunities, whether we acknowledge them or not.

Seeing systems is only the first step. We also need to remember nothing is fixed in place. Systems are dynamic: constantly adapting, shifting, and responding to the choices we make. The next question is not just whether systems evolve, but whether we choose to shape how they do.

Systems Are Not Static

One of the most paralyzing myths about social systems is the idea that they just exist.

We treat them like the weather, beyond our control and inevitable in their outcomes. The rules are the rules. The forms are the forms. The process is the process. And when those rules cause harm, the common refrain is: "That's just the way the system works."

But here's the truth: systems don't just work. They are worked. They don't just exist. We build them. They are created, maintained, and modified by people—by us. By people inside the system, with job descriptions, budgets, authority, and institutional memory. People who inherit rules yet also have the power to question them. People who often feel trapped by the very systems they administer. And they are shaped by people outside the formal system who access services, contribute to their communities, and advocate for change.

Recognizing that systems are designed by us also means recognizing our agency to redesign them. Nowhere is this clearer than in the field of human services—the sector most directly charged with constructing well-being in daily life. This is one of the most liberating truths about human-serving systems: they are not static. They are human constructs, carrying the imprint of the time and values in which we create them, and carrying within them the power to be redesigned.

If we built these systems once, we can rebuild them better.

Constructing Well-Being: A Frame For Human Services

When we talk about *human services*, we mean the systems and infrastructure that shape life journeys as surely as roads or bridges shape travel. These are the systems that show up when life gets complicated: when a parent needs child care to keep working, when a family faces eviction or illness, when someone is aging and needs support. They include child and family supports, food and housing assistance, behavioral health care, aging and disability services, and the community-based organizations that knit these systems together.

Human services are where policy meets people and where public commitments become tangible in everyday life. Yet because these systems are often invisible until they falter or we need them, we tend to see them through a deficit lens: as crisis response, bureaucracy, or "help for other people." In truth, they form the scaffolding that helps all of us weather change and build stable lives. Every person, at some point, will rely on these systems—directly or indirectly—just as we rely on schools, roads, or clean water.

> **Human Services in Plain Sight**
>
> Human services are the structural supports that keep our communities standing and adaptable. They steady individual lives and, together, uphold the framework of our democracy.
>
> - **Child care and family supports** lay the foundation for education, work, and family stability across generations.
> - **Housing assistance** anchors families and neighborhoods, preventing the small cracks from widening into crisis.
> - **Food and nutrition programs** reinforce community strength, circulating resources that nourish both health and local economies.
> - **Behavioral health care** restores balance, strengthening the human capacity to adapt and rebuild.
> - **Aging and disability services** extend the life of our shared structure, ensuring everyone remains part of the whole.
> - **Community organizations and navigators** serve as the connectors—the beams and joints—that hold the system together when pressure mounts.

When human services function well, they reinforce stability and belonging. They prevent crises, support recovery, and make well-being possible across generations. When they fail, the consequences are highly visible: lost financial security, deepened inequity, and fractured trust. Seeing these systems clearly—understanding that well-being is constructed through intentional design, not chance—is the first step toward strengthening them for fairness, reliability, and belonging.

In this sense, human services are not charity or last-resort aid. They are civic infrastructure—the scaffolding that allows communities to adapt, connect, and thrive. The quality of that scaffolding depends on how it is designed and maintained, and on how accessible, reliable, and human-centered it is. Well-being is not something we achieve individually, but something we build together through interdependent systems. And behind those systems is a workforce whose reach is far greater than most people realize.

The Quiet Reach of the Human Services Workforce

To see human services as infrastructure, we also have to see the scale of the workforce that makes that infrastructure real.

Human services are not a niche sector. They sit within one of the nation's largest and most locally rooted public workforces, alongside education, public health, environmental protection, transportation, and other essential civic functions. When we talk about public benefits and social supports, we are also talking about the people and organizations that make up a vast civic workforce.

A major public employer. State, county, and municipal governments together employ more than 19.6 million people across these public functions, making government service one of the largest anchors of local labor markets nationwide. Local governments alone account for 14.2 million workers, providing frontline services in most U.S. communities.[10]

A workforce hidden in plain sight. Within this broader public sector, the human services field is estimated to employ more than 3 million workers—separate from the public health workforce. These are the people who translate policy into practice every day: eligibility workers, social workers, case managers, aging and disability specialists, early childhood administrators, licensing and quality-assurance staff, community navigators, and more.

A broader publicly driven ecosystem. The reach of public systems extends far beyond government payrolls. In the largest U.S. cities, about 31 percent of all jobs are tied to publicly funded sectors—including government, education, health care, and social services.[11] This publicly anchored employment base helps stabilize local economies, especially during downturns when private-sector jobs contract.

A powerful nonprofit partner network. Community-based organizations form the other half of this ecosystem. Nonprofit human and social services providers employed 12.8 million people in 2022—nearly 10 percent of all non-government workers.[12] Many operate under public contracts, extending the economic footprint of government into thousands of neighborhoods.

An engine for local economies. Taken together, this human services ecosystem is an economic force in its own right: it employs tens of millions, anchors local spending, and keeps dollars circulating through neighborhood businesses. What these workers do each day—

support families, stabilize communities, and strengthen well-being—is also what helps local economies remain resilient.

Why it matters. This reach is more than a set of numbers. It is a reminder that human services are part of the nation's core infrastructure—every bit as foundational as schools, transportation, or public safety. When we invest in human services, we invest in the people and institutions that hold communities together.

What We See When We Only See "Programs"

Human services are among the most quietly essential systems in American life and still among the most misunderstood. Public conversation often fixates on a narrow set of programs, such as food assistance or cash support, which are both highly visible and heavily stigmatized. But human services extend far beyond these debates.

They include child protection and foster care, mental health and substance use treatment, disability supports, job training and workforce services, housing assistance and homelessness prevention, elder care, and community development. Together, these systems shape whether children grow up safe, whether families can weather crises, whether older adults can live with security, and whether communities can thrive.

Seen in this fuller light, human services are welfare in its truest sense: investments in our collective well-being. They are not bureaucratic fixes for individual failure, but systems that translate shared values into daily life.

When designed and resourced well, human services are proactive rather than reactive, stabilizing lives before crisis takes hold. When they are framed narrowly or starved of support, they appear fragmented, stigmatized, and ineffective. Design, not intent, makes the difference.

During my years at the American Public Human Services Association, we worked with the National Human Services Assembly and the FrameWorks Institute to develop a more effective way to talk about human services.[13] The metaphor that resonated most powerfully was construction.

Well-Being Is Built

Like buildings, the conditions that support well-being must be designed, resourced, maintained, and updated. Human services are the scaffolding of a healthy society, providing the materials, labor, and tools that help people lay strong foundations and weather life's inevitable storms. Scaffolding is never the end goal. Its purpose is to steady us as we construct something lasting: systems rooted in belonging and well-being for all.

I remember when we first introduced the construction metaphor to sector leaders. Many were skeptical: *What does construction have to do with human beings?* But they quickly learned the power of a metaphor that works. It gave all of us a common vocabulary to describe what human services really do.

When we think about construction, we understand that it requires planning, coordination, skilled workers, and multiple tools. We know that structures don't simply appear; they are assembled piece by piece, through intentional design and care. The stronger the foundation, the stronger the building. Even the idea of designing for resilience—

building to withstand the elements—translates directly to supports that help people weather hardship.

More importantly, this metaphor shifts the focus from deficits to capacity. Instead of asking, *what does someone need to fix about themselves?* it asks: *What systems are—or aren't—in place to support the well-being of all of us?*

That shift matters. It shows how the language we choose can reshape how entire sectors see their work and how the public understands it. It makes the often invisible labor of human services visible as the everyday scaffolding of thriving communities.

> ## Safety Net vs. Scaffolding
>
> **"Safety net"** is often used to describe public benefits or welfare. On the surface, it sounds reassuring. But the metaphor carries hidden limitations:
>
> - A net is used only in emergencies, implying that support is rare and temporary.
> - It imagines catching a single person who has fallen, reinforcing a story of individual failure.
> - Falling into a net suggests stigma, and that help is needed only when something goes wrong.
>
> By contrast, **"scaffolding"** conveys an entirely different picture. Scaffolding is part of every construction project; it surrounds, stabilizes, and supports progress. It stays in place as long as needed, and it can be used whenever structures need repair. It is not shameful or rare—it is expected.
>
> By shifting our language from safety nets to scaffolding, we change how people understand human services. They are not a rescue from a fall, but an everyday structure that helps all of us build strong lives and communities.

A Window Into Our Shared Infrastructure

The pandemic offered a rare moment of narrative clarity: systems are not for *them*. They are for *us*. All of us.

Lines at food banks included families driving SUVs as well as those arriving by bus. Teachers and students alike depended on public broadband to keep classrooms open. Parents who had never applied for assistance suddenly relied on unemployment insurance or financial subsidies.

For a brief window, Americans experienced what many in human services had long known: well-being is built collectively, not individually.

But as with earlier eras, this awakening was temporary. Supports receded. The visibility of systems dimmed once again.

The challenge before us now is to make that visibility permanent. It is to treat human services not as a crisis patch, but as infrastructure for thriving, as essential as roads, power grids, or clean water.

We've done it before. The launch of Medicare in 1965 offers a glimpse of what's possible when systems are permanently restructured. For decades, older Americans who had retired were effectively excluded from the private health insurance market. Within just a few years of Medicare's creation, the uninsured rate for people over age 65 plummeted.[14] What had once seemed like an inevitable hardship—aging without reliable health care—was redefined as an unacceptable failure of the system. By constructing something new, the country reshaped what was possible for older adults' health and well-being, offering a glimpse of what can happen when invisible systems are made visible, and then intentionally redesigned.

From Invisibility to Possibility

Well-being is not earned through grit alone. It is constructed through the systems that surround us. When those systems are visible, the myths of inevitability and blame begin to lose their grip.

But visibility is only the first step. Seeing the scaffolding does not repair its cracks. Understanding systems does not automatically change them. That work requires courage, truth-telling, and imagination. This is the work we turn to next. Chapter 6 takes a wider view and asks: *once systems are visible, how do we confront both the ways they harm and the ways they heal—and summon the will to redesign them for fairness and shared well-being?*

Because systems don't just hold us back: they can also carry us forward to the future we choose.

Reconstructing Well-Being: When A Vision Becomes A Movement

Across the country, communities are proving that well-being can be constructed by design. In San Diego County, California, a vision launched in 2010—Live Well San Diego—has grown into a fifteen-year civic movement that now includes more than 600 recognized partners across cities, schools, businesses, and neighborhoods. Together, partners have tracked meaningful changes across multiple indicators of community well-being over the initiative's first fifteen years, including long-term reductions in deaths from preventable health conditions and progress on education, safety, and other measures that reflect collective impact rather than isolated programs.[15]

What began as a public health framework has become a shared way of civic life. Community leadership teams convene residents to solve problems together, youth and elders collaborate on local projects, and an annual *Live Well Advance & School Summit* draws thousands to celebrate what they've built. When I attended one of those gatherings, the energy was unmistakable with public servants, advocates, and families cheering one another's progress. It was a reminder that when people see themselves as part of the design, systems become movements, and movements become culture.

CHAPTER 6

The Dual Edge of Systems

How They Harm and How They Heal

> We can have all the empathy in the world for a group of people and still participate in the structures and systems that oppress them.
>
> —Valarie Kaur

In the last chapter, we saw how crises make the scaffolding of well-being suddenly visible and how the systems that hold us together can also reveal their cracks. Visibility is only the beginning. The real question is what we do once we can see the beams and bolts of our shared structure. *Do we repair what's broken, or allow the weight to settle unevenly again?*

Once we can see systems clearly, neutrality is no longer an option.

This chapter examines what happens when systems falter, why accountability matters, and why redesign is not just possible but necessary. When we recognize that systems are not static or inevitable but living structures, we also recognize our power to demand change.

The dual edge of systems is not just philosophical: it is practical. Once systems come into view, the question becomes whether we let that visibility fade, or use it to insist on accountability, repair, and redesign.

From Visibility To Accountability

As we've seen, moments of crisis often make the scaffolding of well-being suddenly visible—the breadlines of the Great Depression, the housing collapse of the Great Recession, the mass reliance on food assistance during COVID-19. Each revealed how deeply our well-being depends on more than individual effort. These glimpses matter. They remind us that systems shape opportunity alongside personal grit.

Crises don't create inequity; they expose it. The supports that carry some people through upheaval often existed long before the emergency began: family wealth, stable jobs, reliable housing, inherited networks. For others, that scaffolding has been missing for generations: the result of policies that excluded whole communities from the very foundations of security. Economic shocks make these differences visible for a moment, but they are not temporary problems. They reveal a permanent design gap: a structure built to hold some steady while leaving others to rebuild from scratch each time.

Even recent federal strategies aimed at strengthening economic well-being—such as the Biden administration's *Facing a Financial Shock* framework—frame stability largely in terms of short-term emergencies, noting, for example, that "38 percent of Americans would face difficulty absorbing an unexpected $400 expense."[1] The real task is broader. It is ensuring that scaffolding exists for everyone, not as a temporary fix but as a durable design of shared security. That is not an act of charity. It is a policy choice, and a democratic responsibility.

But as much as this book is about visibility, that alone is not enough. Empathy without action fades quickly. Systems drift back into old patterns. Accountability is what turns recognition into repair. When we hold systems to their promises—by demanding equitable access, redesigning outdated structures, and centering the voices of those most affected—we begin to shift them from harm toward healing.

Accountability opens the door. Redesign walks us through it. True repair means more than preventing harm; it means creating systems that embody presence, care, and belonging.

Each moment of visibility has a shadow. The same programs that reveal our collective capacity to care often ignite backlash once they prove effective. When the New Deal expanded jobs and security, critics warned of dependency. When civil rights legislation widened belonging, opponents called it overreach. When the expanded Child Tax Credit cut child poverty nearly in half, narratives of "undeservingness" re-emerged within months. In our public imagination, progress still triggers a reflex of suspicion. This is the dual edge of systems in action: the very capacity to heal can provoke the fears that undo repair.

The Dual Nature of Systems

When people say "the system is broken," it can sound as if dysfunction is accidental. In truth, systems often work exactly as designed. A program that limits aid, a policy that excludes whole groups, or a law that stigmatizes families may look like failure from one perspective, but from another, it reflects deliberate choices made at particular moments in history. To confront these realities, we need the courage to acknowledge that harm is not incidental. It is structural. And there can be no reconciliation without first accepting that truth.

Human services systems have always carried this dual nature. They can be lifelines that stabilize families and help communities navigate difficult times. As explored in Chapter 2, the creation of Community Action Agencies in the 1960s embodied the idea of "maximum feasible participation," placing communities in the driver's seat of anti-poverty strategies.[2] The launch of the Head Start program similarly recognized that supporting children's well-being must begin in the earliest years and requires attention to families and communities, not just classrooms.[3] These programs showed how design could expand opportunity with inclusion in mind, and they inspired more recent efforts to apply human-centered design to social services, a topic we'll revisit in Chapter 9.

History also reveals that systems can stratify, exclude, and harm. Policy decisions, institutional practices, and cultural assumptions often interact in ways that deepen inequity. The cap on TANF in the 1990s, combined with time limits and restrictions that intensified over the next two decades, did more than alter that one program; it reinforced a mindset that rationed assistance and pushed more families into deep poverty.[4] Housing and lending systems in the mid-twentieth century codified racial segregation through redlining, embedding those practices in banks, zoning boards, and real estate markets and shaping neighborhoods and wealth patterns that endure today.[5] Child support enforcement laws, rooted in presumptions about absent fathers, ignored the diversity of family structures and the realities of what children actually need to thrive.[6]

I have seen this dual nature firsthand in child welfare. Policy changes now allow young people in foster care to remain in care beyond age eighteen—under some state laws, up to age twenty-three or longer if they are still in school.[7] This shift has made a profound difference, ensuring continued access to housing, health care, and other supports as young people step into adulthood. For each young person, it can mean the difference between stability and crisis.

Yet for decades, far too many children have entered foster care in the first place not because of abuse, but because our systems failed to support their families early enough. The absence of adequate income supports, housing stability, and community resources has disproportionately affected families of color, turning child welfare into a system that too often reflects inequity rather than repairing it.[8]

Both realities are true at once. The same system can expand opportunity through thoughtful policy and practice while also reproducing harm through its design and history.

Child Welfare at a Crossroads

- **Extended care matters:** Young people who remain in foster care past age eighteen are more likely to complete high school, pursue higher education, and avoid homelessness.[9]

- **Disproportionate entry:** Black children make up about 14 percent of the U.S. child population but nearly 23 percent of those in foster care. Similar disproportionalities exist for Latinx and Indigenous children.[10]

- **System-driven removals:** Most children enter foster care due to neglect linked to poverty, not abuse, underscoring how unmet basic needs, rather than parental harm, often drive family separation.[11]

- **Policy shift:** The Family First Prevention Services Act of 2018 marked a turning point by allowing federal funds to be used for prevention services that help families stay together. While limited in its scope, and unevenly implemented, the law signaled a growing recognition that systems can—and should—move upstream.[12]

- **A path forward:** Research consistently shows that strengthening front-end supports—income stability, housing, and community resources—reduces unnecessary foster care placements and keeps families intact.[13]

These examples remind us that systems are never neutral. They carry the imprint of the people and politics that shaped them. To move forward, we must tell the truth about where systems have caused harm, not to dwell in blame, but to make room for redesign. When we see systems in their full complexity—both their capacity to connect people to lifelines and their long history of exclusion—we can finally ask the right questions: *What must we deconstruct? And what will we choose to build now?*

As john a. powell reminds us, structural marginalization often operates less through overt acts of bias than through the steady drip of policy, practice, and neglect.[14] Over time, institutions channel opportunity toward some groups while systematically denying it to others. Time, in this sense, is not only lost but stolen. Systemic inequities function like a slow theft of life chances—not always dramatic, but relentless and generational—accumulated through the design and daily operation of our systems.[15]

Derrik Anderson of Race Matters for Juvenile Justice uses a racetrack analogy to describe how this inequity plays out.[16] Not everyone begins at the same starting line. Not everyone runs in the same lane. And not everyone faces the same barriers along the way. Some runners encounter hurdles every few yards, while others sprint on smooth ground.

Over time, these unequal starting points and obstacles compound, producing vastly different outcomes. Education, housing, health care, justice, and employment systems do not operate in isolation; they intersect. For historically marginalized communities, disadvantage accumulates as underfunded schools, unstable housing, limited access to health care, and over-policing reinforce one another. The result is not a single setback, but a lifetime of constrained possibility that is passed down across generations and embedded in the very systems meant to serve us all.

These patterns of cumulative harm are not abstract. They surface most clearly when public systems are tested, and they are too often found wanting. The cases that follow show how design choices, funding structures, and political decisions determine whether systems cushion hardship or compound it.

Case Studies: When Systems Falter

Seeing where systems falter teaches us that harm is not random. It is built into design choices and policy structures. Three examples—TANF during the Great Recession and beyond, the COVID-19 pandemic, and child care supports—show how systems can be revealed as inadequate or misaligned.

TANF: A System Hollowed Out

When the Great Recession struck, unemployment soared and millions of families faced financial collapse. Yet the nation's core cash-assistance program barely moved. Temporary Assistance for Needy Families (TANF) has been frozen at $16.5 billion since 1996, and its real value has eroded by more than 40 percent. Fewer than 1 in 5 families living in poverty now receive any TANF aid; in many states the monthly benefit is less than $500 for a family of three, barely a week's rent. States routinely divert funds to plug budget gaps or finance unrelated initiatives, leaving the people it was created to serve almost invisible.

TANF was not broken during the recession; it was working exactly as designed to limit access and reinforce a narrative that help must be scarce.[17] Unlike unemployment insurance, which expanded automatically with need, TANF's funding had been frozen as a block grant since 1996.[18] In effect, states were expected to meet skyrocketing demand with the buying power of a decade earlier. While a few states accessed emergency funds, most had no new federal resources and many chose not to expand their rolls at all.[19]

That design choice has had lasting consequences. Today, TANF is a shell of its intended purpose.[20] Benefits vary widely depending on where a family lives, and in many states they amount to only a few hundred dollars a month, far below the poverty line.[21] Research shows that states routinely divert TANF funds away from direct cash aid into other programs.[22] Even the program's statutory purposes encode the same restrictive narrative, reflecting policy choices that prioritize regulation over security. The four statutory purposes of TANF, codified in the 1996 Personal Responsibility and Work Opportunity Reconciliation Act, embed the program's underlying narrative of conditionality and moral judgment: (1) to assist needy families so children can be cared for in their own homes; (2) to end dependence on government benefits by promoting job preparation, work, and marriage; (3) to prevent and reduce out-of-wedlock pregnancies; and (4) to encourage the formation and maintenance of two-parent families.[23]

These purposes reveal how behavioral regulation, rather than economic security, was written into TANF's design.

Housing: A Silent Erosion

Housing assistance tells a similar story. Since the 1980s, federal rental-aid funding has fallen steadily in real dollars even as housing costs have soared. Only about one in four households eligible for rental assistance now receives it, and waiting lists in most cities stretch for years. Incremental cuts and shifting priorities have thinned a program once conceived as a stabilizing pillar into a patchwork of scarcity.[24] These reductions rarely make headlines, but they shape lives daily by determining who sleeps safely inside and who does not.

The pandemic underscored this lesson, showing in real time how the strength—or fragility—of public systems shapes who is protected and who is left exposed.

COVID-19 as Teacher

The pandemic laid bare how deeply systems shape well-being. As we have already explored, expanded supports such as the Child Tax Credit briefly cut child poverty nearly in half.[25] Rental assistance helped keep families in their homes, and emergency food benefits reduced hunger. At the same time, COVID revealed how fragile many of these supports were, and how quickly backlash can erase progress. When the expanded Child Tax Credit expired, child poverty nearly tripled within a few years, a stark reminder that gains built on temporary political consensus can vanish the moment that consensus cracks.[26]

School nutrition offers another clear example. Millions of children rely on free or reduced-price school meals. When schools closed, that lifeline was suddenly severed. Districts scrambled to set up grab-and-go sites or shift benefits to SNAP,[27] but many families without reliable transportation or internet access fell through the cracks. Few states could readily connect data on children receiving school meals with families enrolled in SNAP, exposing how poorly connected our education and nutrition systems are, and how essential those connections become during disruption.[28]

COVID-19 also reminded us that systems can adapt quickly when there is political will. But it showed just as clearly how easily thinly constructed or disconnected systems collapse under strain and how quickly protective gains can reverse when supports are temporary rather than structural. Well-being depends not only on the strength of individual programs, but also on how they link together to meet people's needs in real time.

Nowhere is this more evident than in child care—essential to families and the broader economy, yet long treated in the United States as optional.

Child Care Supports

For decades, the United States has underinvested in child care. Families have been left to cobble together fragile arrangements or pay more than they can afford, while the workforce providing care remains among the lowest paid in the economy. The result is a system that functions less as shared infrastructure and more as a private market serving a public necessity.[29] Families who can afford to pay out-of-pocket do; the rest patch together what they can. The child care workforce absorbs the shortfall through chronically low wages.[30]

The consequences are stark. In many states, the cost of full-time, center-based care for an infant exceeds in-state college tuition.[31] Low wages drive high turnover among providers, making reliable care hard to find and further constricting supply.[32]

The pandemic magnified these existing weaknesses. When schools and centers closed, millions of parents—disproportionately women—reduced their work hours or left the workforce altogether. Child care providers operating on razor-thin margins shut their doors permanently. But the truth is that parents were facing these impossible choices long before COVID-19.

Child care is not simply a family concern; it is a cornerstone of the nation's economic and social infrastructure. Like TANF, it shows how system design choices—what we choose to fund, what we leave to private markets, and what we label as "personal responsibility"—shape outcomes for millions of families.

> **Child Care in America:**
> **A Public Good in a Private Marketplace**
>
> Few systems reveal the dual edge of design more clearly than child care. It is a public necessity delivered largely through private markets, exposing how underfunded scaffolding fails families when they need it most. Yet with sustained investment, child care could become one of the nation's strongest foundations of well-being.
>
> **Challenges:**
> - **High cost:** In many states, the cost of infant care exceeds in-state college tuition.
> - **Limited reach:** Only one in six eligible children receives federal child care subsidies.
> - **Underpaid workforce:** Child care workers earn less than $15 an hour on average, and more than 100,000 left the sector during the pandemic, exposing its fragility.
>
> **Potential:**
> - **High return**: Every dollar invested in early childhood programs yields long-term benefits in education, health, and economic mobility.[33]
> - **Stronger economy:** Affordable, stable child care boosts parents' workforce participation and strengthens local economies and communities.

TANF, child care, and the pandemic responses are not isolated examples. They are windows into how our scaffolding of well-being reflects the priorities we set. Seen side by side, they remind us that accountability begins with recognizing this dual nature: the same structures that can cushion families in hardship can also deepen inequality when they are designed—or allowed—to fail.

These more visible breakdowns, however, tell only part of the story. Systems can also falter in quieter ways, through the slow erosion of neglect and avoidance

The Larger Truth

Taken together, these cases show how the scaffolding of well-being can either crack or hold, depending on its design. Some failures are sudden and dramatic—such as the scramble to sustain school meal programs when classrooms closed, or the child care system buckling under COVID-19. Others unfold more quietly, through what we might call drift.

Over time, neglect, underinvestment, or shifting political priorities can hollow out systems without a single new law being passed. TANF's block grant has lost more than 47 percent of its value since 1996 simply through inflation.[34] Child care funding has risen and fallen with political tides, leaving families in chronic uncertainty.

Drift reminds us that design is never static. Choices made—or deferred—accumulate over time, shaping who has access to opportunity and who is left out. Whether through sudden shocks or the slow erosion of neglect, the lesson is the same: systems reveal the values we embed in them. And if we want systems that truly support well-being, we must have the courage to design them that way.

Backlash And The Pull To Invisibility

Visibility alone is never secure. When systems come into view, reform is not guaranteed. Exposure can open the door to redesign, but it can also trigger backlash that pulls systems back into invisibility.

We saw this dynamic after the pandemic. Expanded food benefits, rental assistance, and the Child Tax Credit showed that poverty could be cut dramatically when families are stabilized. As soon as the emergency faded, however, the old narrative of scarcity and personal responsibility reasserted itself. Supports were rolled back with little public debate, treated as a fleeting exception rather than as evidence of what is possible when we invest together.

The same pattern followed the 2020 racial justice movement. For a moment, millions of us acknowledged that policing and criminal justice are not neutral backdrops but powerful systems shaping daily life and opportunity. Conversations about structural racism moved into the mainstream. Yet within months, the pendulum swung back. Legislatures moved to restrict protest, limit how history and systemic racism could be taught, and reinforce punitive law-and-order frames. The system was not "broken"—it was reasserting its design.

History shows this pattern is not new. The War on Poverty produced groundbreaking programs like Head Start and Community Action Agencies, but it also provoked political backlash that fueled decades of rhetoric about dependency and waste. Each cycle teaches the same lesson: visibility is fragile unless it is paired with accountability and redesign.

The pandemic brought that cycle into sharp relief once again. Public investments that kept families afloat were quickly recast as evidence of government excess. Rising inflation became shorthand for a broader claim that we could not afford to invest in people at that scale. But this was never only an economic argument; it was a narrative one, too. It reflected a deep reluctance to imagine abundance—to see shared well-being as infrastructure rather than indulgence. We have long had the means to build systems that sustain stability. What we have lacked is the shared will to name that investment as essential.

Backlash thrives because it draws on familiar cultural stories: that government cannot be trusted, that resources are scarce, and that individuals must succeed or fail on their own. These stories push systems back out of sight, shifting attention away from structures and onto individuals, especially those already bearing the greatest burdens.

Our challenge, then, is not only to bring systems into view but to keep them visible—to illuminate both their harms and their benefits, and to resist the stories that erase them. As Valarie Kaur reminds us, for America to reconcile with itself, we must "push as a nation" to see how "harm runs through generations."[35] If we are the ones to create systems, then we are also the ones with the power and the responsibility to redesign them.

Deconstructing To Rebuild

Seeing systems clearly also requires the courage to confront the harm they have caused. Some structures were never broken; they were built to exclude. The first step in redesign is acknowledging where design itself has failed—or where it has succeeded only for some. Deconstruction is not destruction. It is an act of honesty that clears the ground for rebuilding.

When we deconstruct systems, we are not abandoning the idea of structure; we are reclaiming it. The same scaffolding that once upheld inequity can be rebuilt for equity. Accountability and imagination must work in tandem to take apart what harms us so that we can create what heals us. Every redesign begins with that shared choice: to face what is, and to build what could be.

Deconstruction does not mean tearing down everything. It means telling the truth about the design choices that shaped our systems and then deciding what to keep, what to repair, and what to replace. As Ben McBride writes in *Troubling the Water*, "Deconstruction doesn't just happen for the sake of itself; we deconstruct in order to build a new foundation."[36] This is painstaking work, but it is also liberating. It shifts the conversation from "Is the system broken? " to "What was this system designed to do—and what should we design it to do now?"

Take TANF again. By design, its block grant structure locked in scarcity and placed discretion in state hands. That choice served a political purpose—limiting the reach of cash assistance—while reinforcing cultural narratives about who "deserves" help. When we name that truth together, we reclaim the power to redesign it. TANF can become more than a test of worthiness; it can become a foundation for long-term family success.

Deconstruction also requires us to reconsider power. For too long, many systems have been designed from the top down, with policymakers and administrators making decisions far from the communities most affected. Government inherently holds more structural power than someone seeking help. When a person walks into a benefits office or logs onto an online portal, the system already knows more about them than they know about it. It holds their personal data. It determines whether they qualify for services. It generates cookie-cutter questions with little space to explain what's really happening in their lives. That is *power-over,* not *power-with.*

Redesign means flipping this dynamic: engaging families, frontline workers, and community partners as the architects of new structures. We'll explore how to in Chapter 9, but the following sidebar offers a preview. When communities have a genuine seat at the table, our systems don't just become more effective—they become more resilient, responsive, and legitimate.

Questions for System Redesign

When we take apart what harms, these questions guide how we build what heals:

- Who benefits most from the current design—and who is left out or harmed?
- How do we know? Whose experiences and data are included, and whose are missing?
- Who makes the decisions? Whose voices are at the table, and whose are absent?
- What values are embedded in today's rules and practices, and do they align with our commitments now?
- If we were starting fresh, who should help shape the design—and how would they define success?

Asking different questions is the first step toward building different systems.

Too often, our instinct is to tinker at the margins by simplifying forms here or adjusting funding there, but without confronting the deeper assumptions embedded in design. Tinkering cannot undo structures that were never built for equity in the first place.

Truth-telling, in this sense, is not about blaming or shaming the people who work inside public systems. It is about uncovering the structures that shape their work and the lives of the people at the heart of their mission. We need to distinguish between constructive critique—naming how systems harm so they can be repaired—and the constant, unproductive blasting of government institutions and public servants. As Professor Barbara McQuade warns, "The nonstop narrative of government misconduct can create the impression that the government is mostly dysfunctional and corrupt."[37]

That is precisely why deconstruction requires a counterforce: a way of reframing not only what is broken, but what is possible.

Sociological storytelling offers one such path. By narrating individual experiences in ways that reveal broader social forces, we can connect personal stories to systemic truths. When we listen to families navigating eligibility mazes or workers constrained by rigid rules, patterns emerge that numbers alone cannot capture. These stories invite us to see more clearly, to empathize more fully, and to build systems that work better for all of us.[38]

Abolition as Presence: Designing for What We Need to Exist

At times, redesign requires us to imagine life without certain structures altogether. Abolitionist traditions—whether confronting slavery, prisons, or other harmful institutions—remind us that some systems are so deeply rooted in inequity that they cannot simply be patched. Abolitionist thinking asks not only how to reform what exists, but what new possibilities emerge when we create entirely new alternatives.[39]

From Resistance to Construction

Consider the Free Breakfast for Children program created by the Black Panther Party. Beginning in 1969, local chapters organized before-school meals in church basements and community centers, run entirely by volunteers.[40] The Panthers understood that no child could learn on an empty stomach and that providing nourishment was as much an act of justice as protest. Their program built the structures of care they wished already existed.

Its impact was profound. Historians note that the Panthers' example helped inspire the USDA's School Breakfast Program.[41] What began as radical community care was eventually institutionalized as a public good. This is the power of abolitionist thinking: creating supports so effective and necessary that society adopt them.

We often hear abolition described as removal, as the tearing down of what causes harm. But true abolition, as organizers from the Panthers to today's community-care networks remind us, is an act of construction. As Ruth Wilson Gilmore writes, "Abolition is not absence; it is presence."[42] In this sense, abolition is both imaginative and practical: the creation of structures of care, safety, and well-being robust enough that punitive systems become obsolete.

Designing Presence

Abolition as presence reframes public systems as spaces of possibility rather than of control. It calls us to build the conditions that make caring for one another part of daily life—systems rooted in belonging, where deprivation is unthinkable. Healing does not come from dismantling alone; it comes from replacing absence with abundance.

Presence is not abstract. It is the daily work of designing supports that embed care, safety, and belonging into our civic infrastructure.

Abolition Is Presence
Practical Examples

Presence looks like this:
- **Community Power:** Participatory budgeting, design councils, and community land trusts that keep decisions and assets in community hands.
- **Economic Security:** Guaranteed income and simplified, integrated access to benefits that reduce stigma and volatility (frequent swings in income, benefits, or expenses that make it hard for families to plan, remain housed, or meet basic needs).
- **Housing & Basic Needs:** Housing First approaches with wraparound services, eviction diversion and right-to-counsel, and community hubs for essentials such as food, diapers, and benefits navigation.
- **Health & Healing:** Community health workers, medical–legal partnerships, and school-based health centers that meet people where they are.
- **Family & Child Well-Being:** Family Resource Centers, home visiting programs, and kinship-first supports that keep families together.
- **Education & Youth Justice:** Community schools, restorative justice, and diversion programs that replace punishment with growth.
- **Safety & Crisis Care:** 988 crisis lines, mobile response teams, and community stabilization centers that offer care, not handcuffs.

Abolition in Practice

During my time working with state and local leaders, I saw how deconstruction and redesign can take root when systems invite those most affected to lead change. One vivid example comes from child welfare, where agencies across the country are partnering directly with youth and parents who have experienced foster care to reimagine the system's purpose.

For decades, the child welfare system was built around surveillance and removal, supposedly protecting children by separating families. But across the country, efforts are shifting that design from *proving* harm to *preventing* it. Current and former foster youth are helping design peer navigation programs and youth-led councils that shape policy from the inside. Parent leaders are working alongside caseworkers to co-create family resource centers, home-visiting programs, and kinship-first supports that keep families together.

These are not quick fixes; they are cultural reorientations. Redesign begins when our systems listen differently: when we stop asking, *How do we enforce compliance?* and start asking, *How do we help families thrive?* This is abolitionist thinking in practice: creating structures so responsive and humane that they become common sense.

Redesign is not easy work. It demands both imagination and courage. But without it, we remain stuck patching systems that were never meant for everyone. By facing how we built them, we give ourselves permission—and responsibility—to construct something for all of us.

Toward Redesign And Renewal

Deconstruction is not an end in and of itself. Naming harm, tracing design choices, and exposing gaps are necessary steps, but they are not sufficient. The point of truth-telling is to clear the ground for building anew.

The work ahead is about renewal, reimagining systems not as relics of past choices but as living structures we can reshape for the common good. That means investing in human services as essential infrastructure, designing policies that reflect today's realities, and measuring success by belonging and equity, not just efficiency or growth.

History reminds us that redesign is possible. Programs like Head Start and the expansion of nutrition assistance through SNAP did not emerge by accident; they were built through deliberate choices about the kind of society we wanted to be. The same opportunity is before us now.

Seeing systems clearly is only half the work. The other half is remembering that we have the power to reshape them, and that imagination itself is civic muscle. When we recognize that design belongs to all of us, participation becomes not a burden but an act of shared possibility.

The question is whether we will summon the imagination and the will to do it again. Our social systems are human-made, which means they are human-changeable. They will continue to shape our lives one way or another. The choice before us is whether we allow them to perpetuate inequality—or whether we claim our power to use them to construct well-being for all of us.

From Deconstruction to Design

Every system carries the harm it inherited and the healing it could hold. Seeing that duality clearly is an act of power. Once we understand that design choices created these outcomes, we can choose differently.

The next chapter turns outward, to the forces that test that resolve—economic volatility, disinformation, climate disruption, and more—and to what it will take for our public systems, and for us, to meet them with courage and imagination.

Because the systems we inherit do not define us. The systems we choose to build do.

CHAPTER 7

The Forces We Face

And The Resolve to Face Them

We made the world we're living in, and we have to make it over.
—James Baldwin

The forces we face today may seem new—artificial intelligence, climate displacement, rising disinformation—but they do not meet us on blank terrain. They collide with cultural narratives we have carried for generations. The bootstrap myth tells us to treat technological disruption as an individual problem of "reskilling" rather than a collective challenge of shared security. Radicalized tropes about welfare resurface in debates over who deserves help when families face rising costs, sudden hardship, or forces beyond their control. Fatalism convinces us that global volatility or partisan division are simply the way things are, not problems we can solve together. These modern pressures expose how old stories of deservingness and individualism still script our responses. Unless we confront those stories, they will continue to narrow our imagination of what is possible.

At this point in the book, we have peeled back the narratives that distort our understanding of poverty. We have examined the systems that shape well-being and the ways those systems have been designed, both to help and to harm. We have named the gap between what is and what could be. And we have seen that repairing our social contract requires more than reform. It requires imagination, courage, and truth.

Now we must face the world we are entering, not to fear it, but to prepare for it. We are living in a moment of extraordinary convergence, when multiple forces are reshaping our lives with accelerating speed. Climate instability, racial backlash, population change, digital disruption, economic volatility, and political polarization are not distant threats. They are here. They are colliding. And they are testing every institution—and every narrative—we have inherited.

This is truth-telling, not alarism. And as we saw in Chapter 6, systems cannot change without it.

Facing The Truth—How New Challenges Test Old Narratives

To meet this moment, we must understand the forces reshaping our lives not only as threats but also as tests of who we are and what kind of society we are willing to build. These forces can accelerate harm if left unchecked, but they can also accelerate progress if we design with equity in mind. Artificial intelligence and new technologies, for example, could deepen inequality or become game changers for access and opportunity. A changing climate could widen divides or spark new models of shared resilience. How we act now will determine whether these forces pull us toward retrenchment or push us toward justice, solidarity, and shared well-being.

This chapter is about preparedness, not panic. It is about understanding the world we are entering and recognizing that human services are not peripheral to it, but central.

When designed well, human-serving systems are democracy's connective tissue. They hold communities together through instability and form the scaffolding we need to flourish. They absorb shocks, support mobility, and strengthen resilience. In moments of mass disruption, they can do more than protect us from harm. They can channel change toward greater fairness and belonging. When neglected or politicized, however, these systems weaken. They are easily torn apart and too often blamed for injuries far too many of us endure.

The questions before us are simple: *Are we preparing these systems for the world we are entering? Or are we still organizing them around stories of a past that never included everyone in the first place?*

Each of these forces climate change, technology, shifting demographics, economic volatility, and political polarization is vast in scope. Entire books are devoted to each, and for good reason. My purpose here is not to provide a comprehensive account, but to bring them into focus and connect them to why human services matter. These are the currents already reshaping our daily lives, and they will determine whether our systems are resilient or brittle, equitable or exclusionary. If we fail to see the connections, we risk leaving human services out of the very conversations where they are most essential.

The forces before us are real. So is our power to reshape them.

Global And Economic Volatility: Interdependence Without Infrastructure

In the early 2000s, globalization was often framed as a rising tide: a seamless integration of markets, people, and technology that would lift prosperity and drive innovation across borders.[1] But a series of shocks soon revealed the limits of that optimism—the 2008 financial crisis, waves of refugee displacement, rising authoritarianism, the COVID-19 pandemic, inflation, and increasingly frequent supply-chain breakdowns. Each exposed the same truth: interconnectedness without infrastructure is not resilience. It is fragility.

As in our past, hardship today is too often miscast as individual weakness rather than structural failure. Global volatility, especially during economic downturns, is still narrated as personal failure: another test of resilience instead of a call to strengthen shared infrastructure.

The economic volatility has not stopped.[2] Housing, food, and energy costs continue to climb. Work is increasingly fragmented, with more people navigating contingent, contract, or gig arrangements that offer flexibility for some but little stability or protection for many. AI advancements threaten entire lines of work. Retirement savings shrink. And those already navigating instability are still told to bootstrap their way through systemic disruption. This is not sustainable.

We like to believe that work is the surest route to security, that a job is the ticket to a better life. But in truth, work alone has never guaranteed stability in the United States, and the cracks in that belief are widening. Wages have lagged behind the real cost of living for decades, leaving even full-time workers juggling impossible trade-offs. As *Broke in America* reminds us, work "is often not a way out of poverty" for millions of people.[3] And today, with artificial intelligence transforming jobs at a pace unprecedented in our history, as Emad Mostaque details in *The Last Economy,* the promise that work will protect us is growing even more fragile.[4] When hard work is not enough to keep a family afloat, the story we need to interrogate is not about effort, but about the systems that shape opportunity in the first place. This outcome is not accidental. It stems from treating public systems as marginal rather than central to our collective well-being.

We live in an interdependent world, but we have not built systems that reflect that reality. Our economy can shift in real time, yet human-serving infrastructure remains slow and inflexible, too often constrained by eligibility thresholds, paperwork, and outdated assumptions. The mismatch has consequences. In times of volatility, people need something they can count on. Not just stimulus checks or temporary relief, but durable infrastructure of care and connection. Human services should serve as that infrastructure, yet we have treated them as reactive safety nets rather than essential supports.

Digital disruption adds another layer. Emerging digital currencies and rapid shifts in online banking introduce new forms of volatility, even as households struggle to maintain basic stability.[5] During COVID-19, unemployment insurance systems buckled under record demand. Antiquated technology delayed payments for months, leaving families without income while rent and bills piled up.[6] Human services staff worked around the clock to patch systems never designed for such strain. This was a stark reminder that our care infrastructure must be as resilient as our financial infrastructure.

But what if we built differently? What if we designed human-serving infrastructure with the same urgency and foresight we bring to markets and defense? What if we leveraged the ingenuity of community-based organizations and paid them fairly?[7] What if we invested not merely to mitigate harm, but to maximize resilience? Volatility is not going away. Families are living it every day. And the next major crisis, whether economic, climate-driven, health-related, or geopolitical, is not a matter of if, but when. The question is whether we will be ready.

We can learn from other nations that have built public infrastructure to automatically stabilize households during economic upheaval, rather than waiting for political will after the fact. Many European countries, for example, rely on automatic stabilizers that expand unemployment insurance and social protections when joblessness rises—preventing families from falling into poverty during downturns.[8] Universal health coverage in many nations similarly ensures that access to care is not tied to employment, reducing vulnerability during recessions or pandemics.[9] In Germany, wage subsidies through *Kurzarbeit* allow employers to reduce hours rather than eliminate jobs, with the state covering lost wages. This keeps workers connected to employment and accelerates recovery once conditions improve.[10]

These examples show what resilience looks like when infrastructure is designed to be proactive. By contrast, the United States often waits until a crisis hits, then scrambles to patch holes with temporary fixes.

Building durable infrastructure for well-being means drawing up the plans before the storm arrives.

For human services, this means designing systems that can flex with people's lives—linking income supports, housing, and care networks so help expands automatically when instability rises. When these stabilizers are built into the scaffolding of daily life, human services become not just responders to crisis, but engines of collective security and trust.

Resilience is not luck. It is design.

From Economic Volatility to Fragile Democracy: Economic shocks do more than strain households; they erode trust. When people experience instability without a reliable infrastructure of support, they are more likely to lose faith in institutions and more vulnerable to disinformation that offers simple villains and false certainties.

The Fragility of Democracy and the Rise of Disinformation

We are living through a global crisis of distrust. Democratic institutions—once seen as the bedrock of stability—are now viewed with deep suspicion. Fewer than two in ten Americans say they trust the federal government to do what's right most of the time.[11] Many people can no longer distinguish between fact and weaponized opinion.[12] For some, truth itself has become optional.

Here, too, the old narrative loop echoes. Just as Reconstruction's promise was undone by stories of "undeserving" citizens and nostalgia for a mythical past, disinformation today thrives on similar tropes of blame and longing for a time that never was. Intentional, systematic efforts to distort our historical memory are once again active.[13] The effect is the same: eroding trust in collective solutions.

When people feel alienated or excluded, they become vulnerable to disinformation, not because they are gullible, but because they are searching for a story that explains their pain. Disinformation supplies villains, false certainties, and a sense of control in a chaotic world. The consequences are everywhere. It fueled the January 6th insurrection, shaped responses to the COVID-19 vaccines, and continues to undermine climate science and elections.[14] Beyond politics, it corrodes the very idea of a common good.[15] In this climate of suspicion, public systems, especially those serving marginalized communities, remain easy targets.

And yet, it does not have to be this way. For human services, the challenge is immediate, practical, and civic. We must rebuild trust through daily acts of reliability, fairness, and care. Every accurate benefit payment, every respectful encounter, and every transparent process becomes a small proof point that democracy can still deliver.

During the pandemic, expanded Child Tax Credit payments and the deployment of community health workers to underserved neighborhoods demonstrated how well-designed human services can restore trust. Families reported that, for the first time, they felt government was working *for them*—providing stability and partnership rather than suspicion.[16]

Human services may be one of the most powerful tools we have for rebuilding trust. They are among the few places where government meets people not as voters or consumers, but as human beings. They rely on deep partnerships with community-based organizations, anchoring services in places where people already feel connection.

When we design these encounters around people's real needs, they create ripple effects. People begin to see government not as a cold bureaucracy, but as a capable and caring partner. Trust is not restored by rhetoric; it is restored by experience. In a time of democratic fragility, systems that deliver care with competence are not just a service, they are a demonstration of democracy in action.

From Fragile Democracy to Mass Partisanship: Disinformation thrives where identity divides run deepest. And in today's America, those divides are less about policy and more about who we imagine ourselves to be.

Mass Partisanship and the Normalization of Dehumanization

We are not just divided by policy beliefs, we are also separated by identity. Political identity has become more personal, emotional, and tribal.[17] As partisanship grows more hostile, opponents are no longer merely wrong; they are cast as dangerous. Symbols become flashpoints. Violence becomes thinkable. Public systems do not operate on neutral ground; they either reinforce polarization or interrupt it.

For human services, that choice plays out in thousands of everyday interactions: how eligibility rules are applied, how stories are told, and how people are treated at moments of need. Each encounter can mirror the nation's divisions—or model a different story, one rooted in fairness, respect, and shared responsibility.

The same cultural habits that once allowed politicians to weaponize the "welfare queen" trope now fuel a broader politics of dehumanization, where entire groups are reduced to caricatures and solidarity is replaced by suspicion.

But we can choose another path. Every interaction is an opportunity to counter dehumanization—to say, *You matter. You belong.* This quiet work of democracy repair rarely makes headlines, but it builds trust one encounter at a time. And it's already happening. Across the country, human service agencies are redesigning how people access support, centering belonging and partnership in everything from intake to service delivery. These are not isolated experiments; they are signals of a broader shift toward designing systems that meet people with respect rather than suspicion. We will explore these examples further in Chapters 8 and 9, where they remind us that systems can either harden divisions or practice solidarity in real time.

Research confirms that polarization is not only rhetorical but behavioral. Political scientists Nathan Kalmoe and Lilliana Mason, in *Radical American Partisanship*, document a disturbing rise in the acceptance of political violence. In their surveys, about one in five partisans agreed that violence against opponents could be at least "a little" justified. More than 40 percent described their opponents as "downright evil."[18] These attitudes move beyond disagreement into dehumanization, and we have increasingly seen them play out in national headlines—often with deadly consequences. The normalization of violence heightens the urgency of investing in systems that foster belonging rather than deepen division.

From Partisanship to Technology: These pressures are not contained within politics alone. They are magnified by the technologies we use every day. Algorithms shape what stories we see, what fears are amplified, and how mistrust spreads. Divisions do not end with people; machines accelerate them. The same profit-driven attention loops that shape digital media amplify fear and scarcity, rewarding outrage over context and leaving stories of cooperation and care struggling for airtime.

Technological Acceleration and Algorithmic Power

We live in a period of astonishing technological transformation, one moving faster than our public norms, legal frameworks, and institutions can keep pace with. Artificial intelligence is no longer something happening "elsewhere" or in the future; it is woven into how we search, communicate, learn, work, and make decisions. In human services, algorithms increasingly triage decisions, sorting applications, flagging benefits eligibility, shaping child welfare risk assessments, scheduling appointments, and mediating daily interactions at the front door of public systems. Sometimes technology simplifies. Sometimes it dehumanizes. But always, it shapes the experience.[19]

America's bootstrap mentality makes it too easy to frame job loss from automation or AI as an individual failure—someone who didn't "adapt fast enough." But this is a structural shift requiring a collective response. Biases once held by individuals can now be embedded into code, multiplied at scale, and hidden behind proprietary systems. As Shoshana Zuboff describes, this is "surveillance capitalism":

an economic model that treats human experience as raw material to be harvested and monetized.[20]

Virginia Eubanks warns that this logic has crept deeply into welfare and human services, where algorithms do not eliminate bias—they sanitize it, making inequity harder to see and easier to justify.[21] As AI accelerates, scholars such as Kate Crawford remind us that the entire AI ecosystem rests on extractive practices of data, labor, and community voice.[22] The danger is not only surveillance; it is the outsourcing of public judgment to statistical scores. Algorithms can feel precise, but without public accountability and community governance, they erode human agency and dignity.

The answer, however, is not to reject technology. It is to reclaim it. When designed with equity and humanity in mind, digital tools can simplify access, reduce burden, and strengthen trust. As Safiya Noble, Ruha Benjamin, and Meredith Broussard each remind us, algorithms encode values and power. Noble shows how bias is baked into the architecture of the web itself.[23] Benjamin cautions that without a social infrastructure for justice, technology will deepen inequality.[24] Broussard reminds us that mathematical fairness is not the same as social fairness. Computers can calculate the former, but they cannot define the latter.[25]

When governed with public purpose, technology can advance equity instead of undermining it. As legal theorist Jamie Susskind argues, technology is not just a tool; it is a political actor.[26] If we don't make deliberate choices, those choices will be made by default or by private interests. That's why technology cannot be treated as a back-office upgrade. It is a frontline arena for equity, where public values must be designed in from the start.

Consider two examples. In some jurisdictions, predictive analytics are being used to flag a child's risk of neglect or abuse. While intended to improve safety, these systems raise legitimate concerns about encoded bias and lack of transparency. The lesson is not to abandon such tools, but to co-design them with communities, acknowledging histories of surveillance and addressing risks directly.[27] At the same time, other agencies are investing in human-centered digital redesign of benefits applications to simplify forms, expand multilingual access, improve mobile usability, and reduce administrative burden.[28] Both examples remind us that technology is never neutral. When AI and digital tools are designed with intention and accountability, they can strengthen supports rather than reinforce inequities and expand trust rather than diminish it.

For human services, this is not a theoretical debate; it is daily practice. Every time a caseworker uses a digital tool, a program redesigns an online portal, or an agency decides how data are governed, choices about technology become choices about belonging. Human services sit at the intersection of AI and trust. Our values are either coded into the systems people rely on—or coded out.

Technology as Part of Our Scaffolding

Like the steel supports in a building, technology has become part of the scaffolding that holds up our public systems. It can reinforce fairness and trust, or introduce cracks that weaken the entire structure. What matters is how it is designed, governed, and used.

Risks When Fairness and Access Are Absent

- **Biased algorithms:** Tools used in child welfare or benefits programs can repeat old inequities and make them harder to see.
- **Rigid automation:** Systems that make decisions without human judgment can delay or deny help when flexibility is essential.
- **Excessive data collection:** Monitoring without safeguards erodes privacy and discourages people from seeking support.
- **Unequal digital access:** Families without reliable internet, electronic devices, or digital skills are effectively shut out of essential services.

Possibilities When Fairness and Access Are Centered

- **Simpler digital services:** Clear, multilingual, mobile-friendly applications make it easier for people to get help.
- **Community-shaped data rules:** When people have a voice in how their information is used, transparency and trust grow.
- **Human support alongside technology:** Navigators, caseworkers, and community workers ensure digital tools never replace human connection.
- **Fair and accountable AI:** Algorithms tested for bias and clarity can widen access and protect rights.

The takeaway: Technology is never neutral. It can reinforce the supports people rely on, or undermine them. When we design digital tools with fairness, access, and public purpose in mind, technology becomes part of the scaffolding that helps everyone thrive.

From Technology to Climate: If technology reveals what we code into systems, climate shows what happens when we ignore nature's warnings. Both are accelerants—one digital, one environmental—and both challenge us to ask not only if our systems are resilient, but how we can redesign them to adapt and build shared strength.

Climate Crisis and Environmental Displacement

Among the forces reshaping our collective future, none is more present—or more urgent—than climate change. It affects food, housing, health, mobility, and migration. Rising temperatures, wildfires, floods, droughts, and hurricanes displace families, disrupt economies, and redraw communities. Some disasters arrive suddenly, others build over time, and none and fall evenly. Wealth shapes who can rebuild, race and ZIP code shape risk exposure, and immigration status shapes access to aid.[29] These aren't anomalies. They are previews.

When hurricanes, wildfires, or floods force families from their homes, familiar welfare tropes resurface, shaping who we view as deserving of aid and who we see with suspicion. These dynamics echo exclusions that stretch back to the earliest days of American welfare.

The inequities of disaster response are well-documented.[30] Abraham Lustgarten's 2020 *ProPublica* feature *Where Will Everyone Go?* modeled the human flows likely to follow climate upheaval, projecting cross-border migration that will demand proactive systems of care.[31] A 2025 analysis of the Maui wildfires showed how Native Hawaiian communities, renters, and immigrant families faced disproportionate harm and barriers to recovery.[32] During the 2021 Texas freeze, wealthier neighborhoods often retained power, while low-income and predominantly Black and Brown communities endured prolonged outages and dangerous cold—inequities embedded in energy infrastructure and emergency response.[33]

Human services sit at the center of these stories. When disaster strikes, they are the first responders in social recovery, coordinating housing, distributing food, providing trauma-informed care, and helping families navigate dislocation and return. They also hold untapped potential to lead resilience planning by strengthening neighborhood networks, ensuring benefits are mobile and flexible, building cross-sector partnerships, and equipping residents most vulnerable to climate impacts with agency, not just information.

Some public systems already contain the seeds of resilience, designed to expand through administrative action when disaster strikes. Disaster SNAP allows states to rapidly provide food assistance to households affected by natural disasters, even if they were not previously eligible.[34] Emergency Medicaid waivers enable states to expand eligibility, streamline enrollment, or cover additional services.[35] Unemployment insurance extensions can broaden support during recessions or localized disasters.[36] These examples show that when flexibility is designed into infrastructure—and when that infrastructure is modernized—families can receive timely help rather than waiting months for special legislation or temporary fixes. The lesson is clear: resilience should not be improvised in the moment; it must be built into the scaffolding of well-being in advance.

For human services, this means treating climate adaptation as part of the everyday mission, not a special emergency function. The same systems that stabilize families after a storm can be designed to strengthen them before one, embedding resilience into the daily fabric of community life.

These lessons are not abstract. I have witnessed them firsthand. Over more than twenty-five years in human services, including disaster relief and long-term recovery after Hurricane Katrina and other national disasters, I have seen how quickly communities rally and how rigid systems temporarily adapt, only to snap back within months. I have seen the benefit of programs designed to expand quickly without red tape, and the pain families experience when supports are withdrawn before recovery is complete. These experiences taught me that resilience cannot be built in crisis alone. It must be designed in advance, with an eye toward repairing past harms and rebuilding toward a more just future.

While some cities are developing climate migration strategies and resilient-infrastructure coalitions, too few center human services in climate response. That is a dangerous oversight. In the climate era, human services are not a last resort. They are frontline infrastructure—essential not only for recovery, but for prevention, adaptation, and the restoration of belonging.

As climate change shifts from a series of discrete disasters to a continual condition, our narratives of deservingness will be tested again. When hardship is framed as an "act of God," we rally. When it becomes a slow-moving crisis, compassion contracts. If we fail to expand our sense of shared responsibility beyond emergency response, the inequities of the past will simply reappear in new form.

From Climate to Demographics: Environmental disruption will not unfold in isolation. Climate migration will reshape where people live and with whom, colliding with demographic shifts already underway—an aging society, a rising multiracial generation, and a growing diversity of languages and identities reshaping the public square.

Demographic and Cultural Shifts

America is changing rapidly. By 2045, no racial or ethnic group will constitute a numerical majority. Our society is becoming more multiracial, multilingual, and digitally native—and at the same time older, more isolated, and often more divided. The share of Americans age sixty-five and older is projected to rise sharply in the coming decades, reshaping families, communities, and the demands placed on our public systems.[37]

Shifting the American Mosaic

These demographic turning points illustrate how rapidly America's social and cultural landscape is changing:

By 2034: Adults age sixty-five and older will outnumber children under age eighteen for the first time in U.S. history.

By 2045: No racial or ethnic group will be a numerical majority. The United States will be a multiracial nation, with Latino, Asian, Black, and multiracial populations driving growth.

By 2050: The population age sixty-five and older will grow from about 58 million (17 percent of the population) to more than 82 million (23 percent).

Social fabric: These shifts will reshape families, labor markets, and public systems, bringing both new strengths and new stresses to how we live, work, and care for one another.

This convergence brings both challenges and opportunities. Aging is already straining long-term care, caregiving, and Medicaid as demand for services rises sharply.[38] Rates of loneliness, anxiety, and depression are reaching record levels, especially among youth and older adults.[39] At the same time, growing cultural diversity is testing institutions still built around—and for—one dominant norm. Younger generations expect equity and transparency; older adults expect care and connection. To meet this moment, our human-serving systems must evolve or risk alienating the very people they are meant to serve.

For human services, this evolution begins with design. Every intake form, policy rule, and community partnership can either widen belonging or reinforce exclusion. As the nation's demographics shift, our systems must become translators of shared experience: places where differences are recognized as assets and where connection itself is treated as public infrastructure.

That evolution requires more than "cultural competence."[40] What we now call cultural humility must become a core capacity: an ongoing practice of listening, learning, and adapting with communities. And as loneliness grows, we must also recognize belonging itself as social infrastructure, as essential to well-being as housing or health care. (We'll return to this more deeply in Chapter 9.)

As our nation grows more diverse, an old zero-sum story resurfaces: that expanding belonging for some must mean loss for others. If left unchallenged, this narrative constrains the promise of demographic change as a source of collective strength. But if we tell a different story—one that sees diversity as an engine of resilience—we can build systems that reflect who we truly are and who we are becoming.

These shifts are already reshaping human services in concrete ways:

- **Aging population:** By 2040, the number of Americans over age eighty-five will more than double compared with 2016, straining long-term care, Medicaid, and caregiving supports.[41]
- **Youth diversity:** Generation Z is the first U.S. generation in which fewer than half identify as white, and one in four identify as LGBTQ+.[42]
- **Loneliness as a public health concern:** Nearly 30 percent of adults aged eighteen to thirty-four report frequent loneliness, with similarly high rates among older adults.[43]
- **Language access:** More than 67 million U.S. residents speak a language other than English at home, making multilingual access essential.[44]
- **Workforce pressures:** Direct care and human services jobs are growing faster than almost any other sector, but low wages and high turnover threaten stability.[45]

From Demographics to History: These demographic pressures may feel new, but they echo older struggles over who belongs and how institutions adapt. Every era of expansion—of rights, opportunity, or belonging—has been met with resistance. The lesson of history is not simply that backlash occurs, but that it reveals how systems and stories evolve. If we pay attention, these echoes remind us that today's pressures are not signs of failure. They are signals that we stand once again at a turning point, with the opportunity to build our systems differently.

Historical Echoes and Recurring Pressure Points

The forces pressing on public systems today—economic disruption, racial tension, demographic change, political backlash—are not new. They are recurring pressure points. We have seen them before: the Poor Laws amid fears of disorder, Reconstruction followed by violent retrenchment, the New Deal met with exclusion, and the War on Poverty narrowed by backlash. Each moment of expansion brought resistance, not only over budgets, but over belonging. Today's rhetoric of "makers and takers" or "woke welfare" echoes that longer story.

We should not be surprised that today's systems are caught in the same crossfire. We ask them to serve more people, meet greater needs, and adapt to massive social change, all while navigating culture wars and persistent resource constraints. The strain we see today is not a new test, but a familiar one.

For those working in human services, that familiarity runs deep. Every generation of practitioners has faced versions of the same tension: meeting urgent human need while navigating the politics of deservingness. Their persistence is a reminder that systems evolve not only through policy shifts, but through the steady work of people who keep showing up to serve.

As Timothy Snyder implores us to remember, "History does not repeat, but it does instruct."[46] It tells us that systems built with exclusions cannot simply be stretched wider; they must be redesigned. It tells us that narratives matter, and that justice will always be contested, but that contest is worth entering again and again. Resistance is not proof of failure. It's a sign we are closer to the truth.

The challenges before us are economic, technological, and environmental—but they are also narrative. Again and again, America has met disruption with stories that narrowed our response: hardship is a test of character, some people are less deserving, government is bound to fail. These echoes shape how we interpret job loss in the age of AI, who deserves help after a wildfire, or whether we still trust democracy to deliver on its promises. History may not repeat in identical form, but its narratives endure.

If we want to meet today's forces with resilience rather than resignation, we must claim new stories—stories that expand belonging, honor interdependence, and remind us that welfare, in its truest sense, is about how we fare together. The next chapter turns to that opportunity: how we can rewrite the narrative and design systems that reflect not the limits of the past, but the possibilities of our shared future.

The Opportunity Before Us: Rewriting the Next Chapter

If the forces we face expose the weight of old narratives, they also reveal the chance to tell new ones. Every technological, environmental, demographic, or democratic pressure point invites us to ask: *What stories will we carry forward?* We can continue to fall back on the bootstrap myth, on racialized tropes of deservingness, and on fatalism about systems deemed too broken to fix. Or we can choose differently. We can choose a narrative rooted in solidarity: one that sees public systems not as relics of failure, but as instruments of shared resilience. The opportunity before us is not only to respond to disruption, but to reimagine what welfare—what well-being—means in the twenty-first century.

The story of welfare has always been about more than programs. It has been about who we imagine ourselves to be. For generations, narratives that privileged self-sufficiency over solidarity, sorted deservingness by race and class, and cast government as "them" have constrained what systems we build. The forces we now face make clear that these stories are too small for the challenges ahead.

But this is also our opening. Just as past generations built Social Security, the GI Bill, Medicare, and civil rights protections, we can choose to expand belonging again. We can design systems that meet disruption with resilience, migration with welcome, polarization with connection, and inequity with justice. Doing so will require more than policy reform. It will require a renewed national narrative that understands well-being not as charity, but as infrastructure; not as dependency, but as democracy fulfilled.

The opportunity before us is to reclaim welfare in its truest sense: as the measure of how we fare together—and to write the next chapter of the American story on foundations wide enough for all of us. That path begins with a shift in mindset: from systems as stagnant to systems as dynamic; from people as problems to people as co-creators; from inevitability to imagination.

We already have many of the tools we need—policy evidence, community wisdom, digital infrastructure, and leaders pushing for justice and inclusion. What we need now is alignment and the courage to act. As adrienne maree brown reminds us, transformative futures grow out of small, adaptive acts.[47] And as Rebecca Solnit and Heather

McGhee each argue, hope and solidarity are not luxuries; they are strategies.⁴⁸

Now is the time for us to build a welfare system that is:
- designed for disruption, not just continuity
- centered on human potential, not bureaucratic rules
- grounded in belonging, not mere efficiencies
- accountable to history, and open to repair

We can draw from strategic foresight communities that help us imagine what might go right if we invest in resilience now. And we can use a story—truthful, plural, forward-facing—to widen the lens, challenge fatalism, and remind ourselves of what's possible.

Our future as a nation is not determined by fate. It is the sum of our decisions, designs, and stories. As narratives, systems, and forces collide once again, we are called to a higher purpose for all people now and for the generations to come. This is the opportunity before us: to reclaim welfare in its truest sense as the measure of how we fare together, and to face the forces ahead with resolve equal to their scale.

Facing Forward: The Resolve to Act

Every generation meets its own convergence of forces. They arrive fast, hit hard, and test what we believe about responsibility and belonging. Yet nothing before us is beyond our reach if we choose to meet it together.

Economic volatility reminds us that interdependence is not our weakness, but our strength. Strong nations treat stability as shared infrastructure, not as a private good. When we design automatic stabilizers that expand as need grows, we create predictability in people's lives and trust in our institutions.

Climate disruption asks us to see well-being as a collective ecosystem. Human services agencies are often the first to respond and the last to leave, coordinating food, shelter, and safety when disaster strikes. With foresight, they can do more than repair damage; they can anchor long-term resilience by linking recovery to prevention.

Technological acceleration, driven by the rapid rise of artificial intelligence, demands a new social contract. These tools are reshaping how decisions are made, data is interpreted, and opportunity is distributed. When designed with ethical guardrails, shared governance, and broad digital access, AI can become a force for inclusion rather than control. Used wisely, technology can extend—not erode—human connection, embedding care and fairness into the very code of our systems.

Polarization and disinformation threaten to hollow out trust in one another and in government—the medium in which democracy operates. Human-serving systems can counter that erosion every day: through community centers that convene neighbors, social and health care workers who listen across difference, and agencies that embody fairness and care in real time. Competent care is civic repair.

Demographic and cultural change are not disruptions to endure, but chapters in a continuing story of renewal. Our systems can mirror that renewal by recruiting and supporting a workforce that reflects the full diversity of the nation—linguistically, culturally, and generationally. When people see themselves in the systems that serve them, belonging becomes tangible.

Across all of these forces, one truth holds: the well-being of those who deliver human services shapes the well-being of the systems themselves. The professionals who translate policy into practice—caseworkers, community organizers, benefits processors, and local leaders—are democracy's first responders. Yet too many work under chronic stress, low pay, and public misunderstanding. Investing in their stability, safety, and professional growth is not overhead; it is the foundation of resilience.

The Work Before Us

The forces we face will not wait for consensus. They are already shaping the next era of policy, economy, and daily life. Our resolve must match their scale. To face them is not only to resist harm, but to design for possibility: to treat care, truth, and shared responsibility as forms of national infrastructure. If we do, the scaffolding of human services can once again become the scaffolding of democracy itself.

The chapters ahead turn from possibility to practice—toward how we can design that scaffolding wide enough for everyone to stand upon.

SECTION III

Democracy by Design

Another world is not only possible, she is on her way. On a quiet day, I can hear her breathing.

—Arundhati Roy

Section II brought our systems into view, and now Section III asks what we can build once we refuse to accept systems as fixed in place. Poverty is not destiny; it is design—and design can be changed. The American Dream, so often described as lost or deferred, can be reclaimed, not by returning to a nostalgic past that never fully existed, but by daring to shape a future that fulfills its promise.

This section is about possibility; it is about democracy not as an inheritance, but as a living project that requires imagination, courage, and care. To design differently is to remember that systems are not natural laws but human choices. We can choose belonging over exclusion, connection over division, shared well-being over zero-sum scarcity.

The chapters that follow lay out the work of reclamation: shifting public attitudes, strengthening trust in our institutions, and advancing policies that connect economic security with human flourishing. Together, they show that the foundation of a thriving democracy is not abstract ideals, but the welfare of its people. Section II revealed what lies beneath the surface; Section III turns toward what we can grow next, through deliberate choices that shape the conditions for collective well-being.

CHAPTER 8

The Architecture of U.S.

Designing Social and Economic Policy

The test of our progress is not whether we add more to the abundance of those who have much; it is whether we provide enough for those who have too little.
—President Franklin D. Roosevelt

FDR's words remind us that progress is measured not by excess at the top but by sufficiency for all. The truth is, we are a nation with enough—enough wealth, enough productivity, and enough ingenuity to ensure that every person can live with stability and real well-being. What we lack is not capacity, but the will to align our systems with what we say we value.

For too long, America has told itself a false story that "the economy" and "welfare" occupy separate spheres. Economic policy is framed as serious business—growth, markets, productivity—while social policy is treated as secondary or sentimental, a cost to be contained. One is labeled investment; the other, charity.

This divide is not real, and it has weakened both our economy and our democracy. There can be no durable prosperity without stability, no functioning workforce without care, and no democratic legitimacy without broad-based well-being. When we treat our obligations as zero-sum and our resources as scarce, we narrow the very possibilities our economy depends on. When we recognize that shared prosperity expands collective capacity, we open the door to designing for abundance rather than rationing.

Human services make this connection visible. Programs like child care assistance, SNAP, housing supports, and disability services do more than help individuals meet basic needs. They circulate dollars through local grocers, landlords, child care providers, and small businesses. The human services workforce itself—public agencies and community-based partners—is a major employer and purchaser in every community. These investments stabilize families, anchor local economies during downturns, and strengthen the conditions for growth. In this sense, human services are both the scaffolding of daily life and a quiet engine of economic resilience.

The conclusion is straightforward: social policy is economic policy, and economic policy is social policy. When we deny that connection, we build systems that are fragmented and fragile. When we reclaim it, we can design systems for resilience, shared progress, and democratic strength.

Design is the bridge between the social and the economic. Policy is how our stories about value, responsibility, and belonging become rules, budgets, and institutions. When we imagine these domains as separate, we encode that story into our systems, building walls where bridges are needed. This chapter asks what becomes possible when we design differently—and together.

Policy Is Narrative In Law

Budgets are stories written in numbers. Eligibility rules are stories written into law. Every line item and every threshold signals who is valued—and who is not. When tax cuts for corporations are labeled investment while food assistance is dismissed as handouts, the language does more than reflect priorities; it constructs legitimacy. It tells Americans which supports are strategic and which are suspect, who counts as a contributor and who is cast as a burden.

This isn't semantics. These distinctions shape what gets funded, who qualifies, and how systems treat people at the door. And they collapse under even light scrutiny. Every entrepreneur depends on housing stability and health care. Every parent depends on child care, whether paid or unpaid. Every worker relies on the public infrastructure that makes work possible.

This is not the only story available to us. We have seen what happens when social policy is treated as core economic infrastructure, with systems designed for belonging rather than separation.

Social Security and Medicare have endured for generations precisely because they are universal and largely unconditional.[2] People experience them as earned rights, not handouts, and their broad reach has protected them from stigma and political erosion. The Earned Income Tax Credit (EITC), one of the nation's largest antipoverty programs, delivers annual refunds to low- and moderate-income workers.[3] Families use these dollars for food, rent, car repairs, and school supplies—and because the money is spent quickly and locally, the EITC strengthens neighborhood economies.

SNAP functions in much the same way. It is both a personal lifeline and a community stabilizer, expanding automatically during recessions or disasters. By preventing hunger while channeling billions of dollars into grocery stores and food supply chains, it cushions economic shocks and reinforces the foundations of well-being. Social investment, when designed as infrastructure, does not weaken the economy; it steadies and sustains it.

How Human Services Fuel Local Economies

When people hear "public benefits," they often think only of direct help to families. But the economic ripple effects extend much further:

- SNAP dollars are spent at corner groceries, farmers' markets, and supermarkets, helping keep shelves stocked and workers employed.[4]
- Child care subsidies flow to local providers—many of them small businesses run by women and people of color.[5]
- Housing assistance stabilizes families and sends steady payments to landlords, contractors, and utility providers.[6]
- Disability services sustain organizations that hire local staff, purchase supplies, and contract for transportation, technology, and facilities.[7]

Together, these programs circulate dollars through towns and neighborhoods, supporting jobs and local businesses. Human services are not just about helping individuals; they are part of the economic scaffolding that keeps communities stable and growing.

A next-generation example comes from Michigan. In 2024, state leaders launched Rx Kids in Flint—the nation's first citywide "baby allowance," now expanding to other communities.[8] Every pregnant person receives a $1,500 prenatal grant, followed by $500 per month during the child's first year of life. There are no means tests, no complex eligibility hurdles, and no stigma. Families can use these funds for rent, food, baby supplies, and bills, strengthening both household stability and the local economy.

By making the support universal, Rx Kids reframes care as a shared public good. It is a living example of what becomes possible when leaders act with courage and imagination. This policy is not designed to punish scarcity, but to guarantee presence, the reliable support and security families need, ensuring that every child enters the world with a measure of stability and belonging.

The wall between "economic" policy and "social" policy is an illusion. As economist Darrick Hamilton reminds us, these policies are not side notes to the economy; they *are* the economy.[9] Every investment in housing, food, education, and health is not charity; it is the foundation for people's productivity, innovation, and growth. Shared investments are not abstractions; they are how freedom becomes real in daily life.

Political labels will continue to be invoked as shortcuts for debate. But those labels tell us little about whether families can feed their children, age with security, or weather economic shocks. The real design question is simpler and more consequential: are we building systems that widen belonging, strengthen resilience, and allow all of us to thrive?

The task before us is not to argue over names, but to design on purpose, choosing materials and methods that build belonging at scale. That is the architecture of a democracy that works.

Guaranteed Income: A Simple But Radical Idea

The simplest way to collapse the false divide between social and economic policy is also the most radical: give people cash.

Guaranteed income is not a new idea. During the New Deal, some state and local human services leaders urged federal policymakers to provide direct cash support to families beyond short-term emergency relief, arguing it was the most efficient way to stabilize households.[10] Those proposals were largely set aside in favor of a patchwork of in-kind and contributory programs.

The idea resurfaced in 1969, when President Richard Nixon introduced the Family Assistance Plan, which would have established a modest income floor for nearly every American family.[11] It passed the House twice but failed in the Senate by a narrow margin.[12] Had it succeeded, the United States might have built a far more universal welfare state half a century ago.

Still, the idea never disappeared. In recent years, mayors, governors, and community leaders across the country have launched guaranteed income pilots,[13] testing what happens when people are trusted with flexible resources and freed from the burden of proving their worth. In Stockton, California, families used monthly payments to cover rent, reduce debt, and pursue better jobs, improving health and lowering stress.[14] In Jackson, Mississippi, monthly no-strings-attached cash has helped more than 430 Black mothers meet household needs and strengthen family stability.[15] In Durham, North Carolina, people reentering society after incarceration used the funds to secure transportation and rebuild their lives.[16]

Across these varied contexts, the outcomes are consistent. Guaranteed income does not undermine work; it strengthens it. It reduces the volatility of poverty, eases toxic stress, and creates the breathing room people need to participate fully in family, community, and economic life. As Melvin Carter, former mayor of Saint Paul, puts it: "In a country that works for all of us, no one who works full-time should be stuck in poverty or worry about making ends meet. It's time to reimagine and rethink our economic structures by piloting a guaranteed income."[17]

These results are unfolding in real time across the country. The evidence is striking.

> **What Guaranteed Income Pilots Show Us**
>
> Across the country, guaranteed income pilots reveal what happens when people receive unconditional cash: stability increases, stress declines, and families use funds for essentials that help them move forward.
>
> - **Stockton** *(Stockton Economic Empowerment Demonstration, 2019–2021):* 125 residents received $500 per month for two years. **Results:** reduced income volatility, improved mental health, and increased full-time employment (28 percent to 40 percent, compared with 32 percent to 37 percent in the control group).
> - **Jackson** *(Magnolia Mother's Trust, 2018–present):* Black mothers in subsidized housing receive $1,000 per month for a year. **Results:** sharp reductions in food insecurity, increased savings, and improved parental well-being and engagement with children.
> - **Durham** *(Excel Pilot, 2022–2023):* 109 people released from incarceration received $600 per month for one year. **Results:** reduced food insecurity, better mental health, and improved housing stability during the pilot—though gains faded after payments ended, underscoring the limits of short-term aid.
>
> More recent large-scale demonstrations reinforce these findings. In Compton, a two-year randomized guaranteed income program showed sustained improvements in employment, financial stability, and well-being.[18] In Denver, direct cash support for people experiencing homelessness increased stability and reduced reliance on emergency systems.[19]

Guaranteed income shows what becomes possible when we treat cash not as charity, but as infrastructure. It creates a stable floor beneath every family: a floor that no one falls below and that gives all of us room to rise together.

That floor matters because too often our current system does the opposite. Instead of supporting steady progress, it strips stability away the moment families begin to move forward. These benefit "cliffs" do more than punish effort; they expose a welfare design rooted in scarcity and suspicion rather than security and possibility.

This is more than a policy innovation. It is a correction to the story we have been telling for generations—that people experiencing poverty cannot be trusted with choice. Guaranteed income reverses that assumption. It begins with trust rather than testing, and with possibility rather than punishment.

The Cliff Effect: Punishing Progress

Nowhere is this design flaw more visible—or more painful—than in what we call "the cliff."[20]

A parent receives a small raise and loses the child care support that made the job possible. A worker takes on extra shifts and is cut off from Medicaid. A young adult accepts part-time work and the family's housing voucher shrinks. These are not accidents. They are predictable outcomes of systems designed to regulate access rather than support mobility: systems that keep people in place instead of helping them move forward. The result is chronic uncertainty and instability.

And we're not imagining it. Researchers at the Federal Reserve Bank of Atlanta have documented how a modest raise can push a family over an eligibility threshold and leave them financially worse off—a "benefits cliff"—or no better off—a "benefits plateau." [21] To make these dynamics visible, they developed the CLIFF (Career Ladder Identifier and Financial Forecaster) tools, which allow workers and career coaches to see the real net impact of a promotion before someone says yes.[22]

In Washington, DC, that same research shows how benefit cliffs can impose crushing effective tax rates—sometimes higher than those faced by top earners—creating significant barriers to advancement. The data also points to a clear alternative: better policy design can smooth the path, turning penalties into progress.[23]

National policy organizations echo these findings. The American Public Human Services Association and the National Conference of State Legislatures document how cliffs appear in SNAP, child care, Medicaid, housing, and other programs. They also highlight how states are replacing cliffs with ramps: gradual phaseouts that let families increase earnings without sudden losses.[24]

Another often overlooked lever is refundable tax credits. Analysis from the Urban Institute finds that credits like the Earned Income Tax Credit can offset higher taxes and soften benefit losses as earnings rise, buffering cliffs for many families and making upward mobility more sustainable.[25]

> **From Cliffs to Ramps**
>
> Think of public benefits as part of the scaffolding that helps families climb toward stability.
>
> A **cliff** is like a platform with a sudden drop. You take one small step forward—a raise or a few more hours of work—and the ground disappears beneath you. Supports vanish all at once, leaving families worse off than before and hesitant to keep climbing.
>
> A **ramp**, by contrast, is a steady incline built into the structure. Supports phase out gradually as income rises, giving families the footing they need to keep moving upward. Instead of punishing progress, ramps reinforce it by helping people transition from precarious to solid ground with confidence.

The solutions already exist. The real question is whether we are willing to leave behind the old story long enough to use them, choosing designs that reward progress instead of punishing it. In many cases, the architecture is already in place; it is the story guiding our choices that needs rebuilding.

Money Should Follow The Person

For young people aging out of foster care, this principle is especially powerful. When support follows the person as flexible cash, precarity can become a foothold.

Most public systems are built around programs, not people. Families are sorted into categories and matched to what is available rather than what they actually need. A simple but transformative shift is possible: start with the person, not the program. When money follows the person[26]—as flexible cash or cash-equivalent support—people can address the challenges they face in real time.

We already see how effective this approach can be. Opportunity Passport®, a multisite initiative of the Annie E. Casey Foundation through the Jim Casey Initiative, gives young people aging out of foster care control over funds and matched savings for assets they choose, such as transportation, housing deposits, or credentials. Evaluations show increased savings and targeted purchases that strengthen school and work stability.[27]

Research from Chapin Hall reaches a similar conclusion. Studies of direct cash transfers to youth and young adults at high risk of homelessness find that unrestricted cash, paired with light-touch supports, improves stability and helps sustain exits from homelessness.[28]

In Santa Clara County, a guaranteed income pilot for former foster youth reduced homelessness risk and increased engagement in school and work. Together, these findings confirm what common sense already suggests: youth-directed, flexible dollars build stability faster than compliance forms ever could.[29]

Flexibility is not inefficiency; it is responsiveness. The real measure of accountability is not how well people navigate bureaucratic hoops, but whether they are better off.

Money Follows the Person for Foster Youth

Why it matters

Direct cash and flexible funds act as stability tools for transition-age foster youth. When young people control resources they can use for what matters most—a security deposit, car repair, or certification fee—outcomes improve.

What it does

- Reduces material hardship and toxic stress
- Builds assets, agency, and long-term stability
- Supports housing security
- Helps sustain school and work participation

How we know

- Child welfare research shows that economic and concrete supports lower stress and improve well-being.[30]
- Asset-building models such as Opportunity Passport® increase savings, enable essential purchases, and strengthen financial capability.
- Direct-cash pilots for youth and young adults at risk of homelessness find that unrestricted cash, paired with light supports, improves stability and sustains exits from homelessness.
- Guaranteed-income pilots (e.g., Santa Clara County) report reduced homelessness risk and stronger engagement in school and work.

When money follows the person, the next step is to let services follow our lives into schools, libraries, clinics, workplaces, and the trusted spaces where people already are. This is how systems stop working against us and start moving with us.

Policy In The Places We Live

We change outcomes fastest when policy meets us where we already are—schools, libraries, clinics, workplaces—and when it functions like infrastructure: universal, simple, and dignified. Place matters. When support is woven into daily life, people do not have to clear hurdles to access what keeps them stable. Systems feel real because they are close.

Schools illustrate this most vividly. When meals, health care, and after-school learning are built into the school day, they stop being seen as special services for "those kids" and become part of the ordinary scaffolding every child can count on.

Universal school meals show the power of this shift. When breakfast and lunch are free for all students, participation rises, stigma falls, and meal debt disappears. Attendance improves, and staff spend less time policing lines or collecting fees. California's Healthy School Meals for All demonstrates how universality can become the norm. At the federal level, the Community Eligibility Provision (CEP) makes this approach possible, and once districts adopt it, universal meals prove both simple to operate and difficult to argue against (see sidebar). [31]

School-based health centers bring primary and behavioral health care directly onto campus. Evaluations show they increase access to care, reduce missed class time, and are associated with better attendance, higher grade point averages, improved grade progression, and fewer suspensions. For students managing health concerns like asthma, diabetes, or anxiety, these supports can mean the difference between falling behind and keeping pace.[32]

High-quality after-school and summer programs extend learning and stability beyond the bell. When sustained and intentional, they boost engagement, strengthen literacy and math scores, and give parents confidence that their children are in safe, enriching environments while they work.[33]

Community Schools integrate these strands into a single design. In New York City, evaluations show that schools using this model have higher graduation rates, better attendance, and fewer disciplinary incidents than comparable schools. The lesson is clear: when policy shows up where life already happens, it stops feeling like a program and starts functioning like infrastructure.[34]

Universal Meals Made Simple

The Community Eligibility Provision

What it is: A federal option that allows high-poverty schools and districts to serve free breakfast and lunch to all students—no applications, no paperwork.

Why it works: Reduces administrative burden, eliminates meal debt, removes stigma, and boosts participation so more students are nourished and ready to learn.

Smart design add-on: Pair with breakfast-after-the-bell, which ensures students eat at the start of the day—and normalizes access as part of the school routine.

Libraries with Social Workers, Technology Access, and Cooling Centers

Libraries are among the most trusted civic spaces in America. Free, open to all, and woven into public infrastructure, they offer something many systems struggle to provide: help without stigma. That trust makes libraries uniquely powerful places to reimagine human services—not as distant offices, but as supports embedded in the heart of community life.

Library-embedded social work shows what this looks like in practice. In cities like San Francisco and Denver, libraries have placed social workers on-site to connect patrons directly to housing supports, benefits, and crisis resources. The result has been fewer escalations to security or law enforcement and more constructive engagement in a setting people already know and trust.[35]

Digital access and telehealth offer another path. Delaware's statewide library system has installed private telehealth kiosks and launched device-lending programs that allow patrons to borrow Wi-Fi hotspots, tablets and laptops for home use.[36] These services transform local branches into health and connectivity hubs. A library card becomes a gateway not just to books but to care, bridging digital and health-access gaps in historically underserved communities at relatively low cost.

Cooling centers and resilience hubs point to the future. As climate change accelerates, libraries are increasingly recognized as life-safety infrastructure: air-conditioned, power-enabled spaces that provide clean air, water, charging stations, and reliable information during extreme heat or power outages. Public health guidance now treats libraries as essential in emergency planning, and cities are mapping locations and extending hours to ensure equitable access when communities need them most.[37]

Together, these innovations remind us that libraries are not relics of the past. They are evolving into resilience hubs and community anchors: public infrastructure that adapts alongside us, meeting needs that extend far beyond the stacks.

When we treat trusted community spaces as part of our public well-being infrastructure, we extend the reach of government without expanding its distance. The library's lesson is clear: design follows trust.

Workplaces as Infrastructure for Stability

If schools and libraries are two legs of public life, workplaces are the third leg of the stability triangle. Yet too often, we treat family needs as distractions from work rather than the foundation that makes work possible. When employers invest in care and stability, the benefits flow in both directions: families and businesses thrive together.

Paid family leave (PFL) shows what happens when policy is designed around real lives. In states like California, New Jersey, and New York, PFL programs have increased leave-taking, boosted parental mental health, and supported breastfeeding. Mothers are more likely to remain employed and expand their hours in the year following birth or adoption. Employers benefit as well, through higher retention and lower turnover costs.[38]

On-site or near-site child care shows a similar return. Patagonia, the outdoor apparel store, has a long-standing child care model that reports nearly 100 percent return-to-work rates for new mothers. Independent studies confirm the pattern: when employers provide reliable child care, women are more likely to return to work, increase their hours, and remain with their employer. Far from a "perk," child care is workforce infrastructure that is essential to keeping parents, especially mothers, in the labor force and employers competitive.[39]

Financial coaching as a workplace benefit rounds out the picture. Evaluations show that coaching—often delivered by trusted nonprofit partners—helps employees reduce debt, improve budgeting, and build savings. The result is lower stress, greater stability, and improved productivity. For employers, it is among the most cost-effective supports they can offer.[40]

Workplaces that adopt these practices demonstrate a simple truth: supporting families is not a sideline to economic success; it is the infrastructure that makes it possible. Together, schools, libraries, and workplaces show what happens when scaffolding is woven into the places we already live, learn, and earn. These supports do not feel like programs to apply for. They feel like everyday infrastructure—part of the environment that helps families stay steady and move forward.

Proximity, in other words, does not belong only to public institutions or employers. It also lives in the everyday spaces where trust already exists.

And that is the larger lesson: when policy meets people where they already are, it dissolves stigma, simplifies access, and strengthens trust. The next step is for government itself to embody that principle, not as a distant bureaucracy, but as a partner embedded in daily life.

When Government Shows Up Where We Are

Beyond schools, libraries, and workplaces, government can flip the script from "come to us" to "we'll meet you where you are." Increasingly, agencies are embedding human service navigators in trusted community settings and redesigning their own spaces as neighborhood hubs—so a single visit can address multiple needs.

Take Mecklenburg County, North Carolina. Its Community Resource Centers (CRCs) bring multiple county services under one roof—benefits access, workforce supports, WIC, child support, and more—alongside community partners. The Ella B. Scarborough CRC, for example, offers families an integrated, no-wrong-door experience that feels like a welcoming neighborhood place rather than a bureaucratic maze.[41]

In rural Perry County, Ohio, human services leaders have taken a different but equally effective approach. With limited public transit, Perry County Job & Family Services houses a Mobility Management team that coordinates rides to care for Medicaid members while aligning with Perry County Transit's curb-to-curb services.[42] Co-location at the Perry County Opportunity Center—where OhioMeansJobs operates on the same campus—means residents can connect to benefits and employment support in one place. It is an uncommon but powerful alignment: human services, transportation, and workforce systems operating as a single access point.[43]

When we treat transportation as part of access rather than an afterthought, and when staff meet people in places they already trust, cold handoffs give way to warm handshakes. Trust, once built, becomes the scaffolding for systems that actually work.

Rural Reach: Getting There *Is* the Policy

In rural communities, access is often less about eligibility than geography. The challenge is not only what services exist, but whether people can reach them. Innovative approaches are showing how to close that gap:

- **Mobility management anchored in human services.** A single navigator coordinates rides across programs and providers, so a doctor's appointment or benefits recertification automatically includes the transportation to get there.
- **Curb-to-curb, demand-response transit.** Door-*through*-door service ensures seniors, people with disabilities, and caregivers can reliably reach clinics, caseworkers, or job sites.
- **Co-location with workforce services.** Benefits access is paired with employment support at shared sites, reducing the need for multiple trips.
- **Mobile service units.** Vans and buses equipped for casework, enrollment, and job services meet people in township centers, church parking lots, and other community hubs.

Why it matters: When mobility functions sit within human services, transportation is no longer treated as a separate silo. It becomes infrastructure for access—a recognition that *getting there* is part of the policy. Because a bridge does not matter if people cannot reach it.

When we embed people and braid services this way, government stops acting like a distant gate and starts working as scaffolding—close enough to steady us as we climb.

Why Place Matters

When policy meets us where we live and work, it does three things: it normalizes support, removing stigma; it simplifies access, replacing mazes with clear paths; and it multiplies impact, so one visit can address multiple needs. This is democratic infrastructure in practice—systems we can see, touch, and trust.

Design moves we can make now

- **Default to universal** wherever feasible. Programs like community-wide school meals or Rx Kids show how universality dissolves stigma and builds shared investment.
- **Put care and navigation in the places people already go.** Schools, libraries, and workplaces make support feels routine rather than exceptional.
- **Treat transportation as access infrastructure.** Mobility management, demand-response transit, and rides bundled with appointments make "getting there" part of the policy.
- **Embed human services with partners and redesign public offices as community hubs.** Mobile teams can extend reach to rural and remote areas.

- **Align employer policy with family stability.** Paid leave, child care, and financial coaching sustain both families and businesses.
- **Fund local partners with trust and proximity.** Cover the full cost of service delivery so innovation and relationships can thrive where people have the power to co-design change.

Built this way, systems stand alongside us rather than above us. Government stops being a gate to pass through and becomes the scaffolding we can all lean on as we rise.

Government As Scaffolding

At its best, government is not a fortress but a scaffold—strong enough to provide stability and adaptable enough to let people build upward on their own terms. Its purpose is not to stand forever on its own, but to steady us as we construct something lasting: systems rooted in belonging and well-being for all.

Realizing that vision requires redesigning for accessibility, accountability, and trust through participatory budgeting, co-governance with communities, flexible funding for grassroots organizations, and public roles that value relationships as much as efficiency. This is what democracy by design looks like: power shared.

Social and economic policy are inseparable. Together, they shape the conditions of democratic life. But structure alone is not enough. The blueprints we use—the stories we normalize about who deserves support and why—matter just as much.

And those blueprints are not fixed. They are rewritten through practice. The next chapter turns to the everyday work of changing the welfare story: how we see one another, how we speak, and how we design spaces.

Building on the Blueprint
Further Reading

The works below extend the themes of this chapter, showing what becomes possible when social and economic policy are designed as shared infrastructure. Together, they offer multiple vantage points—personal narrative, policy innovation, rigorous evaluation, and moral vision—on how scaffolding becomes foundation, and how ideas become lived experience.

- **The Deeper the Roots**—Michael Tubbs
  A personal account of growing up in Stockton, California, and leading the nation's first mayor-led guaranteed income pilot—illustrating how lived experience can reshape public policy.
- **Give People Money**—Annie Lowrey
  A journalist's exploration of universal basic income that weaves together global case studies, economic analysis, and human stories to challenge conventional assumptions about poverty and work.

- **The Magnolia Mother's Trust**—Aisha Nyandoro and Springboard to Opportunities
  Findings and reflections from the nation's longest-running guaranteed income program for Black women, offering concrete lessons on trust-based design and family stability.
- **Center for Guaranteed Income Research** (University of Pennsylvania)
  The leading U.S. research hub studying guaranteed income pilots, with evaluations from Stockton, Jackson, Durham, and other communities testing unconditional cash at scale.
- **The Moral Agenda for Economic Rights**—Darrick Hamilton
  A Bellagio Breakthroughs essay for the Rockefeller Foundation, in which Hamilton responds to questions on economic rights, shared prosperity, and why social policy must be treated as core economic infrastructure.
- **The Sum of Us**—Heather McGhee
  An exploration of how racialized narratives of scarcity undermine shared prosperity—and how dismantling them opens pathways toward collective abundance and democratic renewal.

CHAPTER 9

Belonging By Design

Rewriting the Welfare Story Together

What we pay attention to grows.

—adrienne maree brown

For too long, America's welfare story has been told in the language of scarcity: scarcity of money, scarcity of trust, scarcity of imagination. That story has narrowed what we believe is possible and pitted us against one another.

But scarcity is a story, not a fact. The truth is that America has enough—enough resources, enough innovation, enough capacity for care. What we have lacked is belonging: a sense that every one of us counts, every one of us deserves to be seen, and every one of us has a role in shaping our shared future.

If democracy is how we decide who counts and how we care, then belonging is its practice: the daily way we make that promise real. For generations, we have treated democracy as something that happens at the ballot box. Yet its truest form lives in how we show up for one another, in the systems we build, and in the stories we choose to tell.

As historian Timothy Snyder reminds us, freedom is not about defending what is, but about imagining what could be. When we design belonging, we practice that kind of freedom: the kind that turns imagination into shared possibility.

If what we pay attention to grows, then we can choose to cultivate belonging, agency, and enough—on purpose. This chapter is about how we can do welfare differently, and practice a welfare that lives up to its original meaning: our shared well-being.

I outline six practices for designing belonging, each paired with examples and simple moves anyone can take:

1. **See Humanity First**—shifting from labels to people.
2. **Cultivate Curiosity and Complexity**—resisting reduction and asking better questions.
3. **Shift the Frame from Scarcity to Abundance**—designing for enough.
4. **Bridge and Build Belonging**—choosing relationship over distance.
5. **Reimagine Power from Systems *Over* People to Systems *With* People**—moving from compliance to co-creation.
6. **Normalize New Narratives** – repeating better stories until they become common sense.

Each practice is a small democratic act. Repeated together, they can rewrite what welfare means in the American imagination. Because democracy depends on what we normalize, these everyday choices become civic ones—the groundwork for a democracy built on care. And because leadership magnifies practices into stories, this chapter closes with a call to leaders to model these choices at scale.

Practice 1: See Humanity First

Labels don't just describe people; they also prescribe how systems treat them. When intake forms fixate on deficits, when case notes highlight only risks, and when dashboards reduce people to metrics, the message is the same: *you are not expected to succeed.*

We can name this habit and we can change it. Too often, we lead with categories that box people in: "the vulnerable," "the homeless," "the poor," "ex-offenders." These shortcuts freeze people inside problems, and over time, they harden into policy.

A different practice starts with people first: people experiencing homelessness, young people in foster care, people with low incomes, neighbors returning from incarceration. When we add context—such as communities more vulnerable to climate change because of heat islands or disinvestment—we shift the story. We see neighbors before stereotypes, humanity before circumstance. Small changes in language can open much larger shifts in how systems respond.

Quick swaps that move us from deficit labels to people-first framing:
- Use "people experiencing homelessness" — not "homeless people."
- Use "young people in foster care" — not "foster care youth."
- Use "people with low incomes" — not "the poor."
- Use "people returning from incarceration" — not "ex-offenders" or "felons."
- Use "people receiving disability benefits" — not "the disabled."

These are not cosmetic changes. The words we choose shape how people are treated, how policies are written, and what futures are imagined. Language is civic infrastructure. It builds or erodes democracy one sentence at a time. Choosing words with care is one way we build belonging.

And this practice extends beyond language. Whether we are neighbors, parents, students, voters, business owners, or policymakers our choices shape the culture around public systems and the people who navigate them. We can greet families in their preferred language, especially now that translation tools make this easier than ever. We can write policies and job descriptions that center relationships rather than surveillance. We can design processes that introduce a neighbor to a human, not a number to a screen. Seeing humanity first does not instantly change structural conditions, but it is where change begins.

To see humanity first is to practice narrative freedom: the freedom for each person to author their own story rather than live inside someone else's. When we use language that recognizes agency and dignity, we expand the boundaries of belonging and how democracy feels.

Simple Moves We Can Make

- Lead with a person's name in daily encounters—at the checkout counter, in parent group meetings, at the post office.
- Swap labels for people-first language in emails, posts, and meetings.
- When a stereotype surfaces, interrupt it with a story that widens the lens and reveals a fuller human picture.

As we reclaimed welfare in Chapter 1—as our promise to one another—we saw how historic labels harden into enduring policy. Seeing humanity first is that reclamation, practiced person by person. And as Chapter 6 showed, systems can harm or heal; this practice tips them toward healing.

We begin by recognizing one another in everyday interactions. Every greeting, every rephrased sentence, is a democratic act—small, ordinary, and world-shaping. Reclaiming welfare starts with recognition and continues with curiosity.

Practice 2: Cultivate Curiosity and Complexity

If seeing humanity first is where change begins, curiosity is how we listen long enough to understand one another. It is the practice that turns empathy into understanding and keeps us from slipping into judgment. By resisting reduction, curiosity interrupts our tendency to fall into the blame and fatalism traps. It is also a democratic discipline: an act of staying open when our culture rewards certainty.

Curiosity asks different questions: *What happened? What systems shaped the choices here? What strengths have helped this family endure? What tradeoffs are at play?* Complex lives rarely fit a checkbox. Poverty, trauma, disability, caregiving, and displacement intersect. Listening for another person's story of themselves—and their story of us—is the work. Curiosity is how we make room for that story to unfold.[2]

Curiosity is imagination in motion: the quiet courage to ask before we assume, to look for what connects before we decide what divides. When we wonder instead of judge, defensiveness drops and attention widens. Curiosity slows our snap judgments ("Threat!") and opens space for us to see fuller context ("Welcome!"). Practically, this means we ask better questions, build on strengths, notice more options, and reconnect to our shared humanity. This is not softness; it is how we arrive at wiser choices together. Looking back, I wish I had discovered the power of curiosity much earlier in my own life.

As Brené Brown maps in *Atlas of the Heart*, awe, wonder, and curiosity are places we go when life feels bigger than us; they help us slow down and make meaning together.[3] Psychologist Dacher Keltner adds that awe orients us beyond the individual self, opening our minds to wonder about "the systems of life and our small part in them."[4] Beyond the personal, research summarized in *Harvard Business Review* finds that curiosity boosts engagement, reduces conflict, and improves decision-making, exactly the capacities public life now demands.[5]

In a democracy tested by mistrust, curiosity rebuilds the civic reflex to seek understanding instead of victory. Science confirms what practice teaches us. Curiosity slows our snap judgments, widens our attention, focuses us on context rather than blame, and leads us to wiser, more humane choices.

> **Simple Moves We Can Make**
> - With people: Before offering advice, ask *"What happened?"* and *"What would make this doable?"*
> - With news: Before reposting outrage, look for patterns and context, not just a single story.
> - With policy debates: Before making snap judgments, name two tradeoffs you hadn't considered, and name one upside for someone unlike you.

Curiosity refuses the old scripts that blame people (Chapter 3 or shrug at inevitability (Chapter 4. It is the discipline that keeps us designing for real lives, not imagined ones. Reclaiming welfare requires inquiry. Curiosity is democratic muscle memory—the habit of seeking understanding across difference.

When we practice curiosity, we loosen the grip of judgment. To build differently, we must also loosen the grip of scarcity. If what we pay attention to grows, then turning our attention toward abundance is how we grow futures worth sharing.

Practice 3: Shift The Frame From Scarcity To Abundance

If curiosity opens our minds, abundance expands our field of vision. Scarcity thinking tells us there isn't enough for all of us, at least without conditions. It shrinks imagination and fuels zero-sum politics. Behavioral scientists Sendhil Mullainathan and Eldar Shafir remind us that scarcity does not just describe a lack of resources; it consumes attention.[6] When people are forced to navigate constant shortages, their minds lock onto the next bill, the next crisis, the next deadline. Urgent needs crowd out everything else, leaving little mental space to plan, learn, or trust.

A story of scarcity always carries an excuse for who gets left out. It justifies rationing and suspicion. A story of abundance—and belonging—tells a different truth: everyone has worth, everyone can contribute, and there can be enough when what we have is shared. That is the quiet revolution of abundance. It invites us to measure prosperity not by accumulation, but by participation and by how widely well-being is spread.

Our response must be to design for slack—time, cash, and hassle-free access—so people can focus on building, not just surviving. Abundance reframes the work. It shifts the question from *How little can we get by with?* to *What would it take for everyone to thrive?* We invest for enough, not scarcity. We measure the cost of doing nothing, not only the price tag of doing the right thing. We lift up what is already working—universal benefits that recognize shared worth, flexible supports that stabilize—and we scale them. Or, as economist Mariana Mazzucato argues, we shape markets through mission-oriented public investment rather than simply "fixing" failures.[7]

Abundance is not wishful thinking; it is measurable. Global research on flourishing now tracks not only income, but also purpose, connection, and hope. Gallup's 2024 Global Flourishing Study finds that people thrive when they experience belonging and believe the future can improve.[8] These findings mirror what human services work to build every day: the social and emotional infrastructure that allows people to imagine and pursue new possibilities together.

Abundance is both a design choice and an investment strategy. It begins with imagination. One of my favorite exercises in strategic planning is to "dream big." At APHSA, we often began new planning cycles this way, asking teams to write the headline they hoped to see in their community, organization, or nation ten years from now. The only rules were to focus on outcomes, think abundantly, and dream beyond current constraints.

It takes encouragement to let go of the limits we have been taught to accept, but once we do, our visions sound strikingly alike. We imagine communities that flourish, inequities erased, and human-serving systems that heal rather than harm. That alignment reminds us that abundance grows when we act together, or what Heather McGhee calls the solidarity dividend.[9]

This is democracy practiced as mutual investment: the shared belief that what lifts one of us helps lift us all.

Simple Moves We Can Make

- Tell one local story this month of a public system that works; invite an unexpected messenger—business, faith, or frontline—to share it.
- When someone says "We can't afford it," respond with: "What's the cost of doing nothing?"—and name the human potential lost.
- Swap a scarcity label ("a drain on taxpayers") for an investment frame ("shared scaffolding that pays community dividends").

Chapter 2 reminded us that the American Dream has been rationed. Chapter 8 showed that our policies are blueprints for the economy itself. Choosing abundance means refusing to ration belonging and instead building for enough—a common floor sturdy enough to hold us all.

Reclaiming welfare means designing not just for survival, but for flourishing. It means choosing to grow possibility on purpose and recognizing that the future we imagine together is one we can, in fact, build. Abundance, like democracy, expands with use.

Practice 4: Bridge and Build Belonging

Bridging begins not with grand gestures but with everyday encounters—with listening across difference, noticing kindness in our neighbors, and forming new relationships. Psychologists describe the feeling this can evoke as *moral elevation*: the warmth and expansion we experience when we witness goodness or courage in others. It reminds us that connection is not abstract; it is something we create each time we meet one another with openness and respect.[10]

As john a. powell reminds us in *The Power of Bridging,* bridging begins by asking, *"What is the other's story of themselves—and their story of us?"* He notes that *"us versus them"* is simple, while *"we and we"* is complex and full of surprises.[11] Bridging requires curiosity and a willingness to engage that complexity. Because people are layered and always changing, we should not expect to fully understand one another—or even ourselves. Our work is to keep listening, keep learning, and keep widening the "we." In doing so, we practice one of the most ordinary and essential forms of democracy: relationship.

Belonging is more than inclusion. It is not just having a seat in the room; it is being accepted as you are and having a voice in shaping the structures you are part of. Bridging creates the conditions for that belonging. It does not require agreement; it requires staying in relationship while we do the work.[12]

Bridging also makes imagination visible. Every conversation that holds difference without hostility expands the space of what is possible. I think of bridging as a way to move beyond the binaries that divide daily life—us versus them, left versus right, public versus private. When we bridge, we do more than imagine futures big enough for all of us; we co-create them. This is the quiet architecture of democracy, built not in marble halls but in the moments when we choose connection over contempt.

Bridging in Action: The Future Caucus

Future Caucus is a cross-partisan network of young state legislators—Republicans, Democrats, and Independents—committed to tackling issues that matter to rising generations, from the economy to democratic reform. At a time when polarization so often stalls progress, these lawmakers model a different way forward by building trust across party lines, centering generational challenges over partisan talking points, and collaborating on practical solutions.[13]

Their work offers a clear example of bridging in action. By creating space for shared values and fresh ideas, the Future Caucus demonstrates that political differences need not lead to political paralysis. Legislators can reframe their work around what connects them: care for constituents, concern for the future, and a commitment to democratic possibility. In a moment when scarcity and polarization dominate our national story, the Future Caucus shows that choosing relationship over division is not only possible, it is essential to rebuilding belonging in civic life.

Bridging also happens closer to home. Across the country, organizations are designing for relationship and connection:

- **Deep Canvassing:** Volunteers knock on doors not to persuade but to listen. By sharing personal stories and asking open-ended questions, they create space for reflection and connection, including across partisan divides.[14]
- **Braver Angels Workshops:** "Reds" and "Blues" come together for structured dialogue that builds empathy and understanding.[15]
- **Story Circles:** Small group discussions with guiding questions and timed sharing (no interruptions), building trust among people who don't usually meet.[16]
- **Community Gardens:** Neighbors grow food side by side, bridging cultural divides while cultivating nourishment and connection.[17]
- **Libraries as Bridging Hubs:** Neutral, trusted spaces in which neighbors connect through dialogues, classes, and community gatherings.[18]

Bridging does not demand sameness. It asks for curiosity, humility, and the willingness to stay in relationship while we do the work together. These practices remind us that belonging is not built by policy alone; it grows through how we show up for one another every day. And when public systems adopt the same posture—designing for relationship rather than transaction—they reinforce that belonging at scale.

> **Simple Moves We Can Make**
>
> - Attend one public meeting—school board, city council, or library board—not to persuade, but to listen across difference. Then share what you learned.
> - When a conversation heats up, ask, "What's at stake for you here?" Reflect back what you heard before responding.
> - Host a 60-minute story circle with neighbors unlike you: Ask two shared questions, allow five minutes per person, and listen without interruption.

Fatalism isolates us, and the forces we face (Chapter 7) exploit that isolation. Bridging is democracy's repair work for the human infrastructure that keeps institutions from collapsing under mistrust.

To be *in relationship* is not to agree or to resolve differences quickly. It is the practice of staying present, listening across tension, and continuing to show up even when outcomes are uncertain. Reclaiming welfare requires that kind of relationship. It asks us to practice the courage of connection long enough to imagine a future together—and to keep building it, side by side.

Practice 5: Reimagine Power from Systems *Over* People to Systems *With* People

Every system runs on power—who sets the rules, who enforces them, and who gets left out. For too long, our human-serving systems have operated through *power over*: rules written far away and compliance policed up close. But power is not fixed. It can be shared, built, and used to repair. In democratic design, power is meant to circulate, moving through communities rather than accumulating at the top. We can design for *power with*.

Power with begins by naming the power systems already hold. As I wrote for APHSA's *Policy & Practice* in 2022, structural power lives inside every public agency, but it is rarely acknowledged, let alone shared.[19] Shifting that power requires more than voice. It means communities have real authority, access to resources, and accountability mechanisms that make participation consequential. As one agency leader put it, leaders must sometimes "let go of decisions and power they have held too tightly."

In practice, *power with* looks like co-creation rather than consultation, governance rather than guidance, partnership rather than permission. It is present when people with lived and learned experience hold equal standing in designing solutions—when policy tables reflect the full breadth of community wisdom. The Full Frame Initiative's Community Bill of Rights and Centering Community Self-Assessment offer practical tools for this shift: embedding shared ownership, resourcing communities with the same information agencies hold, and tracking accountability together.[20]

Across the country, we are beginning to see what this looks like in motion (see sidebar). The shift is incomplete, but it is underway, showing that public systems can be rebuilt *with* the people they serve. This is institutional freedom in action: structures that enable participatory imagination rather than merely enforce compliance.

Globally, governments are testing what shared governance can look like at scale. In Leuven, Belgium, for example, the city has adopted participatory models of civic decision-making that bring residents, government, and business to the same table.[21] In the United Kingdom, public sector design frameworks increasingly treat design as a democratic act—one that values collective knowledge and co-creation in policymaking.[22] We are beginning to see similar experiments emerge in the United States: a shift from consultation to co-creation, from power *over* to power *with*.

Power With—in Action

- **Child Welfare Co-Design** (Multiple States): State agencies embed parents and youth with foster care experience as paid staff and design partners. Their leadership has reshaped reunification supports, kinship care, and extended foster care, shifting from compliance-driven "case plans" to youth- and family-led plans.[23]

- **L.A. REPAIR Participatory Budgeting** (City of Los Angeles, CA): The city launched L.A. REPAIR, allocating approximately $8.5 million across nine REPAIR Zones—neighborhoods identified for high need and historic underinvestment. Residents directly decide how funds are spent on local priorities.[24]

- **Participatory Budgeting Pilot** (Los Angeles County, CA): The county piloted a $1 million participatory-budgeting process using discretionary funds from one supervisorial district. Residents proposed and voted on community projects—an early test of shared fiscal decision-making at the county level.[25]

- **System of Care Framework** (Pennsylvania): Counties implementing this framework require youth and families to serve as decision makers in policy, funding, and governance roles, moving beyond advisory positions to co-governance.[26]

Each of these efforts moves beyond consultation. They change how decisions are made, who defines the problem, who allocates the resources, and who is accountable. Some operate locally; others reshape entire systems. Together they show that shared governance is not theoretical or optional; it's an essential practice for systems change.

These shifts in power are reshaping not only individual programs but the identity of the social sector itself. A growing movement of community organizations and national networks is calling for a new story that defines the sector by its impact, imagination, and partnership with government rather than by the absence of profit. This is democracy as shared authorship: institutions learning to govern *with* rather than *for*.

When communities hold equal footing, trust stops being a hurdle and becomes a product of the process itself. *Power with* is not chaos; it is co-creation that deepens through co-discovery, co-incubation, co-implementation, and co-refinement—a feedback loop that keeps systems responsive and alive. It rests on a simple belief: all of us have agency, and that agency grows stronger every time we design, build, and learn together.

Leading this way changes how systems see people. We stop treating communities as problems to manage and start recognizing them as partners in making systems work for everyone.

Simple Moves We Can Make

- Participate in—or help initiate—a shared decision-making process in your community, and invite two neighbors to join you.
- Co-author a public comment with people most affected by the policy. Don't speak *for*; speak *with*.
- Serve on a local board, advisory council, or working group—and practice sharing the mic.
- Ask in every meeting: "Who's not here—and what will we change so they are next time?"

If well-being is constructed (Chapter 5) and systems cut both ways (Chapter 6), then *power with* is the design choice that makes scaffolding (Chapter 8) real. When decisions are shared, public systems become sites of belonging and agency. Reclaiming welfare means democratizing design and treating participation itself as public infrastructure.

And when we share power, we also share authorship. That leads to the next frontier of design: narrative. The stories we tell determine what becomes possible. Systems built *with* people must also be narrated *by* people. Every new policy, partnership, or practice begins as a story someone believes can be true. If *power with* makes democracy tangible, narrative makes it durable. It's how we turn moments of participation into movements of belonging.

Practice 6: Normalize New Narratives

Narratives don't shift just because we debunk a myth. They shift when truer stories of shared possibility become normal. That takes repetition, visibility, and practice—in newsrooms, classrooms, city halls, and living rooms. As the Narrative Initiative puts it plainly, "The future of our country depends on millions of everyday narrators."[27]

Narrative change is democratic work. It is how a society renews the meaning of "us." Each time we tell a truer story, we expand who belongs inside it.

We need to be clear-eyed about narrative power. The way we frame an issue shapes the solutions we build. Wrong assumptions produce the wrong fixes. Starting from a shared drive for well-being challenges stories of deviance or deficiency and invites a broader "we."

We can tell a different story. Poverty is not an individual flaw; it is a policy failure we can fix. People do not need fixing. What we need is infrastructure that gives all of us a fair shot and the freedom to thrive. Public systems can be places of belonging and agency. Well-being is a responsibility we share.

When a debate forces a false binary—such as capitalism versus socialism—we can name the tactic and reframe the value: "We're focused on designs that measurably improve well-being and expand freedom in daily life." Then we point to outcomes and invite action: "Here's what works. Here's how we scale it."

Normalizing new narratives is freedom in practice. It is the collective act of imagining aloud—again and again—until possibility becomes common sense.

Spreading the Story of Us

Stories don't spread on their own; people do. Each time we tell a truer story about what welfare means, one grounded in belonging and shared well-being, we chip away at the old one.

Narrative change isn't abstract. It happens when enough of us repeat truer stories until they become common sense. We normalize belonging by living it out loud through the stories we share, the examples we lift up, and the language we choose in our daily lives and professional roles.

If policy is narrative in action, then our everyday words and choices are the material that gives it form. Whether we're speaking at a community meeting or posting online, writing a headline or drafting a grant proposal, telling a child about the American Dream or greeting a neighbor in need, we are always reinforcing a story. We either repeat scarcity and suspicion or help rewrite the story toward shared possibility.

When we narrate care as strength and describe public systems as scaffolding for well-being, we practice democracy through language. Culture shifts this way, one conversation, one post, one headline at a time.

In today's attention economy, the stories that travel farthest are rarely the ones that heal. Digital platforms reward outrage, fear, and division, the emotional triggers that keep people scrolling but also keep us stuck. Stories of cooperation, repair, and shared well-being struggle to compete when relevance is measured by conflict. To normalize new narratives, we must attend not only to what we say, but to the systems that amplify it, and choose, again and again, to reward curiosity, connection, and care as signals of what matters.

Share Stories that Reveal Human Services as Public Infrastructure

Repetition builds reality. When we speak about human services as democratic infrastructure, as the connective tissue of our shared life, we make visible what has long been hidden. Stories of thriving systems, trusted relationships, and collective well-being travel farther than policy papers. And when more of us tell them, they begin to reshape what we expect as the norm.

Each of us is a messenger. In a culture saturated with cynicism, telling truer stories is not a small act; it is a civic practice. It reminds people that government is us, that care is infrastructure, and that belonging is not sentimental but structural. Narrative work is the everyday maintenance of democracy. It keeps the beams of belief from rusting and holds open the possibility of a future we build together.

Narrative Resources—Changing the Story Together

Changing culture requires both repetition and resourcing. The organizations below advance narrative change in practice by offering language, research, and storytelling tools for anyone ready to help rewrite the American welfare story.

- **ideas42:** *Shifting Harmful Narratives about Poverty in the U.S.*
  A behavioral science initiative reframing poverty as a systemic challenge rather than an individual failure, with applied insights for policymakers, advocates, and communicators.
- **FrameWorks Institute:** *Multiple Resources and Toolkits*
  Evidenced-based research and tools about public systems, democracy, and collective problem-solving.
- **Social Current:** *Five & Rising Campaign*
  A national effort to reframe the social sector itself, not as "nonprofit," but as essential civic infrastructure, inviting communities to rise with a new story of care, trust, and shared well-being.
- **The Opportunity Agenda:** *Shifting the Narrative, Advancing Equity*
  Practical guidance for telling stories that connect opportunity,

equity, and belonging, helping advocates move hearts as well as minds.
- **Narrative Initiative:** A networked movement organization supporting change makers to align stories across sectors, centering values of interdependence, justice, and collective care.

These are starting points, not scripts. The most powerful narrative shift begins where you are, with the stories you choose to tell and repeat.

Simple Moves We Can Make

- **Flood the zone with belonging.** Algorithms amplify what is repeated. Share stories of universal school meals, guaranteed income pilots, or human-centered service redesigns that affirm care for one another as democratic strength.
- **Practice public gratitude.** Thank the social workers, public servants, and community partners who hold the fabric of belonging together. Public appreciation shifts what we value.
- **Be a bridge online.** Follow and share voices across lines of difference. Highlight cooperation and collaboration that remind us democracy is built through relationship.
- **Model narrative change at work.** Swap words like "clients" or "cases" for "participants" and "partners." In budgets and reports, frame investments in care as investments in community stability and shared prosperity.

Changing a national narrative can feel daunting, but every post, meeting, and story is a chance to widen the "we." When enough of us practice it, at kitchen tables and conference tables, in congregations and classrooms, the new story of American welfare becomes not only believable, but visible.

We began by reclaiming the word *welfare* (Chapter 1) and unmasking the rationing of the American Dream (Chapter 2). We named the forces we face (Chapter 7) and the scaffolding we need (Chapter 8). Normalizing new narratives is how those truths become common sense. It is how democracy learns to speak again.

Belonging becomes the headline, not the footnote. Reclaiming welfare means reclaiming the story of us.

Leading the Story Forward

Each practice in this chapter—seeing humanity, cultivating curiosity, designing for abundance, bridging divides, reimagining power, and normalizing new narratives—is a small democratic act. Repeated together, they become a movement.

Leadership is what magnifies these practices into culture. When leaders model belonging through how they listen, frame issues, and share power, they reshape what the public expects of systems and what people expect of one another. And the truth is, we are all students of belonging. We will not get it right every time, but we can keep learning. Every policy briefing, team meeting, media interview, and community forum is an opportunity to tell a larger truth: our shared well-being is the architecture of democracy.

The story of American welfare is ultimately the story of us: how we show up, what we make visible, and what we choose to grow. When leaders at every level claim that story and live it out loud, belonging becomes both a value and a design principle.

That is where the next chapter begins. Imagine what democracy itself can look like when we build it with care, courage, and the conviction that everyone counts.

Drawing the New Blueprint

We can write a different story, one grounded in enough for all of us and built on relationships. A story where systems are designed *with* us, not done *to* us. A story we practice in daily interactions until it becomes the way we live.

Reclaiming welfare is not a slogan; it is a practice. It is recognition, inquiry, enough, relationship, shared power, and stories that make belonging and agency normal. When we live these practices in homes, headlines, and halls of government, we redraw the blueprint of what America believes it owes itself. Narratives do not change because myths are debunked, but because new stories take hold. Stories of abundance. Stories of belonging. Stories that feel less like aspiration and more like common sense.

The question is not whether stories will change, but whether we will change them together. If policy is scaffolding and practice is habit, then narrative is blueprint. It is time to draw a new one.

When we draw that blueprint together, we are not only rewriting the welfare story—we are redesigning democracy itself.

Building What We Imagine

Every blueprint is a promise waiting for structure. What we imagine here, the systems, relationships, and stories of shared well-being, becomes real only when we build it. The next chapter turns that promise into architecture: *Democracy by Design*, where belonging becomes the foundation and care for one another becomes the frame of a new American Dream.

Carrying the Story Forward
Further Reading

- **See No Stranger**—Valarie Kaur
  A call to practice "revolutionary love" as both a personal discipline and a public ethic—showing how courage, curiosity, and care can reshape how we belong to one another.

- **The Power of Bridging**—john a. powell
  Explores bridging as a core practice of belonging, moving beyond "us versus them" toward a larger, more resilient "we" capable of holding difference without division.

- **Hope for Cynics**—Jamil Zaki
  Draws on psychology and neuroscience to show that empathy, trust, and optimism are not naïve ideals, but learnable practices that strengthen connection and collective resilience.

CHAPTER 10

Democracy by Design

A New American Dream

Democracy is not a state. It is an act.

—John Lewis

If narrative is the blueprint, then democracy is what we build together. It is not something fixed behind glass, but a structure renewed by our choices. We often mistake it for a finished house—checks and balances, a Constitution, a vote every few years. Yet democracy lives only through the acts we take with and for one another.

At its core, democracy rests on a simple belief: every person matters, and our shared life should reflect and protect that truth. It is tested daily in our systems—schools, workplaces, hospitals, and human services—and in whether they affirm the agency and possibility of every one of us. When systems nurture belonging, democracy becomes tangible. When they do not, democracy erodes from within. At the very moments when democracy should feel strongest—times of vulnerability, transition, and need—our systems too often ask people to prove their worth. Paperwork replaces care. Suspicion replaces support. Shame replaces belonging.

No matter where we sit politically, most of us sense that something vital has thinned in our shared life. The question is how we thicken it again through care, connection, and design.

This thinning is not only a policy failure; it is a failure of democratic vision. And yet, because democracy is an act of humans, it is also something we can remake. We are not bound to repeat what no longer serves us. We can choose a different future, one in which caring for one another is not peripheral to the American Dream, but its foundation.

Democracy as Infrastructure

Democracy is more than ballots and branches of government. It is the everyday architecture of belonging. Its strength depends on the reliability of our shared systems that feed, house, educate, heal, and connect us.

Just as bridges and roads enable commerce, civic infrastructure enables trust. When public systems are fair, inclusive, and dependable, they generate confidence that government works and that participation matters. When they are brittle or inequitable, trust erodes, and democracy weakens from within.

Designing democracy, then, means designing the conditions for collective well-being:

- **Civic trust**—Systems that keep promises and meet needs reliably.
- **Inclusion**—Policies that expand who belongs and who decides.
- **Shared well-being**—Institutions that treat care as a public good.

Together, these form the scaffolding of a healthy democracy and the idea that freedom is not only the right to participate, but the capacity to thrive together.

Reimagining welfare as shared infrastructure reframes democracy not only as the right to participate, but as the right to thrive together.

When my son asked me what the American Dream means today, I paused because the answer felt both deeply personal and profoundly public. This chapter is my response to his homework. The dream is not secured by wealth or luck or grit alone. It will be secured—or lost—by how we choose to care for one another, and by the systems we design to make that care real.

So let us imagine what that future could look like. We each hold a piece of the redesign. Imagine waking up in an America where systems are designed for everyone to thrive.

Reimagining The Possible: A Counterfactual American Dream

To imagine differently is an act of freedom. As historian Timothy Snyder writes, freedom is not the defense of what is, but the imagination of what could be.[1] Our democracy depends on that collective imagination and the courage to design what we have yet to realize.

Democracy by design begins with a simple question: *What if our public systems actually reflected the values we claim to hold—where care, connection, and possibility are the structure of daily life, not side projects?*

Across the country, glimpses of that future already exist.

Imagine a school that functions as a true community hub. A young mother, finishing a night shift, drops her son off early. He heads to a warm breakfast and before-school program while she speaks with a nurse about his asthma and then rests briefly in a parent room before heading home. In New York City, community schools like this already exist. They show graduation rates 5 to 7 points higher than comparable schools and significantly lower chronic absenteeism, especially among students facing housing instability.[2] In Cincinnati, Community Learning Centers have narrowed the achievement gap between Black and White students from 14.5 percent to 4.5 percent, while boosting third-grade reading and family engagement.[3] These examples show what becomes possible when schools serve as scaffolding for care and belonging.

Imagine a state where economic disruption does not immediately spiral into an emergency. A newly unemployed father logs into an online portal, updates his income, and checks whether his family qualifies for food, housing, health care, or child care through one streamlined application. Research from Georgetown University's Digital Benefits Network shows that integrated eligibility systems are evolving, allowing families to apply for multiple supports in one place.[4] These designs are not yet seamless, but they move us closer to stability arriving sooner, before hardship cascades into deeper instability.

Innovation is already shaping this work. States are experimenting with artificial intelligence to translate policy text into software code, making rules easier to align across programs.[5] The American Public Human Services Association is studying how AI can modernize SNAP processing, reduce burdens on staff, and improve timely access.[6] National partners are also helping states build the public capacity needed to govern AI responsibly, advancing projects that equip agencies with the tools, frameworks, and guardrails to use technology in service of equity and democratic purpose.[7] These are early efforts, but they show what happens when technologists, advocates, and human service leaders design together: systems that are more human, responsive, and democratic by design.

Imagine a generation of children for whom lunch is simply part of the day, not a marker of status. In states from California to Colorado to Maine, universal school meals are normalizing a shared floor: nourishment as a public good that belongs to all of us.[8]

Imagine a state where child care is treated as a public good rather than a private burden. In 2022, New Mexico voters approved a constitutional amendment directing a portion of the state's Land Grant Permanent Fund—fueled by oil and gas revenues—into early childhood education and child care. By late 2025, the state began rolling out universal child care for all families, regardless of income, marking the nation's first constitutional guarantee of permanent public funding for early learning.[9]

Imagine a frontline workforce honored as bridge-builders rather than gatekeepers. In New Mexico, community health workers stand beside families as trusted navigators.[10] In North Carolina, family navigators open doors instead of guarding them.[11] Success is measured not by cases closed but by trust built.

Imagine local leadership redefined. A human services director walks alongside faith leaders, small-business owners, and neighborhood organizers to weave connections that strengthen community scaffolding. Across the country, communities are planning for climate impacts in this way, bringing human services into resilience planning alongside emergency managers and measuring not only dollars saved, but trust earned and resilience gained.[142]

Counterfactual in Practice:

Where It's Already Happening

These examples show that the future we imagine is not fantasy. It already exists in places today:

- **Community schools:** Higher graduation rates, reduced chronic absenteeism, narrowed racial achievement gaps, and stronger family and community engagement.
- **Integrated eligibility systems:** Single applications across food, health, and child care programs reduce barriers and delays. AI tools are also freeing staff time for working with families, not paperwork.
- **Universal school meals:** Free breakfast and lunch for all students reduce stigma, improve attendance, and normalize public goods.
- **Libraries as civic anchors:** Social workers, peer navigators, telehealth kiosks, and legal aid clinics embedded in trusted public spaces.
- **Community health workers and family navigators:** Trusted bridge-builders who measure success by trust built, not cases closed.
- **Climate and human services planning:** Human services at the table with emergency managers to strengthen resilience before disasters strike.

This is not utopia. It is a counterfactual grounded in evidence and lived practice—visible in communities that have chosen to build differently and in systems already showing us what is possible. We have the ingenuity. What we need is scale, and the collective will to make care, belonging, and well-being the norm rather than the exception.

What It Will Take To Get There

Visions do not become reality on their own. They require will. Design. Courage. Alignment. They require that we act not only with imagination, but with intention.

To build the kind of human well-being system that democracy demands, we will need more than redesigned programs. We will need to reclaim our shared purpose.

And we can, because the pieces are already here. Each of us participates in the architecture of democracy through the stories we tell, the policies we support, the institutions we lead, and the ways we show up for one another.

We write democracy into being through five design choices.

1. Narrative Shift: From Shame to Solidarity

We must flood the zone with stories that center human ingenuity, belonging, and agency—not deficiency. Culture shifts slowly, but it does shift. We have seen it before, when seatbelts moved from personal choice to law and a shared norm, and when the Americans with Disabilities Act made ramps and captions a basic expectation. In both cases, stories of collective care reshaped what we designed, and design reshaped what we believed.

The same can be true for human services. A growing coalition of mayors, county officials, and legislators is championing guaranteed income as a means of stability and opportunity.[13] Their efforts and the stories of families whose lives are strengthened by unconditional cash support are advancing a new narrative that direct investment in people works.

These stories make policies not only imaginable, but expected. Systems follow stories. And when the story changes, so does what becomes possible.

2. Policy Design: Simple, Universal, Flexible

We must enact policies that reflect what we already know works: unconditional supports, common access points, and flexibility by default. Human services leaders across the country are integrating eligibility and benefits so families no longer face endless applications. The expanded Child Tax Credit in 2021 showed how quickly unconditional income can reduce poverty at scale.[14]

Momentum is also building behind universal systems that reduce stigma and increase trust, including the national movement for free school meals, with entire states now guaranteeing them for all children. As Michigan's Rx Kids program demonstrates, when support is universal and stigma-free, belonging becomes a design feature, not an aspiration.[15]

This isn't about more bureaucracy. It's about smarter, more human design.

3. Institutional Courage: Centering Proximity and Co-Design

Redesigning systems begins with redesigning who gets to build them. Across the nation, people with lived experience are gaining seats at policymaking tables as co-designers and co-implementers. Their leadership shows how governance changes when proximity, trust, and lived wisdom guide the work.

Networks of community health workers, family navigators, and grassroots organizers demonstrate what happens when that wisdom is put into practice. Organizations like Think of Us, led by Sixto Cancel, are reimagining foster care by bringing those who lived its failures into the design of solutions rooted in belonging.[16]

Counties such as Fairfax, Virginia, are part of a growing movement treating climate resilience as a human services issue, ensuring readiness and community care before disasters strike.[17]

This is how government earns trust, not through distance or decree, but through proximity, shared authorship, and care.

4. Political Strategy: Invest in Scaffolding for Care and Connection

A nation that can mobilize trillions for defense or financial bailouts can mobilize just as forcefully for well-being and the building blocks that sustain it—housing, child care, and economic security. During COVID-

19, federal action temporarily expanded unemployment insurance, nutrition benefits, and cash supports, demonstrating that rapid investment in human infrastructure is possible.[18]

But urgency alone isn't enough. We also need a different story about how value is created. As Mariana Mazzucato argues, public institutions are not passive responders to markets. They are co-creators of value, shaping possibility through investment, innovation, and shared purpose.[19]

Today, cross sector coalitions are advancing this shift. Code for America's Safety Net Innovation Lab is helping states redesign benefit delivery so supports are dependable and user-friendly.[20] The Care Economy Business Council calls for child care and paid leave as essential to growth.[21] National coalitions like Care Can't Wait and Caring Across Generations are aligning caregivers, labor, and advocates around a shared vision of care as a public good.[22]

Philanthropy is accelerating this shift through large-scale investments, including the $50 million CARE Fund backing grassroots coalitions of care workers and organizers.[23] Together, these efforts signal more than policy reform. They reflect a political and cultural reorientation toward caring for one another as the scaffolding of democracy and prosperity, not charity at the margins.

5. Leadership—At Every Level

Rewriting the welfare story also requires rewriting the story of the social sector itself. For decades, community-based organizations—the backbone of service delivery—have been defined by what they are not:

"nonprofits." That framing has reinforced chronic underfunding and invisibility.

In truth, this sector is not peripheral. It is central. It is where policy meets lived experience, where belonging is either affirmed or denied.

The Social Current Five & Rising campaign, launched in 2025, is among the boldest efforts to change this narrative.[24] Inspired in part by the film *UnCharitable*,[25] the campaign calls for discarding the "nonprofit" label and embracing a new vision of the social sector measured by impact rather than scarcity. Through pilot communities, it is testing new models of funding, governance, and partnership designed to unlock innovation and scale.

We need leaders who hold both truth and possibility: who can name the past, face the present, and help shape the future.

Leadership is showing up everywhere. Human services executives are reorienting agencies toward community building. Legislators are advancing guaranteed income and child allowances. Philanthropies are funding narrative change. Youth activists are reframing climate justice as inseparable from social well-being.

Richmond, Virginia offers a vivid example. Its Office of Community Wealth Building, sustained across administrations, has built a durable model for economic mobility and neighborhood resilience. By centering community leadership and long-term investment, Richmond demonstrates what it looks like when cities treat well-being as core civic infrastructure.[26]

This is what scholars describe as *leadership in place*. It is leadership rooted in context, accountable to community, and shaped by proximity rather than position. Leadership is not reserved for the elected or appointed. It is practiced daily by parents raising curious children, neighbors organizing for safer housing, and caseworkers refusing to treat families as numbers.

We do not need to start from scratch. The scaffolding is already here. What we need is the courage to align it, and the vision to build beyond what we inherited. The future will be shaped by what we normalize, what we fund, and what we demand.

History reminds us that change rarely begins with majority support. It begins with a committed few, telling a new story, building a new model, and refusing to believe that what we have is all there is.

Leadership as Narrative in Action

Narratives don't shift on their own. We carry them, repeat them, and decide—often without realizing it—which stories become normalized. That's why leadership is about more than budgets or policy. It is about what we choose to name, the values we lift up, and the practices we normalize.

I saw this dynamic firsthand during my time leading APHSA, when we partnered with Leadership for a Networked World at Harvard University's Technology and Entrepreneurship Center to reimage how the human services sector saw itself. Together with Executive Director Dr. Antonio Oftelie, creator of the Human Services Value Curve, we convened human service leaders from across the nation to explore how agencies could move from compliance-driven practices toward creating public value.[27]

That shift required changing not only what we measured, but how we spoke about our work. Research from the FrameWorks Institute helped give us the language to do it. When leaders reoriented from administering programs to generating people-centered solutions—and paired that shift with language focused on constructing well-being and human potential—it filtered into daily practice. Staff communication changed. Partners began to see agencies differently. Even the public started to glimpse human services not as last-resort programs but as scaffolding for thriving communities.

Those moments reminded me how powerful leadership can be in setting a different story in motion. By choosing goals and words rooted in possibility, we gave permission for systems to see themselves differently—and to act differently.

These experiences taught me that when we, as leaders and practitioners, normalize belonging instead of blame, and abundance instead of scarcity, we change the story of what human services can be. And when the story changes, the system changes.

This is the quiet but powerful work of building belonging: not only changing policies, but reshaping the stories that guide them. If we can create this kind of shift within a single agency, imagine what becomes possible when we design every system with belonging at its core.

Leadership, at its best, is narrative in action: the daily practice of aligning story and structure until they reinforce one another. When leaders tell a truer story of who we are and what we owe each other, they help democracy remember itself.

That same principle applies at every level of public life. What we normalize, repeat, and design ultimately determines the story we live by.

The Story We Carry Forward

This book began with a word—*welfare*. Once, it meant well-being, care, and shared responsibility. Then it was twisted into shame and weaponized into division, shrinking the horizon of what we thought was possible.

But we know better now. Welfare was never the problem. It was always the promise.

We've traced how these narratives were constructed—by politics, by racism, by fear. We've seen how they hardened into systems that punish instead of support. Blame became policy. Suspicion became design. Belonging was denied at scale.

And still, across these pages, we've also seen something else:
- Leaders daring to tell a truer story.
- Public officials advancing once-radical ideas like guaranteed income and universal school meals.
- Coalitions of parents, youth, and organizers demanding a role in co-designing the systems that shape their lives.
- Communities preparing for climate disruption and insisting that resilience must include social care and human services.

These glimpses remind us that another way is not only possible; it is already being built.

Rebecca Solnit writes that we live and die by the stories we tell: stories that trap us or free us.[28] What matters is remembering that we have the power to be storytellers, not just listeners.

The final truth of this book is this: We *get to choose the story*. The story of who we are to one another. The story of what public systems should feel like. The story of what we owe one another as co-authors of a shared democracy.

The systems we live with today were imagined and designed by people. They can be redesigned—by us. We can choose to make well-being visible, belonging undeniable, and democracy stronger in the very places where it now feels most fragile.

A story we tell truthfully, build collectively, and live daily can change everything. It can become policy. It can become culture. It can become the new normal. But only if we choose it, again and again. In boardrooms and break rooms. In budgets and ballot boxes. In classrooms, congregations, and community centers. In the quiet choices of daily life and the loud echoes of the public square.

When my son Sean prepared his school presentation on the American Dream, he and his classmates chose to believe in it, even while naming the gap between promise and reality. As Sean reminds us: *"It's something we must aspire to."*

That is the work before us now: to make the dream whole by building systems that embody care, belonging, and the well-being of all of us.

To reclaim the word *welfare* is to reclaim its truth—that the strength of our democracy rests on how well we care for one another.

That is the invitation—

to tell the fuller story,

to design the better system,

to shape the more abundant future.

Not just for some. **For all of U.S.**

EPILOGUE

The Story We Write Together

We are at an inflection point, not unlike those that came before—the end of the Civil War, the Great Depression, the Civil Rights Era, and the upheaval of COVID-19. Each of those moments revealed how fragile our systems were and offered a chance to expand the circle of belonging. Sometimes we rose to meet it; other times we retreated. Today, we face another choice. Will we allow fear, division, and scarcity thinking to shrink our democracy? Or will we claim this moment to build systems worthy of the American Dream we have too long rationed? History shows that in times of fracture, bold strides are possible—if we summon the will.

The future of our democracy depends on whether we do.

TECHNICAL AUTHOR'S NOTE

Notes on Sources

This book draws on a wide range of materials, including historical texts, contemporary research, published articles, public records, and my professional experience. Because readers may encounter these works in different formats, a few clarifications may be helpful:

Books. Print editions are cited with page numbers. For e-books, citations reference chapter or section headings rather than page numbers, since pagination varies by device and platform. Because chapter or section identifiers are consistent across formats, specific e-book editions (such as Kindle or Apple Books) are not noted.

Online sources. URLs are provided when available. Access dates are included only when an online source lacks a clear publication date or when the content is subject to change, update, or removal.

Selective bibliography. The bibliography is intentionally selective rather than comprehensive. It is offered as a guide for readers who wish to explore further, highlighting works that were especially influential in shaping the book's analysis and arguments.

Quotations from other published works are used in accordance with U.S. fair use principles and are fully cited in the endnotes.

ENDNOTES

Epigraph

1. Rebecca Solnit, foreword to *Hope in the Dark: Untold Histories, Wild Possibilities*, 3rd ed. (Haymarket Books, 2016).

Welfare Wasn't a Bad Word

1. The phrase "general Welfare" is used twice in the U.S. Constitution: once in the Preamble and again in Article I, Section 8, which grants Congress the power "to provide for the common Defence and general Welfare."

2. The official name change from the American Public Welfare Association (APWA) to the American Public Human Services Association (APHSA) occurred after the 1996 welfare reform legislation known as the Personal Responsibility and Work Opportunity Act.

3. "Welfare." Online Etymology Dictionary, accessed July 19, 2025, https://www.etymonline.com/word/welfare

4. In eighteenth-century English, capitalizing abstract nouns was a way of emphasizing their importance. David Crystal, *The Stories of English* (Overlook Press, 2004), 318–20. Crystal explains eighteenth-century conventions in capitalization, especially in formal and legal writing, and how they reflected emphasis and rhetorical style.

5. Chimamanda Ngozi Adichie, "The Danger of a Single Story," filmed July 2009 at TEDGlobal, Oxford, UK, *TED* video, posted October 2009.
https://www.ted.com/talks/chimamanda_ngozi_adichie_the_danger_of_a_single_story.
Adichie notes that stereotypes aren't necessarily untrue, but incomplete, making "our recognition of equal humanity difficult."

6. See Chapter 3, "The Five-Decade Drift: How Blame and Shame Took Root."

7. See Chapter 3, "The Hidden Harm of Tropes."

8. Some communications scholars and psychologists have long cautioned that repeating false or stigmatizing narratives can unintentionally reinforce them—a dynamic sometimes called the "backfire effect." While more recent research suggests this effect is less universal than once believed, it remains true that familiarity itself can make a story feel credible, even when it is wrong. This is why advocates stress the importance of using stronger, alternative narratives can replace harmful frames than simply negate them. See Stephen Lewandowsky et al., "Misinformation and Its Correction: Continued Influence and Successful Debiasing," *Psychological Science in the Public Interest* 13, no. 3 (2012): 106–31, https://doi.org/10.1177/1529100612451018

9. john a. powell, director of the Othering & Belonging Institute at the University of California, Berkeley, intentionally spells his name in lowercase as an expression of his belief in the importance of community over the individual and to de-emphasize ego in academic and social discourse.

10. john a. powell, *The Power of Bridging: How to Build a World Where We All Belong* (Sounds True, 2024), chap. 1.

11. I was introduced to the power of social norms through the work of Dr. Betsy Levy Paluk, professor of psychology and public affairs at Princeton University and recipient of a MacArthur Genuis Grant. My podcast co-host, Karen Heller Key and I had the privilege of interviewing Dr. Paluk in 2023. See Tracy Wareing Evans and Karen Heller Key, *Our Dream Deferred*, episode "Unwritten Rules that Shape Us," podcast, APHSA, July 12, 2023, Libsyn, https://aphsa.libsyn.com/unwritten-rules-that-shape-us

12. Social psychologists distinguish between descriptive norms—what people commonly do—and injunctive norms—what people believe they ought to do, based on social approval or disapproval. This distinction was introduced in Robert B. Cialdini, Raymond R. Reno, and Carl A. Kallgren, "A Focus Theory of Normative Conduct: Recycling the Concept of Norms to Reduce Littering in Public Places," *Journal of Personality and Social Psychology* 58, no. 6 (1990): 1015–26, https://doi.org/10.1037/0022-3514.58.6.1015

13. I was first introduced to the science of framing and cultural narratives through the work of the FrameWorks Institute. Their research on human services and child welfare opened new ways of thinking that reshaped my approach to leadership in the sector. I explore this more deeply in Chapter 5 and reference other narrative scholars throughout the book. For further discussion, see my podcast interview with FrameWorks CEO Nat Kendall-Taylor: Tracy Wareing Evans and Karen Heller Key, *Our Dream Deferred*, episode "Cultural Mindsets: Understanding the Lenses that Shape the Way We See the World," podcast, APHSA, September 6, 2023,

https://aphsa.libsyn.com/cultural-mindsets-understanding-the-lenses-that-shape-the-way-we-see-the-world-part-1

14. For more on the racialized evolution of the public image of welfare, see Chapters 3 and 4.

15. The English Poor Laws were a series of laws enacted at the turn of the sixteenth century under Queen Elizabeth to address widespread unemployment and rising social unrest. John E. Hansan, "Poor Relief in Early America," *Social Welfare History Project*, Virginia Commonwealth University, accessed July 21, 2025,

https://socialwelfare.library.vcu.edu/programs/poor-relief-early-amer/

16. Hansan, "Poor Relief in Early America."

17. Lesley Kennedy. "How 'Poor Laws' Tried to Tackle Poverty in Colonial America." *History.com*, last updated May 27, 2025,

https://www.history.com/articles/colonial-america-poor-laws

18. Individuals deemed "undeserving" were usually sent to workhouses, which were harsh facilities in which shelter was exchanged for labor. People who refused to work faced punishment or incarceration. Hansan, "Poor Relief in Early America."

19. Following the American Revolution, the poor-law framework persisted, but its administration shifted. Because the new constitutional order separated church and state, responsibilities once held by parish churches were transferred to secular county officials, especially in states like North Carolina, South Carolina, and Virginia. This marked an important transition: poverty relief moved from a religious duty to a civic function, embedding it more firmly within governmental authority and social regulation. James W. Ely, Jr., "Poor Laws of the Post-Revolutionary South," 1776–1800, *Tulsa Law Journal* 21, no. 1 (1985): 4–5,

https://digitalcommons.law.utulsa.edu/tlr/vol21/iss1/1

20. William P. Quigley, "Reluctant Charity: Poor Laws in the Original Thirteen States," *University Richmond Law Review* 31, no. 4 (1997): 111-12, http://scholarship.richmond.edu/lawreview/vol31/iss1/4

21. Quigley, "Reluctant Charity," 121-23.

22. For a general overview of nineteenth-century poorhouses and their role in local poor relief, see David Wagner, "Poor Relief and the Almhouse," *Social Welfare History Project*, Virginia Commonwealth History Project, accessed July 21, 2025, https://socialwelfare.library.vcu.edu/issues/poor-relief-almshouse

23. Oliver asks not for himself, but for another boy who is so hungry that he fears he might harm the child sleeping next to him. Charles Dickens, *Oliver Twist* (first published 1838; repr., 1867), chap. 2.

24. Jane Addams, *Democracy and Social Ethics* (1902; Project Gutenberg transcription), chap. 2.

25. Walter I. Trattner, *From Poor Law to Welfare State: A History of Social Welfare in America*, 6th ed. (Free Press, 1999), chap. 8.

26. Stephanie Saulnier, "The Progressive Era's Response to Social Needs," in *Social Welfare Policy History* (Salk: Pressbooks, 2025), chap. 5, https://saalck.pressbooks.pub/social-welfare-policy/chapter/chapter-5-the-progressive-eras-response-to-social-needs/. See also Jane Addams, *Twenty Years at Hull-House: With Autobiographical Notes* (Macmillan, 1910), 109-115.

27. Addams, *Democracy and Social Ethics*, chap. 1.

28. Kathryn Kish Sklar, *Florence Kelley and the Nation's Work: The Rise of Women's Political Culture, 1830–1900* (Yale University Press, 1995), 205–208.

29. John Bodnar, "Jane Addams, Hull House, and Immigration."*Bill of Rights Institute*, accessed July 29, 2025, https://billofrightsinstitute.org/essays/jane-addams-hull-house-and-immigration

30. Historians note that Hull House reflected the racial boundaries of its neighborhood and rarely included Black families in its early decades. "Segregation at Hull-House: A Closer Look," *Jane Addams Papers Project Blog*, July 21, 2021,

https://janeaddams.ramapo.edu/2021/07/21/segregation-at-hull-house-a-closer-look/.

See also John E. Hansen, "Settlement Houses: An Introduction," *Social Welfare History Project*, Virginia Commonwealth University, accessed September 23, 2025,

https://socialwelfare.library.vcu.edu/settlement-houses/settlement-houses/.

Dr. Harriet Alleyne Rice, who started working at Hull House as early as 1893 was the first and (for a long time) only Black resident. Stacy Lynn, "Dr. Harriet Rice: First Black Resident at Hull-House," *Jane Addams Papers Project Blog*, August 11 2021,

https://janeaddams.ramapo.edu/2021/08/dr-harriet-rice-first-black-resident-at-hull-house/

31. See Isabel Wilkerson, *Caste: The Origins of Our Discontent* (Random House, 2020), chap 3, noting that "over time colonial laws granted English and Irish indentured servants greater privileges than the Africans who worked alongside them."

32. Martin Luther King Jr., *Where Do We Go from Here: Chaos or Community?* (Beacon Press, 1967), chap. 3.

33. David Treuer, *The Heartbeat of Wounded Knee: Native America from 1890 to the Present* (Riverhead Books, 2019), prologue. Treuer dismantles the myth of Native disappearance and instead emphasizes continuity and survival. He does so by confronting the brutal foundations of American expansion: the seizure of land, the breaking of treaties, and the destruction of communities, all legitimized by law and celebrated in settler narratives.

34. Heather McGhee, *The Sum of Us: What Racism Costs Everyone and How We Can Prosper Together* (One World, 2021), chap. 1.

35. Wilkerson, *Caste*, chap. 4.

36. Joanne Goldblum and Colleen Shaddox, *Broke in America* (BenBella Books, 2021), chap. 1. See also Mark Rank, Lawrence M. Eppard, and Heather E. Bullock, *Poorly Understood: What America Gets Wrong About Poverty* (Oxford University Press, 2021).

37. Snyder writes "The task begins with rescuing the word [freedom] from overuse and abuse... we speak of freedom without considering what it is." Timothy Snyder, *On Freedom* (Crown, 2024), preface.

An American Illusion

1. James Truslow Adams, *The Epic of America* (Little, Brown, 1931), chap. 1.

2. Adams cautioned that neither government nor corporate leaders could deliver a "satisfying and humane existence" unless individuals themselves cultivated a deeper sense of what constitutes "a genuinely satisfying life." He saw material accumulation as an insufficient measure of national strength and urged that the American Dream must be rooted in collective values and purpose, not just private gain. Nearly a century later, his words resonate in a nation still prone to equating economic expansion with social progress, even as widening inequality and fraying trust reveal the limits of prosperity without shared well-being. Adams, *The Epic of America*, epilogue.

3. Langston Hughes, "Harlem," in *The Collected Poems of Langston Hughes*, ed. Arnold Rampersad (Vintage Classics, 1994), 426.

4. James Baldwin, debate remarks at the Cambridge Union Society, Cambridge, UK, February 18, 1965, video, YouTube, posted by "BBC Newsnight," April 7, 2014,
https://www.youtube.com/watch?v=VOCZOHQ7fCE.
See also James Baldwin, "The American Dream and the American Negro," *New York Times Magazine*, March 7, 1965, reprinted in *Collected Essays*, ed. Toni Morrison (Library of America, 1998), 714-19. In that essay, he wrote: "Until the moment comes when we, the Americans, are able to accept the fact that my ancestors are both black and white, that on that continent we are trying to forge a new identity, that we need each other, that I am not a ward of America, I am not an object of missionary charity, I am one of the people who built the country—until this moment comes there is scarcely any hope for the American dream."

5. Reverend Dr. William J. Barber II, *White Poverty: How Exposing Myths About Race and Class Can Reconstruct American Democracy*, (Liveright Publishing, 2024), chap. 10.

6. The Opportunity Agenda defines this kind of narrative as "a Big Story, rooted in shared values and common themes, that influences how audiences process information and make decisions." The Opportunity Agenda, *Shifting the Narrative*. 2021, accessed August 11, 2025,
https://opportunityagenda.org/messaging_reports/shifting-the-narrative/

7. Susanne Jungerstam and Annika Wentjärvi, "Country Portrait Finland—The Finnish Welfare State: Principles and Economic Impact," *Socialnet.de*, accessed October 20, 2025,

https://www.socialnet.de/en/international/Finland

8. "New Zealand—Implementing the Wellbeing Budget," *Wellbeing Economy Alliance*, accessed October 20, 2025,

https://weall.org/resource/new-zealand-implementing-the-wellbeing-budget

9. Scottish Government, *National Performance Framework: About Us*, accessed October 20, 2025,

https://blogs.gov.scot/national-performance-framework/about-us

10. Frameworks Institute, "Six Things to Know About Cultural Mindsets," November 21, 2024, https://www.frameworksinstitute.org/articles/fact-sheet-6-things-to-know-about-cultural-mindsets/.

This analysis helps explain why the cultural mindset of the American Dream is so resilient: it draws heavily on the deeply rooted mindset of individualism, making it especially difficult to interrupt or reframe.

11. In France, the revolutionary cry of *liberté, égalité, fraternité* continues to shape national debate, though its meaning remains contested. As Réjane Sénac observes, the motto endures as historical symbolism and as an active framework for defining who counts as a citizen within French society. Réjane Sénac, "The Contemporary Conversation about the French Connection 'Liberté, Egalité, Fraternité': Neoliberal Equality and 'Non-brothers'," *Revue française de civilisation britannique*, vol. 21, no. 1 (2016),

https://journals.openedition.org/rfcb/840.

French far-right leaders, meanwhile, have sought to appropriate republican discourse itself. Emile Chabal notes how figures like Marine Le Pen present themselves as defenders of the Republic's values, invoking *liberté, égalité, fraternité* in exclusionary ways that recast immigrants and minorities as threats. Emile Chabal, *France's Identity Crisis* (Polity Press, 2024).

12. In South Africa, the postapartheid ideal of the "Rainbow Nation" continues to inspire, yet it collides with stark realities of inequality. As the International Monetary Funds shows, the top 20 percent of South Africans still capture more than two-thirds of national income, while the bottom 40 percent hold only 7 percent. International Monetary Fund, "Six Charts Explain South Africa's Inequality," January 30, 2020,

https://www.imf.org/en/News/Articles/2020/01/29/na012820six-charts-on-south-africas-persistent-and-multi-faceted-inequality.

The Carnegie Endowment similarly observes that the "rainbow miracle" has been undermined by deep divides that persist across race, class, and geography, challenging social cohesion and fueling disillusionment. Carnegie Endowment for International Peace, "South Africa: When Strong Institutions and Massive Inequalities Collide," March 25, 2021,

https://carnegieendowment.org/research/2021/03/south-africa-when-strong-institutions-and-massive-inequalities-collide

13. The Freedmen's Bureau was officially known as the Bureau of Refugees, Freedmen, and Abandoned Lands. U.S. Senate, "The Freedmen's Bureau Acts of 1865 and 1866," Art & History, accessed August 11, 2025,

https://www.senate.gov/artandhistory/history/common/generic/FreedmensBureau.htm.

For more on its role and impact, see Social Welfare History Project, "Freedmen's Bureau," Virginia Commonwealth University Libraries, accessed August 11, 2025,

https://socialwelfare.library.vcu.edu/federal/freedmen%e2%80%99s-bureau/.

Historically Black Colleges and Institutions like Howard and Fisk Universities still stand as living testaments to this ambitious—if incomplete—vision.

14. Indeed, as Reverend Barber notes: "Decades before any American politician would propose the possibility of universal healthcare, Reconstruction experimented with providing it to Black and white people in the postwar South. Barber II, *White Poverty*, chap. 10.

15. Jim Crow Museum, "Black Codes." Ferris State University, accessed August 11, 2025, https://jimcrowmuseum.ferris.edu/links/misclink/blackcode.htm.

In two landmark rulings, the Supreme Court gutted federal protections for Black civil rights. *Slaughter-House Cases*, 83 U.S. (16 Wall.) 36 (1873), held that the Fourteenth Amendment's Privileges or Immunities Clause protected only rights of national citizenship, not most civil rights, thereby sharply limiting federal protection against state infringement. *United States v. Cruikshank*, 92 U.S. 542 (1876), further weakened Reconstruction protections by ruling that the Fourteenth Amendment did not apply to the actions of private individuals and that the federal government could not prosecute perpetrators of the Colfax Massacre under the Enforcement Act, leaving protection of civil rights largely to the states. By shielding those who committed racial terror from prosecution, the law itself became a tool of white supremacy.

16. Equal Justice Initiative, *Reconstruction in America: Racial Violence After the Civil War, 1865-1876*. Equal Justice Initiative (Montgomery, AL), 2020,

https://eji.org/report/reconstruction-in-america/

17. Social Welfare History Project, "Freedmen's Bureau," VCU Libraries; Equal Justice Initiative, "President Withdraws Federal Troops from Last Southern State House, Ending Reconstruction." *A History of Racial Injustice*, accessed August 11, 2025,

https://calendar.eji.org/racial-injustice/apr/24

18. Heather Cox Richardson, *Democracy Awakening: Notes on the State of America* (Penguin Random House, 2023), chap. 4.

19. Fredrick Douglass Papers, "Address to the 1876 Republican National Convention," June 14, 1876,

https://frederickdouglasspapersproject.com/s/digitaledition/item/17976

20. Equal Justice Initiative, *Reconstruction in America*, chap. 2. Following President Lincoln's assassination, Vice President Andrew Johnson took office and rescinded the order granting Black farmers land tracts.

21. For details on sharecropping, see Equal Justice Initiative, *Reconstruction in America*, chap. 2. For an example of debt peonage see La Toya Tanisha Francis and Patrick Rael, "Mentha Morrison: A Story of Debt Peonage in Jim Crow Georgia," *Black Perspectives* (blog), African American Intellectual History Society, October 4, 2018, https://www.aaihs.org/mentha-morrison-a-story-of-debt-peonage-in-jim-crow-georgia/. For details of the convict-leasing system in which Southern states "leased" prisoners to private railways and mines, see Equal Justice Initiative, "Convict Leasing." November 1, 2013, https://eji.org/news/history-racial-injustice-convict-leasing/. For a deeper analysis of how Southern states recast incarceration and penal codes after Reconstruction as mechanism of racial control, see Susanne Schwarz, "The Spawn of Slavery? Race, State Capacity, and the Development of Carceral Institutions in the Postbellum South," *Studies in American Political Development* 37, no. 2 (October 2023): 181-98.
https://doi.org/10.1017/S0898588X22000281

22. Equal Justice Initiative, *Reconstruction in America*, chap. 2.

23. For analysis of how eugenic thought infused U.S. public policy by linking racial hierarchy to ideas of biological "fitness" and "dependency" see Alexandra Minna Stern, *Eugenic Nation: Faults and Frontiers of Better Breeding in Modern America* (University of California Press, 2005); and Dorothy Roberts, *Killing the Black Body: Race, Reproduction, and the Meaning of Liberty* (Vintage Books, 1997). See also Stephen Jay Gould, *The Mismeasure of Man*, rev. ed. (W. W. Norton, 1996), for discussion of the scientific rationales that gave eugenics intellectual legitimacy.

24. Washington Post, *How the Lost Cause Narrative became American History*. Video, YouTube, August 11, 2020,

https://www.youtube.com/watch?v=9Y6luq3aUvc&t=150s.

See also Alan T. Nolan, "The Anatomy of the Myth," in *The Myth of the Lost Cause and Civil War History*, ed. Gary W. Gallagher and Alan T. Nolan (Indiana University Press, 2000), chap. 1.

25. For background on how the Lost Cause myth made its way into southern schools, see Greg Huffman, "Twisted Sources: How Confederate Propaganda Ended up in the South's Schoolbooks," *Facing South*, April 10, 2019,

https://www.facingsouth.org/2019/04/twisted-sources-how-confederate-propaganda-ended-souths-schoolbooks

26. See Franklin D. Roosevelt Presidential Library, "Great Depression Facts," accessed August 15, 2025, https://www.fdrlibrary.org/great-depression-facts ("24.9% of the total workforce—or 12,830,000 people—was unemployed by 1933"); and Federal Reserve Bank of St. Louis, "How Bad Was the Great Depression? Gauging the Economic Impact," Great Depression Curriculum, accessed August 15, 2025,

https://www.stlouisfed.org/the-great-depression/curriculum/economic-episodes-in-american-history-part("the unemployment rate reached a peak of 25% in 1933"). For analysis of housing distress during the Great Depression, see David C. Wheelock, "The Federal Response to Home Mortgage Distress: Lessons from the Great Depression," *Federal Reserve Bank of St. Louis Review* 90, no. 3 (May/June 2008): 133-48,

https://ideas.repec.org/a/fip/fedlrv/y2008imayp133-148nv.90no.3%2Cpt.1.htm

27. As then-governor of New York, FDR said: "[T]he country needs—and, unless I mistake its temper, the country demands bold, persistent experimentation." Franklin D. Roosevelt, "Address at Oglethorpe University, Atlanta, Georgia," May 22, 1932, The American Presidency Project, University of California, Santa Barbara,

https://www.presidency.ucsb.edu/documents/address-oglethorpe-university-atlanta-georgia

28. Like FERA, the CARES Act of 2020 provided direct cash payments (in the form of stimulus checks) to individuals and families in the face of the global health crisis. Coronavirus Aid, Relief, and Economic Security (CARES) Act, Pub. L. No. 116-136, 134 Stat. 281 (2020).

29. Jill Quadagno, *The Color of Welfare: How Racism Undermined the War on Poverty* (Oxford University Press, 1994), 19-20.

30. Frances Perkins said "The people are what matter to government, and a government should aim to give all the people under its jurisdiction the best possible life." See "The Woman Behind the New Deal," Frances Perkins Center, accessed August 30, 2025,

https://francesperkinscenter.org/learn/her-life/

31. For more on Perkins' legacy, see Tracy Wareing Evans, "The Courageous Leader: Frances Perkins' Legacy," *Cornerstone Solutions Blog*, March 5, 2025,

https://cornerstonesolutions.blog/2025/03/05/the-courageous-leader-frances-perkins-legacy/

32. Eleanor Roosevelt, *My Day* (syndicated newspaper column, 1935–1962), Eleanor Roosevelt Papers Project, George Washington University,

https://erpapers.columbian.gwu.edu/my-day

33. Quadagno, *The Color of Welfare*, 20; see also Mark Robert Rank, Lawrence M. Eppard, and Heather E. Bullock, *Poorly Understood: What America Gets Wrong About Poverty* (Oxford University Press: 2021), chap. 2.

34. Richardson, *Democracy Awakening*, chap. 30.

35. Throughout this book, I use the term Brown to describe communities racialized as non-white and excluded through systems that privileged whiteness, including but not limited to Latino, Indigenous, and immigrant communities. This language reflects shared exposure to exclusionary design, not a claim of uniform experience.

36. Quadagno, *The Color of Welfare*, 20.

37. Quadagno, *The Color of Welfare*, 23. For a detailed understanding of the impact of redlining, see Richard Rothstein,*The Color of Law: A Forgotten History of How Our Government Segregated America* (Liveright, 2017).

38. Leaders from state and local jurisdictions founded the American Public Welfare Association (APWA) in the early 1930s and worked closely with emerging federal agencies during the development of the New Deal. Archival records from APWA suggest that, while some early New Deal measures provided emergency cash assistance to families, federal policymakers resisted incorporating sustained cash-assistance approaches into later New Deal legislation. American Public Welfare Association. "10-Year Anniversary Documentation." American Public Welfare Association Records, Social Welfare History Archives, University of Minnesota.

39. For evidence on how postwar prosperity widened racial gaps—including through the GI Bill, suburban development, and discriminatory labor and housing policies—see Ira Katznelson, *When Affirmative Action Was White* (W. W. Norton, 2005); Rothstein, *The Color of Law* ; and Hilary Herbold, "Never a Level Playing Field," *Journal of Blacks in Higher Education* 6 (1994): 104–08, https://doi.org/10.2307/2962479

40. On the role of civil rights–era violence and media coverage in shaping national consciousness, see Timothy B. Tyson, *The Blood of Emmett Till* (Simon & Schuster, 2017); and Taylor Branch, *Parting the Waters* (Simon & Schuster, 1988).

41. On how the Civil Rights Movement reframed inequality and laid groundwork for the War on Poverty, see Martha J. Bailey and Sheldon Danziger, eds., *Legacies of the War on Poverty* (Russell Sage Foundation, 2013), and Michael B. Katz, *The Undeserving Poor*, 2nd ed. (Oxford University Press, 2013).

42. When first published in 1962, Michael Harrington's *The Other America* shocked the nation by exposing the persistence of poverty in an age of prosperity. As Maurice Isserman notes in his foreword, in the 2012 edition Harrington's short book (just 186 pages) advanced a simple but powerful thesis: poverty in the United States was both more extensive and more entrenched than most Americans imagined. By documenting that more than 40 million people—roughly one in four Americans—lived below the poverty line, often in rural isolation or urban slums hidden from middle-class view, Harrington revealed an "invisible land" of the poor. His warning that "the poor are invisible" gave urgency to the idea that neglect was not merely rhetorical but also structural, and it captured the attention of policymakers, including President John F. Kennedy. In 1964, Harrington was called to Washington, D.C., where he worked with Sargent Shriver as a consultant to President Lyndon Johnson in preparing antipoverty legislation. Maurice Isserman, foreword to Michael Harrington, *The Other America: Poverty in the United States* (Scribner, 1962; reprint, Simon & Schuster, 2012).

43. The full quote is: "Unfortunately, many Americans live on the outskirts of hope—some because of their poverty, and some because of their color, and all too many because of both. Our task is to help replace their despair with opportunity. This administration today, here and now, declares unconditional war on poverty in America. I urge this Congress and all Americans to join with me in that effort." See Lyndon B. Johnson, "Annual Message to the Congress on the State of the Union," January 8, 1964, *The American Presidency Project*, University of California, Santa Barbara,

https://www.presidency.ucsb.edu/documents/annual-message-the-congress-the-state-the-union-25,

and LBJ Foundation, *LBJ State of the Union: War on Poverty*, video, YouTube, January 8, 2014, https://www.youtube.com/watch?v=lx8BMnteNfw

44. For photographs of President Johnson's April 1964 "poverty tour" visit with Tom Fletcher and his family in Inez, Kentucky, see Ben Cosgrove, "War on Poverty: Portraits from an Appalachian Battleground, 1964," *Time*, January 7, 2014, https://time.com/3878609/war-on-poverty-appalachia-portraits-1964/; see also *Seeing Appalachia*, "President Lyndon B. Johnson Visit to Tom Fletcher Residence During Poverty Tour of Appalachia," April 24, 1964, Cecil Stoughton, White House Photo Office, Serial No. 215-21-WH64,

https://seeingappalachia.org/overview

45. The War on Poverty encompassed a sweeping array of legislation, including the Economic Opportunity Act of 1964, the Food Stamp Act, The Social Security Act, and the Child Nutrition Act, among others. For a concise overview, see Executive Office of the President, *The War on Poverty 50 Years Later* (White House, January 2014),

https://obamawhitehouse.archives.gov/sites/default/files/docs/erp_2014_chapter_6.pdf,

and Robert Haveman et al., "The War on Poverty: Measurement, Trends, and Policy," *Journal of Policy Analysis and Management* 34, no. 3 (Summer 2015): 593–638,

https://pmc.ncbi.nlm.nih.gov/articles/PMC4822720

46. The Housing and Urban Development Act of 1965 established new housing subsidy programs and promoted increased federal funding for public housing. The Elementary and Secondary Education Act provided funding for primary and secondary schools, emphasizing the need for high standards and equal opportunity for students who were economically disadvantaged. The Higher Education Act of 1965 provided support for college and university students through scholarships, low-interest loans, and work study programs. See Executive Office of the President, *War on Poverty 50 Years Later*; Haveman et al., "War on Poverty."

47. The War on Poverty focused on "upstream" preventions – funding to schools, job training, health coverage, and quality early care. These were not focused on expanding "welfare doles," but on the systemic and structural inequities that prevented many families from moving ahead. Scholars Strategy Network, "The Accomplishments and Lessons of the War on Poverty," April 4, 2014. Summary of essays in *Legacies of the War on Poverty*, edited by Martha J. Bailey and Sheldon Danziger,

https://scholars.org/contribution/accomplishments-and-lessons-war-poverty

48. Council of Economic Advisers, *War on Poverty: 50 Years Later*, Table 1.1.

49. Programs created under the Economic Opportunity Act of 1964 and related legislation were bound by Title VI of the Civil Rights Act, which prohibited exclusion from federally funded activities "on the ground of race, color, or national origin." Civil Rights Act of 1964, Pub. L. No. 88-352, Title VI, 78 Stat. 252 (1964). Moreover, several War on Poverty–era laws carried explicit nondiscrimination provisions, extending the reach of the Civil Rights Act into social welfare programs. The Food Stamp Act of 1964 required that benefits be distributed without discrimination on the basis of race, religion, national origin, or political beliefs. *Food Stamp Act of 1964*, Pub. L. No. 88-525, § 2(b), 78 Stat. 703, 704 (1964). The Social Security Amendments of 1965 (creating Medicare and Medicaid) likewise prohibited exclusion or denial of benefits "on the ground of race, color, or national origin." *Social Security Amendments of 1965*, Pub. L. No. 89-97, § 508, 79 Stat. 286, 354 (1965). Together, these provisions made antidiscrimination an explicit condition of participation in landmark antipoverty programs.

50. U.S. Congress, *Economic Opportunity Act of 1964*, Pub. L. No. 88-452, § 202(a)(3), 78 Stat. 508, 516 (1964). Sargent Shriver, the first director of the Office of Employment Opportunities, believed solutions should come from the communities most affected. His vision for community action programs required that residents be included in designing and overseeing programs—a radical shift from traditional top-down approaches. Black leaders, in particular, gained entry into local political structures through these programs, laying the groundwork for a new generation of civic leadership. Sargent Shriver Peace Institute, "War on Poverty," accessed August 2025, https://www.sargentshriver.org/about-sargent-shriver/war-on-poverty

51. See Quadagno, *The Color of Welfare*, 37, 40-44.

52. Shriver Institute, "War on Poverty," accessed October 15, 2025, https://www.sargentshriver.org/about-sargent-shriver/war-on-poverty

53. One of the most consequential provisions of the Economic Opportunity Act was its requirement that community action programs be administered with the "maximum feasible participation" of the people it was intended to benefit. U.S. Congress, *Economic Opportunity Act of 1964*, Pub. L. No. 88-452, § 202(a)(3), 78 Stat. 508, 516 (1964). This mandate became a flashpoint, as local officials often resisted sharing power with poor and minority residents. James T. Patterson, *America's Struggle Against Poverty, 1900–1985* (Harvard University Press, 1986), 146–50; see also Quadagno, *Color of Welfare*, 35-37.

54. See Quadagno, *The Color of Welfare*; and Alice O'Connor, *Poverty Knowledge: Social Science, Social Policy, and the Poor in Twentieth-Century U.S. History* (Princeton University Press, 2001).

55. The "war" metaphor that had first galvanized support soon became a liability. As Gareth Davies observes, the failure to deliver a quick "victory" against poverty made it easier for opponents to brand Johnson's programs as expensive, ineffective, and indistinguishable from welfare dependency. Gareth Davies, *From Opportunity to Entitlement: The Transformation and Decline of Great Society Liberalism* (University Press of Kansas, 2004), 63–65. Ronald Reagan seized on this rhetoric in his 1966 campaign for governor, deriding the War on Poverty as "a war that is being lost." Quoted in Annelise Orleck and Matthew Lassiter, eds., *The War on Poverty: A New Grassroots History, 1964–1980* (University of Georgia Press, 2011), 12.

56. Martin Luther King, Jr., *Where Do We Go from Here: Chaos or Community?* (Beacon Press, 1967), chap. 3.

57. Johnson reportedly told Shriver that his only guiding principle was "No doles!" Sargent Shriver Peace Institute, "Empowerment & the War on Poverty," SSPI Blog, January 7, 2014,

https://www.sargentshriver.org/blog/empowerment-the-war-on-poverty.
Historians also note that the War on Poverty's resources were limited, competing with military spending and other domestic priorities. Miller Center, University of Virginia, "LBJ on Sargent Shriver, Politics, and the War on Poverty," accessed September 26, 2025,
https://millercenter.org/the-presidency/educational-resources/lbj-on-sargent-shriver-politics-and-the-war-on-poverty

58. The findings and purpose of the Equal Opportunity Act clearly state its intent, which ring eerily true to this day: "[P]overty continues to be the lot of a substantial number of our people. The United States can achieve its full economic and social potential as a nation only if every individual has the opportunity to contribute to the full extent of his capabilities and to participate in the workings of our society. It is, therefore, the policy of the United States to eliminate the paradox of poverty in the midst of plenty in this Nation by opening to everyone the opportunity for education and training, the opportunity to work, and the opportunity to live in decency and dignity." *Economic Opportunity Act of 1964*, Pub. L. No. 88-452, § 2, 78 Stat. 508 (1964).

59. U.S. Department of Labor, Office of Policy Planning and Research. *The Negro Family: The Case for National Action* (Government Printing Office, March 1965). The full report can be read st https://www.blackpast.org/african-american-history/moynihan-report-1965/

60. U.S. Department of Labor, *The Negro Family*, chap. 4.

61. Ronald Reagan, "Radio Address to the Nation on Welfare Reform," February 15, 1986, Ronald Reagan Presidential Library and Museum, https://www.reaganlibrary.gov/archives/speech/radio-address-nation-welfare-reform

The Blame Trap

1. Although there was widespread support, the Great Society programs did face early resistance, criticized by some conservatives as wasteful expansion of federal power and resources. "War on Poverty," *Research Starters: Politics and Government*, EBSCO, accessed September 26, 2025, https://www.ebsco.com/research-starters/politics-and-government/war-poverty.
In one early example, Representative John Byrnes (R-WI), ranking minority member of the House Ways and Means Committee, dismissed Johnson's antipoverty initiative as "a political slogan in search of a program" during 1964 hearings on the Economic Opportunity Act. U.S. Congress, House Committee on Education and Labor, *Economic Opportunity Act of 1964: Hearings on H.R. 10440*, 88th Cong., 2nd sess., May–July 1964 (Government Printing Office, 1964), 412.

2. Martin Luther King, Jr. announced the Poor People's Campaign in December of 1967 at the Southern Christian Leadership Conference in one of his last speeches. It is worth reading MLK's powerful words, capturing this call to action. His wife would lead the first march of the campaign on Washington just five weeks after his assassination. Martin Luther King Jr., "Statement by Martin Luther King Jr., President, Southern Christian Leadership Conference," December 4, 1967,

Civil Rights Movement Archive, https://www.crmvet.org/docs/6712_mlk_ppc-anc.pdf

3. Jill Quadagno, *The Color of Welfare: How Racism Undermined the War On Poverty* (Oxford University Press, 1994), 78.

4. See Chapter 2 "The War on Poverty (1964-1973): Ambition Undermined."

5. Rachel Black and Aleta Sprague, "The Rise and Reign of the Welfare Queen," *New America Weekly*, September 22, 2016, https://www.newamerica.org/weekly/rise-and-reign-welfare-queen/

6. President Richard Nixon first appealed to "the great silent majority" in his televised address on the Vietnam War, November 3, 1969. Richard Nixon, "Address to the Nation on the War in Vietnam," November 3, 1969, *The American Presidency Project*, University of California, Santa Barbara, https://www.presidency.ucsb.edu/documents/address-the-nation-the-war-vietnam.
While Nixon initially invoked the silent majority in his call for national solidarity on the Vietnam War effort, the message also became a signal to support his domestic policies for "Middle America." As historian Rick Perlstein observes, Nixon's invocation of a silent, patriotic mainstream was not just about Vietnam policy but also about constructing a durable political identity rooted in cultural division. Rick Perlstein, *Nixonland: The Rise of a President and the Fracturing of America* (Scribner, 2008), 371–75; see also Quadagno, *The Color of Welfare*, 12.

7. Quadagno, *The Color of Welfare*, 12. See also Perlstein, *Nixonland*.

8. Nixon Foundation, "President Nixon's Family Assistance Plan," *Nixon Foundation Blog*, June 17, 2014, https://blog.nixonfoundation.org/2014/06/family-assistance-plan-families-can-succeed/

9. Quadagno, *The Color of Welfare*, 133.

10. Reagan first used the welfare queen trope on the campaign trail. See Ronald Reagan, campaign speech, January 1976, audio, *Slate Voice*, SoundCloud, https://soundcloud.com/slate-articles/ronald-reagan-campaign-speech.
See also Black and Sprague, "Rise and Reign of the Welfare Queen."

11. Josh Levin, *The Queen: The Forgotten Life Behind an American Myth* (Little, Brown and Company, 2019), author's note. Levin's book traces the details of her complicated life, noting "[t]he legend of the Cadillac-driving welfare queen ultimately overwhelmed Taylor's own identity."

12. Ronald Reagan, "Remarks at a White House Briefing for Supporters of Welfare Reform," February 9, 1987, Ronald Reagan Presidential Library and Museum,

https://www.reaganlibrary.gov/archives/speech/remarks-white-house-briefing-supporters-welfare-reform

13. Reagan's 1981 and 1982 budgets reduced funding for the Aid to Families with Dependent Children (AFDC) program—federal cash assistance originally established under the Social Security Act of 1935—along with cuts to food stamps and Medicaid. For detailed discussion of these reductions and their framing in welfare politics, see Quadagno, *The Color of Welfare*, 162; Jerry D. Marx, "The Conservative Transition in American Social Policy," *Social Welfare History Project*, Virginia Commonwealth University Libraries, accessed August 21, 2025,

https://socialwelfare.library.vcu.edu/eras/1980s-beyond/the-conservative-transition-in-american-social-policy/

14. Lou Cannon, "Ronald Reagan: Domestic Affairs," Miller Center, University of Virginia, accessed August 21, 2025,

https://millercenter.org/president/reagan/domestic-affairs .
This narrative shift happened despite that overall government spending rose under Reagan.

15. Clinton first introduced the phrase "end welfare as we know it" in late 1991 as part of his "New Covenant" speeches at Georgetown University, framing it as both a moral and practical reform. The slogan quickly became a centerpiece of his 1992 presidential campaign, signaling a break from the traditional Democrats' defenses of welfare and appealing to voters skeptical of government programs. See Steven M. Gillon, *The Pact: Bill Clinton, Newt Gingrich, and the Rivalry that Defined a Generation* (Oxford University Press, 2008), 50–52.

16. *Personal Responsibility and Work Opportunity Reconciliation Act of 1996*, Pub. L. No. 104-193, 110 Stat. 2105 (1996). For summaries of the law, see U.S. Department of Health and Human Services, Office of the Assistant Secretary for Planning and Evaluation, *The Personal Responsibility and Work Opportunity Reconciliation Act of 1996*, August 31, 1996,

https://aspe.hhs.gov/reports/personal-responsibility-work-opportunity-reconciliation-act-1996 ;
and U.S. Department of Health and Human Services, Administration for Children and Families, *Major Provisions of the Welfare Law*, updated May 20, 2019,

https://acf.gov/ofa/policy-guidance/major-provisions-welfare-law

17. *PRWORA*, Pub. L. No. 104-193 (1996). Despite its passage, PRWORA was controversial, and several senior officials within President Clinton's own administration resigned in protest. Most notably, Mary Jo Bane and Wendell Primus, both assistant secretaries at the Department of Health and Human Services, stepped down after Clinton signed the law. They and other critics argued that the new time limits and work requirements would push families deeper into hardship rather than reduce poverty. Their resignations underscored how divisive welfare reform was—even among those who had championed Clinton's broader agenda of economic opportunity. For a visual history of this moment, see Retro Report, *Welfare and the Politics of Poverty*, video, 13:38, New York, May 1, 2016,

https://retroreport.org/video/welfare-and-the-politics-of-poverty/.

See also Mary Jo Bane and David T. Ellwood, *Welfare Realities: From Rhetoric to Reform* (Harvard University Press, 1994).

18. PWORA ended the individual entitlement to cash assistance under Aid to Families with Dependent Children (AFDC) and replaced it with the Temporary Assistance for Needy Families (TANF) block grant, giving states wide discretion to restrict access even further. Arizona, for example, reduced its TANF lifetime limit to just 12 months. Center for Law and Social Policy, "Arizona Cuts TANF Lifetime Limit to 12 Months, Harshest in the Country," CLASP blog, May 20, 2015,

https://www.clasp.org/blog/arizona-cuts-tanf-lifetime-limit-12-months-harshest-country

19. See e.g., *Deficit Reduction Act of 2005*, Pub. L. No. 109-171, 120 Stat. 4 (2006) and *One Big Beautiful Bill Act*, H.R. 1, 119th Cong. (2025), Pub. L. No. 119-21, 139 Stat. 72 (2025).

20. While welfare overpayments were not uncommon in the 1990s and 2000s—SNAP error rates hovered around 9.9 percent in 1999—these mistakes were predominantly administrative or unintentional. A 2003 analysis by the Center on Budget and Policy Priorities noted that few errors were due to recipient dishonesty. Center on Budget and Policy Priorities, "Food Stamp Overpayment Error Rate Hits Record Low," revised July 8, 2003,

https://www.cbpp.org/sites/default/files/archive/4-30-01fs.htm.

A Congressional Research Service report similarly concluded that SNAP fraud was relatively rare and that many questionable cases (e.g., duplicate enrollments) could be attributed to error rather than intent. Randy Alison Aussenberg, "Errors and Fraud in the Supplemental Nutrition Assistance Program (SNAP)," Congressional Research Service, updated September 28, 2018, https://sgp.fas.org/crs/misc/R45147.pdf

21. Linda Tirado, *Hand to Mouth: Living in Bootstrap America* (Penguin Group, 2014), introduction.

22. Daniel Markovits, *The Meritocracy Trap: How America's Foundational Myth Feeds Inequality, Dismantles the Middle Class, and Devours the Elite* (Penguin Press, 2019), introduction.

23.*APA Dictionary of Psychology*, s.v. "fundamental attribution error," American Psychological Association,
https://dictionary.apa.org/fundamental-attribution-error

24.*The Little Engine That Could* is a 1930 American folktale by Arnold "Watty Piper" Munk, best-known for its signature motif: "I think I can!" Watty Piper, *The Little Engine That Could* (Platt & Munk, 1930, repr. 1961).

25.*Oxford English Dictionary*, s.v. "moocher," accessed August 21, 2025,
https://www.oed.com/dictionary/moocher_n?tab=factsheet#3597603

26.*Oxford English Dictionary*, s.v. "freeloader," accessed August 21, 2025,
https://www.oed.com/dictionary/freeloader_n?tl=true

27. One notable usage was in the title in the book by Nicholas Eberstadt, *A Nation of Takers: America's Entitlement Epidemic* (Templeton Press, 2012). See also Jane Mayer, "No Takers," *New Yorker*, January 21, 2013,
https://www.newyorker.com/news/news-desk/no-takers

28. The ideal of helping people "stand on their own" has shaped U.S. social policy for decades, from the 1962 Public Welfare Amendments and their emphasis on self-support to the 1996 Personal Responsibility and Work Opportunity Reconciliation Act, which explicitly tied assistance to personal responsibility and independence. See U.S. Department of Health, Education, and Welfare, *Public Welfare Amendments of 1962* (Government Printing Office, 1962); and Personal Responsibility and Work Opportunity Reconciliation Act of 1996, Pub. L. 104–193.

29. Tracy Wareing Evans and Karen Heller Key, "Misunderstanding Poverty: Changing American Mindsets," *Our Dream Deferred*, podcast, APHSA, August 16, 2023, Libsyn, https://aphsa.libsyn.com/misunderstanding-poverty-changing-american-mindsets

30. Robert B. Reich, *The System: Who Rigged It, How We Fix It* (Vintage Books, 2021), chap. 3.

31. Victim-blaming assigns the blame for trauma or hardship to the victim instead of the perpetrator or systemic issues. William Ryan, a social psychologist, introduced the term "blaming the victim" in his 1971 book by the same name. He argued that American society often attributes poverty and racial inequality to individual failings rather than to structural barriers. Ryan wrote this book as a direct response to Daniel Patrick Moynihan's 1965 government report on the Black family, which claimed that a "tangle of pathology" within African American communities sustained poverty. Ryan argued that such reasoning shifts responsibility away from systemic racism and discriminatory institutions, thereby reinforcing inequality under the pretense of objective analysis. William Ryan, *Blaming the Victim* (Vintage Books, 1971).

32. *APA Dictionary of Psychology*, s.v. "just-world hypothesis," https://dictionary.apa.org/just-world-hypothesis; Melvin J. Lerner, *The Belief in a Just World: A Fundamental Delusion* (Plenum Press, 1980).

33. Federal officials in the War on Poverty focused on preparing people for jobs versus finding jobs for people. Quadagno, *The Color of Welfare*, 67.

34. Ife Floyd, Ashley Burnside, and Jeniece Jones, *TANF Policies Reflect Racist Legacy of Cash Assistance*, Center on Budget and Policy Priorities, August 4, 2021, https://www.cbpp.org/sites/default/files/8-4-21tanf.pdf

35. Sociologist Stanley Cohen is credited with coining the phrase *moral panic* in his influential 1972 book, *Folks Devils and Moral Panics: The Creation of Mods and Rockers*, 3rd ed.(Routledge, 2011). Cohen used the term to describe the societal reactions to two youth subcultures—two groups of British teenagers—whose occasional altercations were sensationalized by the media in the 1960s.

36. See Mark Robert Rank, Lawrence M. Eppard, and Heather E. Bullock, *Poorly Misunderstood: What America Gets Wrong About Poverty* (Oxford University Press, 2021), chap. 5; Joanne Samuel Goldblum and Colleen Shaddox, *Broke in America: Seeing, Understanding, and Ending US Poverty* (BenBella Books, 2021), chap. 1.

37. Heather McGhee, *The Sum of Us: What Racism Costs Everyone and How We Can Prosper Together* (One World, 2021), chap. 1.

38. William J. Barber II, *White Poverty: How Exposing Myths About Race and Class Can Reconstruct American Democracy* (Liveright, 2024).

39. Rubén G. Rumbaut, "Zombie Ideas and Moral Panics: Framing Immigrants as Criminal and Cultural Threats," *Russell Sage Foundation Blog*, November 2, 2016,

https://www.russellsage.org/news/zombie-ideas-and-moral-panics-framing-immigrants-criminal-and-cultural-threats; American Immigration Council, *Debunking the Myth of Immigrants and Crime*, fact sheet, updated 2024,

https://www.americanimmigrationcouncil.org/fact-sheet/debunking-myth-immigrants-and-crime; "Debunking the Myth of the 'Migrant Crime Wave,'" *Brennan Center for Justice*, May 29, 2024,

https://www.brennancenter.org/our-work/analysis-opinion/debunking-myth-migrant-crime-wave

40. The trope of the "deadbeat dad" first crystallized publicly in 1986, when a CBS exposé profiled a man who bragged about fathering multiple children without supporting them—a narrative that, like the welfare queen, became highly exaggerated, triggering the enactment of the Bradley Amendment, which forbade forgiving child support debt even in cases of financial hardship. By the late 1990s, failure to pay child support was treated as a criminal act through federal law—reinforcing stigma and penalizing poverty. See Anne Kim, "Punishing Fathers for Being Poor," *Washington Monthly*, April–June 2020,

https://washingtonmonthly.com/2020/04/05/punishing-fathers-for-being-poor/;

and Ann Cammett, "Deadbeat Dads & Welfare Queens: How Metaphor Shapes Poverty Law," *Boston College Journal of Law & Social Justice* 20, no. 1 (May 2014): 1–37.

41. Abe Bortz, "Mother's Aid," *Social Welfare History Project*, Virginia Commonwealth University Libraries, accessed August 22, 2025,

https://socialwelfare.library.vcu.edu/programs/mothers-aid

42. In recent years, many states and the federal Office of Child Support Enforcement have shifted toward more supportive, family-centered approaches, emphasizing employment services, co-parenting, and debt compromise rather than purely punitive enforcement. Pilot programs that forgive arrears in exchange for consistent payments, mediation efforts to improve father engagement, and recognition of noncustodial parents' economic struggles mark a notable departure from the earlier "deadbeat dad" era. See Office of Child Support Enforcement, *CSPED Characteristics and Implementation: Highlights from the Evaluation of the Child Support Noncustodial Parent Employment Demonstration* (U.S. Department of Health and Human Services, March 2020),

https://acf.gov/sites/default/files/documents/ocse/csped_characteristics_and_implementation_reports_highlights.pdf

43. Matthew Desmond, *Poverty, By America* (Crown, 2023), chap. 1.

44. Joe Jones, *2024 Impact Report* (Center for Urban Families, 2024), accessed August 22, 2025, https://www.cfuf.org/

45. The phrase "at-risk youth" gained widespread use after the 1983 report *A Nation at Risk* by the National Commission on Excellence in Education, which warned that the nation's students—and, by extension, the country—were in danger from declining academic performance. The report popularized "at-risk" as a way to describe children vulnerable to school failure, and it soon became a key part of education reform discussions, shaping policy, funding priorities, and research agendas over the following decades. National Commission on Excellence in Education, *A Nation at Risk: The Imperative for Educational Reform* (U.S. Government Printing Office, 1983).

46. Sociologist Victor Rios has been a leading voice in challenging the label "at-risk" and advocating for the alternative term "at-promise." In his TEDx talk, he describes how the language we use pathologizes young people and argues for reframing them as full of potential rather than deficit. Victor Rios, "From 'At-Risk' to 'At-Promise': Supporting Teens to Overcome Adversity," TEDxUCSB, June 2016, video, 15:39,

https://youthrex.com/video/from-at-risk-to-at-promise-supporting-teens-to-overcome-adversity-victor-rios-at-tedxucsb/;
and Victor Rios, *My Teacher Believes in Me!: The Educator's Guide to At-Promise Students* (Corwin, 2021).

47. Ruha Benjamin, *Viral Justice: How We Grow the World We Want* (Princeton University Press, 2022), chap. 3.

48. The origins of the term "nanny state" are contested. It is most often attributed to British political discourse, with Conservative MP Iain Macleod using the phrase in a 1965 *Spectator* column to criticize government overreach. John Coggon, *The Nanny State Debate: A Place Where Words Don't Do Justice* (Cambridge University Press, 2018), 7. Its appearance in U.S. debates is harder to date, though it began circulating more widely in the late 20th century as a pejorative shorthand against regulation and public benefit programs. Regardless of its precise origin, the phrase functions as a cultural metaphor that infantilizes citizens and frames government intervention as overprotective or illegitimate.

49. See Ronald Reagan, *Radio Address to the Nation on Welfare Reform*, February 15, 1986, The American Presidency Project, https://www.presidency.ucsb.edu/documents/radio-address-the-nation-welfare-reform-0; and Ronald Reagan, *Address Before a Joint Session of Congress on the State of the Union*, February 4, 1986, The American Presidency Project, https://www.presidency.ucsb.edu/documents/address-before-joint-session-congress-the-state-the-union.
Both speeches illustrate how social supports, family structure, and moral language became bound together in the political framing of welfare policy.

50. john a. powell, *The Power of Bridging: How to Build a World Where We All Belong* (Sounds True, 2022), chap. 1.

51. For a compelling argument for how heuristics (i.e., rules of thumb) can enable people to simplify information and make good decisions see Antoinette Schoar and Saugato Datta, *The Power of Heuristics*, ideas42, January 2014,
https://www.ideas42.org/wp-content/uploads/2015/05/ideas42_The-Power-of-Heuristics-2014-1.pdf

52. The American Psychological Association defines confirmation bias as "the tendency to gather evidence that confirms preexisting expectations, typically by emphasizing or pursuing supporting evidence while dismissing or failing to seek contradictory evidence." *APA Dictionary of*

Psychology, s.v. "confirmation bias,"
https://dictionary.apa.org/confirmation-bias

53. The concept of cognitive dissonance was first introduced by social psychologist Leon Festinger, who described it as the mental discomfort people experience when holding two contradictory beliefs at once. Leon Festinger, *A Theory of Cognitive Dissonance* (Stanford University Press, 1957). Fifty years later, Joel Cooper reflected on how the theory has evolved and why it remains one of psychology's most enduring explanations of human behavior. Joel Cooper, *Cognitive Dissonance: Fifty Years of a Classic Theory* (Sage, 2007).

54. Mahzarin R. Banaji and Anthony G. Greenwald, *Blindspot: Hidden Biases of Good People* (Delacorte Press, 2013), chap. 1.

55. The term "hegemonic narrative" refers to the dominant story that justifies and stabilizes the social order—what Antonio Gramsci described as cultural hegemony, the way ruling groups secure consent by shaping common sense. Antonio Gramsci, *Selections from the Prison Notebooks*, ed. and trans. Quintin Hoare and Geoffrey Nowell Smith (International Publishers, 1971). Cultural theorists like Stuart Hall have extended this idea, showing how ideology works through narrative to naturalize inequality. Stuart Hall, "The Problem of Ideology: Marxism without Guarantees," *Journal of Communication Inquiry* 10, no. 2 (1986): 28–44,
https://doi.org/10.1177/019685998601000203

The Fatalism Trap

1. Economic Innovation Group, *The Geography of Persistent Poverty* (Economic Innovation Group, 2019),
https://eig.org/persistent-poverty/

2. The phrase "inner city" has long operated as coded shorthand for Black poverty, segregation, and urban decline—language shaped less by the communities themselves than by the policies that constrained them. Leaders and thinkers across generations have described how this coding emerged. In his *The Other America* speech (1967), Martin Luther King Jr. invoked "rat-infested, vermin-filled slums" to expose the structural conditions produced by discrimination, not to reinforce stereotypes. James Baldwin, in *The Fire Next Time* (1963), wrote that urban ghettos were intentionally constructed to contain Black Americans. And William Julius Wilson later traced how economic restructuring, segregation, and policy decisions hardened the "inner-city" as a symbol in American discourse rather than a neutral description of place. See Martin Luther King Jr., "The Other America" (speech, Stanford University, April 14, 1967), para. 3; Martin Luther King Jr., *Where Do We Go from Here: Chaos or Community?* (Beacon Press, 1967); James Baldwin, *The Fire Next Time*, in *Collected Essays*, ed. Toni Morrison (Library of America, 1998), 300–302; William Julius Wilson, *The Truly Disadvantaged: The Inner City, the Underclass, and Public Policy* (University of Chicago Press, 1987).

3. The "rural South" has often served as coded shorthand for poverty, backwardness, and racial division—language shaped by the region's history of extraction and caste, not by the people who live there. Scholars and writers have long described how these narratives took root. After Reconstruction, the Lost Cause myth romanticized the antebellum South while obscuring the economic exploitation and racial hierarchy that defined it. W.E.B. Du Bois argued that the region's social and economic conditions could not be separated from the legacy of slavery and racial caste. James Baldwin later wrote that Southern poverty and racial hatred were intertwined products of a system that trapped both Black communities and poor white communities. Contemporary research by Kathryn Edin, H. Luke Shaefer, and Timothy Nelson shows how entrenched disadvantage in many rural Southern counties reflects this long arc of exploitation and ongoing neglect by illustrating how "place" continues to function as shorthand for persistent poverty and division. See David W. Blight, *Race and Reunion: The Civil War in American Memory* (Harvard University Press, 2001); W. E. B. Du Bois, *Black Reconstruction in America, 1860–1880* (Free Press, 1998 [1935]); James Baldwin, "Nobody Knows My Name," in *Collected Essays*, ed. Toni Morrison (Library of America, 1998), 197; Kathryn J. Edin, H. Luke Shaefer, and Timothy J. Nelson, *The Injustice of Place: Uncovering the Legacy of Poverty in America* (Mariner Books, 2023).

4. Appalachia has often been framed through coded portrayals of cultural deficiency and dependence—an image that reduces a complex region to "a problem people" and obscures the structural forces that shaped its conditions. Scholars and journalists have long described how this narrative emerged. During the War on Poverty, widely circulated photographs and documentaries spotlighted severe hardship in eastern Kentucky and West Virginia, but often without the context of the coal companies, absentee landownership, and resource extraction that drained the region's wealth. Historians such as Dwight Billings, Kathleen Blee, and Ronald Eller later traced how economic exploitation, environmental degradation, and political marginalization produced the very circumstances now stereotyped as cultural failings. Their work underscores that Appalachia's story is not one of inherent deficiency, but one of resilience in the face of long-standing structural harm. See Dwight B. Billings and Kathleen M. Blee, *The Road to Poverty: The Making of Wealth and Hardship in Appalachia* (Cambridge University Press, 2000); Ronald D. Eller, *Uneven Ground: Appalachia Since 1945* (University Press of Kentucky, 2008); *Hunger in America*, directed by Martin Carr (CBS News, 1968), television documentary,

https://www.cbsnews.com/video/hunger-in-america-the-1968-cbs-documentary-that-shocked-america/

5. Native communities—especially those on reservation lands—have often been portrayed as places of inevitable poverty, isolation, or dependence, images that mask the federal policies and forced removals that harmed them. Historians and Native scholars have shown how these narratives emerged from the long arc of land seizure, confinement, and assimilation. Andrés Reséndez documents how systems of enslavement, displacement, and coercion undermined Native economies and sovereignty well into the nineteenth and twentieth centuries. Roxanne Dunbar-Ortiz explains how settler-colonial narratives cast Native peoples as vanishing or deficient in order to legitimize the reservation system and the dispossession that preceded it. David Treuer argues that portraying reservations as "basins of perpetual suffering" erases the resilience, self-governance, and cultural renewal that define contemporary Native life. Together, these works show that the conditions often stereotyped as inevitable are the result of deliberate policy design, not cultural deficiency. See Andrés Reséndez, *The Other Slavery: The Uncovered Story of Indian Enslavement in America* (Houghton Mifflin Harcourt, 2016); Roxanne Dunbar-Ortiz, *An Indigenous Peoples' History of the United States* (Beacon Press, 2014); David Treuer, *The Heartbeat of Wounded Knee: Native America from 1890 to the Present* (Riverhead Books, 2019), prologue.

6. Edin et al., *The Injustice of Place*.

7. For images circulated at that time, see Ben Cosgrove, "War on Poverty: Portraits from an Appalachian Background, 1964," *Life*, accessed September 10, 2025,

https://www.life.com/history/war-on-poverty-appalachia-portraits-1964/ ; *Hunger in America*, CBS News, 1968.

8. The Kerner Commission later criticized news media for focusing overwhelming on violence in Black neighborhoods rather than their social context. See National Advisory Commission on Civil Disorders (Kerner Commission), *Report of the National Advisory Commission on Civil Disorders* (U.S. Government Printing Office, 1968); KABC-TV, *Watts Riots Coverage, 1965* (television news broadcast), uploaded by "Real Time 1960s," YouTube video, posted August 11, 2015, https://www.youtube.com/watch?v=BDAv2XcG06s;

CBS News, *Lost Coverage of the Newark Race Riots, 1967* (television news broadcast), uploaded by "tvdays," YouTube video, posted July 15, 2020,

https://www.youtube.com/watch?v=4yUYaAiWZpw .

For photographic images circulated at that time, see Bill Syken, "Race in the 1960s: The Photography of Frank Dandridge," *Life*, accessed September 10, 2025,

https://www.life.com/history/race-in-the-1960s-the-photography-of-frank-dandridge/

9. The impoverished rural South has long been a subject of satire and caricature, often depicted in political cartoons, jokes, and popular entertainment as culturally deficient and backward. Scholars trace how the "redneck" and "hillbilly" stereotypes emerged as enduring shorthand for poverty, ignorance, and rural decline, reinforced across media from cartoons to reality television. See Patrick Huber, "A Short History of Redneck: The Fashioning of a Southern White Masculine Identity," *Southern Cultures* 1, no. 2, 145-166 (Winter 1995),

https://www.southerncultures.org/article/short-history-redneck-fashioning-southern-white-masculine-identity/

10. Tribal Nations and communities have likewise been rendered invisible or portrayed through narrow stereotypes, often framed as "forgotten places" disconnected from modern prosperity. Media scholarship shows that Native Americans remain underrepresented and, when visible, are frequently cast through outdated tropes of poverty, victimhood, or historical relics rather than as contemporary, thriving communities. See Casey Ryan Kelly, "Representations of Native Americans in the Mass Media," *Oxford Research Encyclopedia of Communication* (Feb. 27, 2017), https://oxfordre.com/communication/display/10.1093/acrefore/9780190228613.001.0001/acrefore-9780190228613-e-142;

Peter A. Leavitt, Rebecca Covarrubias, Yvonne A. Perez, and Stephanie A. Fryberg, "'Frozen in Time': The Impact of Native American Media Representations on Identity and Self-Understanding," *Journal of Social Issues* 71, no. 1 (March 2015): 39-53, https://doi.org/10.1111/josi.12095;

Arianne E. Eason, Laura M. Brady, and Stephanie A. Fryberg, "Reclaiming Representations & Interrupting the Cycle of Bias Against Native Americans," *Dædalus* 147, no. 2 (Spring 2018): 70-81, https://www.amacad.org/publication/daedalus/reclaiming-representations-interrupting-cycle-bias-against-native-americans

11. Julie Sweetland and Marisa Gerstein Pineau, "Talking about Young People in a Time of Manufactured Controversy," *FrameWorks Institute*, August 15, 2025, https://www.frameworksinstitute.org/articles/talking-about-young-people-in-a-time-of-manufactured-controversy/

12. Martin Luther King Jr., "Beyond Vietnam: A time to Break Silence," speech delivered April 4 1967, Riverside Church, New York City, https://www.americanrhetoric.com/speeches/mlkatimetobreaksilence.htm

13. The term is believed to have been popularized in the U.S. around the mid-twentieth century. The earliest known use in print is from a 1949 *Nebraska State Journal* article in which a rancher, describing the harsh conditions of his life, stated: "It is what it is." Fred R. Shapiro, *The Yale Book of Quotations* (Yale University Press, 2006), s.v. "It is what it is."

14. Tristan Harris, "How a Handful of Tech Companies Control Billions of Minds Every Day," filmed April 2017 at TED2017, Vancouver, BC, *TED*, video, https://www.ted.com/talks/tristan_harris_how_a_handful_of_tech_companies_control_billions_of_minds_every_day

15. Psychologists describe this tendency as negativity bias—the human inclination to give more weight to bad experiences than good ones. See Roy F. Baumeister, Ellen Bratslavsky, Catrin Finkenauer, and Kathleen D. Vohs, "Bad Is Stronger Than Good," *Review of General Psychology* 5, no. 4 (2001): 323–70; Daniel Kahneman, *Thinking, Fast and Slow* (Farrar, Straus and Giroux, 2011).

16. The "finite pool of worry" is a psychological concept introduced by Elke U. Weber in 2006, suggesting that humans can only emotionally manage a limited number of threats at once—so when one concern, like economic instability, surges, another, like environmental change, may recede. See Elke U. Weber, "Experience-Based and Description-Based Perceptions of Long-Term Risk: Why Global Warming Does Not Scare Us (Yet)," *Climatic Change* 77, no. 1–2 (2006): 103–20;

https://doi.org/10.1007/s10584-006-9060-3.

For a more accessible discussion, see Rebecca Leber, "There's Been a Shift in How We Think About Climate Change," *Vox*, August 31, 2023,

https://www.vox.com/climate/2023/8/31/23849730/climate-public-views-emotions-hope-concern

17. See FrameWorks Institute, "Talking About Immigration Now: Moving Beyond the 'Worthiness Trap,'" July 21, 2025,

https://www.frameworksinstitute.org/articles/talking-about-immigration-now-moving-beyond-the-worthiness-trap/;

and Sweetland and Gerstein Pineau, "Talking about Young People." Both articles show how fear-based narratives directed at individuals or groups—whether about immigrants or urban youth—divert public attention from shared, solvable problems and reduce support for policies that promote community well-being.

18. Jamil Zaki, *Hope for Cynics: The Surprising Science of Human Goodness* (Grand Central Publishing, 2024), chap. 2.

19. Pew Research Center, "Public Trust in Government: 1958-2024," June 24, 2024,

https://www.pewresearch.org/politics/2024/06/24/public-trust-in-government-1958-2024/

20. Trust started falling in the late 1960s during the Vietnam War and Watergate scandal, briefly rebounded in the 1980s and after 9/11, but has remained depressed since the 1970s. Today, partisan polarization exacerbates the problem. Registered Democrats tend to trust the government more when their party is in power, while registered Republicans trust the government more when theirs is, but both sides have seen trust decline overall. See Pew Research Center, "Public Trust in Government."

21. The idiom "good enough for government work" originally referred to the high standards needed for successful completion of the World War II effort. See Federal Managers Association, "Reclaiming 'Good Enough for Government Work,'" accessed September 25, 2025,

https://www.fedmanager.com/news/reclaiming-good-enough-for-government-work

22. By the 1960s and 1970s, however, it had devolved into a disparaging remark about poor or just-barely-adequate work. Grammarist, "Good Enough for Government Work and Close Enough for Government Work," accessed September 25, 2025,

https://grammarist.com/idiom/good-enough-for-government-work-and-close-enough-for-government-work/

23. The concept of internalized oppression has long been used to describe how marginalized groups absorb negative cultural messages about themselves, a theme explored in Paulo Freire, *Pedagogy of the Oppressed*, 30th anniversary ed. (Continuum, 2000 [1970]); and Suzanne Pharr, *Homophobia: A Weapon of Sexism* (Chardon Press, 1988). Scholars of organizational change and equity have extended this idea to institutions themselves—showing how workers within public systems may internalize cultural narratives of ineffectiveness, leading to diminished morale and innovation. See also Camara Phyllis Jones, "Levels of Racism: A Theoretic Framework and a Gardener's Tale," *American Journal of Public Health* 90, no. 8 (2000): 1212–15.

24. Deborah Winograd and Beth Cohen, *Workaches: The Neuroscience Guide to Surviving and Thriving at Work* (The Mind Press, 2019).

25. See James W. Loewen, *Sundown Towns: A Hidden Dimension of American Racism* (The New Press, 2005). Loewen documents thousands of communities across the United States that maintained formal and informal policies excluding Black residents and other minorities well into the twentieth century, revealing how the idealized image of "small-town neighborliness" often coexisted with segregation and enforced silence.

26. Nostalgia is politically perilous. Jason Stanley shows in *How Fascism Works* that fascist politics rely on mythologizing the past to divide people and suppress truth. Timothy Snyder likewise warns in *On Freedom* that when plural futures collapse into a single imposed vision, "fake cheerfulness and real determinism give way to nostalgia and resentment," a pattern he connects to Russia and the United States. Jason Stanley, *How Fascism Works: The Politics of Us and Them* (Random House, 2018), chap. 1; Timothy Snyder, *On Freedom* (Crown, 2024), chap. on mobility.

27. U.S. Census Bureau, "National Poverty in America," accessed August 24, 2025, https://www.census.gov/newsroom/stories/poverty-awareness-month.html;

Peter G. Peterson Foundation, "7 Key Trends in Poverty in the United States," November 26, 2024, https://www.pgpf.org/article/7-key-trends-in-poverty-in-the-united-states/; Matthew Desmond, *Poverty, By America* (Crown, 2023), prologue.

28. Reverend Dr. William J. Barber II, *White Poverty: How Exposing Myths About Race and Class Can Reconstruct American Democracy*, (Liveright, 2024) chap. 1; Colleen Shaddox and Joanne Samuel Goldblum, *Broke in America: Seeing, Understanding, and Ending U.S. Poverty*, (Bella Books, 2021), chap. 1.

29. Paul Slovic, "Psychic Numbing and Genocide," *Judgment and Decision Making* 2, no. 2 (April 2007): 79–95.

30. PolicyLink is "a research and action institute that is working to build a future where all people in the United States can participate in a flourishing multiracial democracy, prosper in an equitable economy, and live in thriving communities," accessed August 24, 2025, https://www.policylink.org/

31. Barber, *White Poverty*, chap. 5.

32. Jacob Harold, *The Toolbox: Strategies for Crafting Social Impact* (Wiley, 2023), 99.

33. Harold, *The Toolbox*, 100.

34. The 2021 Child Tax Credit (CTC), expanded under the American Rescue Plan, temporarily increased the benefit for families with children to up to $3,600 per child under age 6 and $3,000 per child ages six to seventeen. For the first time, it was fully refundable, meaning families with very low or no income qualified. Half of the credit was delivered as monthly payments from July through December 2021. *Policy Basics: The Child Tax Credit*, Center on Budget and Policy Priorities, accessed September 10, 2025,
https://www.cbpp.org/research/policy-basics-the-child-tax-credit

35. The U.S. child poverty rate, as measured by the Supplemental Poverty Measure, was cut almost in half in 2021 driven by the expanded Child Tax Credit (CTC). Overall, 5.3 million people — including 2.9 million children — were lifted out of poverty that year. *The Expanded Child Tax Credit Dramatically Reduced Child Poverty in 2021* (U.S. Congress, Joint Economic Committee, 2022), accessed September 10, 2025,

https://www.jec.senate.gov/public/_cache/files/dd209a98-c23b-4b2e-8478-61a55ec2b647/the-expanded-child-tax-credit-dramatically-reduced-child-poverty-in-2021-final-1-.pdf

36. The expanded Child Tax Credit expired at the end of 2021, and efforts in Congress to extend it were unsuccessful. See Brendan McDermott, *Selected Issues in Tax Policy: The Child Tax Credit* (IF12820), Congressional Research Service, November 19, 2024,

https://www.congress.gov/crs-product/IF12820

37. Heather McGhee describes this as the "zero-sum paradigm"—the belief that progress for some must come at the expense of others. She traces how this narrative has been deliberately racialized in U.S. history to pit communities against each other and prevent investments that benefit everyone. Heather McGhee, *The Sum of Us: What Racism Costs Everyone and How We Can Prosper Together* (One World, 2021).

38. Social Security enjoys extraordinary public trust. A June 2025 AARP poll finds that 74% of Americans view it as one of the most important government programs—a rare point of cross-partisan agreement. Among adults fifty and older, the sentiment is even stronger: 85% regard it as critical, and 93% say it helps older Americans stay independent. *Social Security: What You Need to Know*, AARP, August 2025, accessed September 10, 2025,

https://datastories.aarp.org/2025/social-security/

39. Over the twentieth century, *Social Security* dramatically reduced elderly poverty (e.g., the poverty rate for those 65 and older fell from ~35 % in 1960 to ~10 % by 1995). National Bureau of Economic Research. "Social Security and Elderly Poverty," *The Bulletin on Aging & Health*, no. 2 (2004), accessed September 10, 2025,

https://www.nber.org/bah/2004number2/social-security-and-elderly-poverty.

Kathleen Romig, *Social Security Lifts More People Above the Poverty Line Than Any Other Program* (Center on Budget and Policy Priorities, updated January 21, 2025),

https://www.cbpp.org/research/social-security/social-security-lifts-more-people-above-the-poverty-line-than-any-other

40. Karen Davis, Cathy Schoen and Farhan Bandeali, "Medicare: 50 Years of Ensuring Coverage and Care," *The Commonwealth Fund*, April 2015, accessed September 12, 2025,

https://www.commonwealthfund.org/publications/fund-reports/2015/apr/medicare-50-years-ensuring-coverage-and-care

41. The phrase "breaking the cycle of poverty" appears to have emerged in the rhetoric of the War on Poverty, particularly in the language surrounding the Economic Opportunity Act of 1964 and the programs of the Office of Economic Opportunity. States and local initiatives, such as Operation Breakthrough in North Carolina, adopted the phrase as they implemented antipoverty programs, and it quickly became a common way to describe their objectives. See *Economic Opportunity Act of 1964*, Pub. L. No. 88-452, 78 Stat. 508; and "Operation Breakthrough (anti-poverty movement)," Wikipedia, accessed September 25, 2025,

https://en.wikipedia.org/wiki/Operation_Breakthrough_(anti-poverty_movement)

42. During the 1996 welfare reform, versions of both of these metaphors were used, depicting Aid for Dependent Children as an expensive failure that trapped families stuck in a *cycle of dependence*. Premilla Nadasen, "Welfare Reform and the Politics of Race: 20 Years Later," *Perspectives* (AHA), August 22, 2016,

https://www.historians.org/perspectives-article/welfare-reform-and-the-politics-of-race-20-years-later-september-2016/

43. The poverty line refers to the official measure the federal government uses to determine who is considered poor. It was first developed in the 1960s by Social Security Administration economist Mollie Orshansky, who calculated the minimum cost of a nutritionally adequate diet and multiplied it by three to account for other household expenses. Although adjusted each year for inflation, the formula has changed little since, and many experts argue it underestimates what families need to make ends meet today. Gordon M. Fisher, "The Development of the Orshansky Poverty Thresholds and Their Subsequent History as the Official U.S. Poverty Measure" (U.S. Census Bureau, September 1997), accessed September 26, 2025,

https://www.census.gov/library/working-papers/1997/demo/fisher-02.html

44. One hundred million people in the United States—roughly one in three—live in households with incomes below 200% of the federal poverty level, a common benchmark for economic insecurity. See Abbie Langston, "100 Million and Counting: A Portrait of Economic Insecurity in the United States" (PolicyLink, 2018), accessed September 26, 2025,
https://www.policylink.org/resources-tools/100-million

45. See Ascend at the Aspen Institute and FrameWorks Institute. *Framing Two-Generation Approaches to Supporting Families*, September 3, 2019.
https://www.frameworksinstitute.org/articles/framing-two-generation-approaches-to-supporting-families/ee

46. See Lizabeth Cohen, *A Consumers' Republic: The Politics of Mass Consumption in Postwar America* (Alfred A. Knopf, 2003); and Jill Lepore, *These Truths: A History of the United States* (W. W. Norton, 2018). Both describe how postwar skepticism toward large corporations and private profiteering gradually gave way to distrust of government. As deregulation and antigovernment rhetoric gained traction, the locus of blame for systemic failure shifted from private industry to the public sphere, deepening civic fatalism and weakening belief in collective solutions.

47. Framework's research found that "government is understood as a separate body that stands in opposition to what people want and need." See e.g., FrameWorks Institute, "Understanding Mindsets about Government Can Help Us Advocate for Children," *FrameWorks Institute*, August 6, 2024, accessed September 10, 2025, https://www.frameworksinstitute.org/resources/understanding-mindsets-about-government-can-help-us-advocate-for-children/

Well-Being Is Constructed

1. A social system refers to the interconnected institutions, relationships, and norms that shape how people live and interact. It includes formal structures like schools, health care, housing, and human services, as well as informal networks such as families, neighborhoods, and community organizations. Social systems operate in the background of daily life, often unnoticed, but they powerfully determine opportunities, risks, and outcomes. They are not fixed—they are human-made and can be redesigned, which is why understanding them is key to improving well-being. See Donella H. Meadows, *Thinking in Systems: A Primer* (White River Junction, VT: Chelsea Green Publishing, 2008).

2. When I refer to COVID-19, I am describing the social and economic impacts of the widespread closures that accompanied the pandemic, not the direct health crisis. The loss of more than one million lives in the United States to COVID-19 remains one of the most devastating public health tragedies in our history. My focus here is on how the shutdowns made the scaffolding of our social and economic systems more visible.

3. Elaine Waxman et al., *Documenting Pandemic EBT for the 2020–2021 School Year: State Perspectives on Implementation Challenges and Lessons for the Future* (Urban Institute, 2021), https://www.urban.org/sites/default/files/publication/104949/documenting-pandemic-ebt-for-the-2020-21-school-year_1.pdf

4. See APHSA, Administration for Children and Families (U.S.), and W.K. Kellogg Foundation, *COVID Response Project: Lessons Learned from State Adaptations and Federal Flexibilities*, January 2021,

https://acf.gov/sites/default/files/documents/oro/APHSA_COVIDresponseProject_011921_FINAL_1.pdf;

see APHSA and National Community Action Partnership, *Aligning Systems to Advance Family and Community Partnership: A Partnership Playbook for Community Action and Human Service Agencies*, January 2022,

https://aphsa.org/wp-content/uploads/2024/07/f090af97-105e-4c18-a000-6f980a770607.pdf

5. Reverend Dr. William J. Barber II, *White Poverty: How Exposing Myths About Race and Class Can Reconstruct American Democracy* (Liveright, 2024) chap. 8.

6. See Chapter 6 "Case Studies: When Systems Falter."

7. Leon Festinger, *A Theory of Cognitive Dissonance* (Stanford University Press, 1957).

8. Mariana Mazzucato, *The Value of Everything: Making and Taking in the Global Economy* (New York: PublicAffairs, 2018); Elizabeth Anderson, *Private Government: How Employers Rule Our Lives (and Why We Don't Talk About It)* (Princeton University Press, 2017).

9. United States National Park Service, "Sacrificing for the Common Good: Rationing in WWII," National Park Service, accessed July 30, 2025,

https://www.nps.gov/articles/rationing-in-wwii.htm

10. Sarah Andersen et al., *Annual Survey of Public Employment & Payroll, 2023* (U.S. Census Bureau, 2024), accessed December 10, 2025,

https://www.census.gov/library/publications/2024/econ/g24-aspep.html

11. Brett Theodos and Brady Meixell, *Public Sector Employment and Its Role in Local Economic Development* (Urban Institute, April 2024),

https://www.urban.org/research/publication/public-sector-employment-and-its-role-local-economic-development

12. U.S. Bureau of Labor Statistics, "Nonprofits accounted for 12.8 million jobs, 9.9 percent of private-sector employment in 2022," *TED: The Economics Daily*, August 16, 2024,

https://www.bls.gov/opub/ted/2024/nonprofits-accounted-for-12-8-million-jobs-9-9-percent-of-private-sector-employment-in-2022.htm

13. See research from the Frameworks Institute on why the metaphor of construction works to explain human services. Michael Baran et al., *Talking Human Services: A FrameWorks MessageMemo,* Frameworks Institute, January 8, 2015,

https://www.frameworksinstitute.org/resources/talking-human-services-a-frameworks-multi-media-messagememo/

14. See Chapter 4 "The Zero-sum Game Narrows Our Imagination" for a fuller discussion of Medicare's impact.

15. County of San Diego Health and Human Services Agency, *Live Well San Diego Annual Impact Report 2024–2025* (County of San Diego, 2025),

https://www.livewellsd.org/about/annual-report

The Dual Edge of Systems

1. White House Office of Management and Budget. *U.S. Strategy on Reducing Poverty and Building Economic Security* (White House, 2023). See also Performance.gov, "Facing a Financial Shock,"

https://www.performance.gov/cx/life-experiences/facing-a-financial-shock/

2. U.S. Congress, *Economic Opportunity Act of 1964,* Pub. L. No. 88-452, § 202(a)(3), 78 Stat. 508, 516 (1964).

3. U.S. Department of Health and Human Services, Administration for Children and Families, Office of Head Start, "History of Head Start," last updated June 30, 2024,

https://acf.gov/ohs/about/history-head-start

4. For impact of TANF on deep poverty, see Marianne Bitler and Hilary Hoynes, "The State of the Social Safety Net in the Post-Welfare Reform Era," *Brookings Papers on Economic Activity,* Fall 2010, 71–127,

https://gspp.berkeley.edu/assets/uploads/research/pdf/Bitler-Hoynes-BPEA-2010.pdf

5. Richard Rothstein, *The Color of Law: A Forgotten History of How Our Government Segregated America* (Liveright, 2017).

6. Legal scholars have shown that the nation's child-support system grew out of cultural assumptions, especially the belief that fathers, particularly Black fathers and fathers with low incomes, were likely to be absent or irresponsible. These assumptions shaped policies that valued only formal, wage-based support and treated informal or in-kind contributions as if they did not count. In doing so, the system reinforced harmful stereotypes and ignored the many ways families actually organize care and resources. For deeper analysis, see Sergio Maldonado, "Redefining Child Support for Poor Fathers," *UC Davis Law Review* 39 (2005): 991–1045; and Osagie K. Rambert, "The Absent Black Father: Race, the Welfare–Child Support Complex," *UCLA Law Review* 68, no. 6 (2021): 1242–1323.

7. Annie E. Casey Foundation. "Extended Foster Care Explained." *The Annie E. Casey Foundation Blog*, updated October 19, 2025,
https://www.aecf.org/blog/extended-foster-care-explained; Child Welfare Information Gateway, *Extension of Foster Care Beyond Age 18*. (U.S. Department of Health and Human Services, Administration for Children and Families, Children's Bureau, March 2022),
https://www.childwelfare.gov/resources/extension-foster-care-beyond-age-18/

8. Emma Kahle Monahan, Yasmin Grewal-Kök, Gretchen Cusick, and Clare Anderson, *Economic and Concrete Supports: An Evidence-Based Service for Child Welfare Prevention* (Chapin Hall at the University of Chicago, April 2023),
https://www.chapinhall.org/wp-content/uploads/ECS-and-FFPSA-Brief_FINAL-4.13.23.pdf;
Casey Family Programs, *How Are Child Welfare Systems Using Flexible Funds to Support Families and Prevent the Need for Foster Care?* (Strategy Brief, updated January 2024),
https://www.casey.org/media/24.07-QFF-TS-Economic-supports-strategies.pdf

9. Mark E. Courtney, Nathanael J. Okpych, and Sunggeun (Ethan) Park, *Report from CalYOUTH: Findings on the Relationship between Extended Foster Care and Youth's Outcomes at Age 21* (Chapin Hall at the University of Chicago, November 2018), iii–iv,
https://www.chapinhall.org/wp-content/uploads/Impacts-of-extended-care-age-21.pdf

10. The Annie E. Casey Foundation, KIDS COUNT Data Center, "Child Population by Race and Ethnicity," last updated July 2024, accessed September 4, 2025,

https://datacenter.aecf.org/data/tables/103-child-population-by-race-and-ethnicity; The Annie E. Casey Foundation, KIDS COUNT Data Center, "Children in Foster Care by Race and Hispanic Origin," last updated August 2025, accessed September 4, 2025,
https://datacenter.aecf.org/data/tables/6246-children-in-foster-care-by-race-and-hispanic-origin

11. U.S. Children's Bureau. *The AFCARS Report* #29 (U.S. Department of Health and Human Services, 2022), table "Circumstances Associated With Child's Removal,"
https://www.acf.hhs.gov/sites/default/files/documents/cb/afcars-report-29.pdf

12. *Family First Prevention Services Act of 2018*, Pub. L. No. 115-123, 132 Stat. 64 (2018).

13. Monahan et al., "Economic and Concrete Supports."

14. john a. powell, "Deepening Our Understanding of Structural Marginalization," *Poverty & Race* 22, no. 5 (September/October 2013): 3–4, 13,
https://www.prrac.org/pdf/SeptOct2013PRRAC_powell.pdf

15. For a compelling look at the way systems steal chances see Ruja Benjamin, *Viral Justice: How We Grow the World We Want* (Princeton University Press, 2022).

16. I had the privilege of getting to know Derrik during my time at the APHSA when he graciously joined the association's board of directors. I am grateful for all the things he taught me and for helping inspire leaders in the human services sector to always be "truthtellers." For more on his work, see Tracy Wareing Evans and Karen Heller Key, "We Have to Be Truthtellers," *Our Dream Deferred*, podcast, APHSA, October 26, 2021, Libsyn,
https://aphsa.libsyn.com/we-have-to-be-truthtellers

17. Bitler and Hoynes, "State of the Social Safety Net in the Post-Welfare Reform Era," 98.

18. The TANF block grant has remained at its original nominal funding level losing 47% of its value to inflation over time. Richard Kogan, Kiran Rachamallu, Josephine Cureton, and David Reich, *History Shows That Block-Granting Low-Income Programs Leads to Large Funding Declines Over Time* (Center on Budget and Policy Priorities, July 29, 2025),
https://www.cbpp.org/research/federal-budget/history-shows-that-block-granting-low-income-programs-leads-to-large

19. Bitler and Hoynes, "State of the Social Safety Net in the Post-Welfare Reform Era," 98; see also Heather Hahn et al., *Why Does Cash Welfare Depend on Where You Live? How and Why State TANF Programs Vary* (Urban Institute, June 2017),
https://www.urban.org/sites/default/files/publication/90761/tanf_cash_welfare_0.pdf

20. As of the latest data, only about 20% of families living in poverty receive TANF cash assistance. Victoria Bowden, Diana Azevedo-McCaffrey and Maria Manansala, "AFDC and TANF Caseload and Poverty Data, 1978-2023," Center on Budget and Policy Priorities, April 11 2025, https://www.cbpp.org/research/income-security/afdc-and-tanf-caseload-and-poverty-data. In absolute terms, approximately 2.4 million people receive TANF benefits (cash or noncash). Adrianne R. Brown, *Temporary Assistance for Needy Families (TANF): 2022 Survey of Income and Program Participation Snapshots*, P70FS-208 (U.S. Census Bureau, January 2025).

21. As of July 2024, TANF benefit levels for a family of three ranged from $1,694 per month in California to just $204 per month in Arkansas, with most states clustered between $300 and $700. In recent years, many states have used their own funds to raise benefit levels; even with these increases, assistance still falls well below the poverty line. Diana Azevedo-McCaffrey and Tonanziht Aguas, *Continued Increases in TANF Benefit Levels Are Critical to Helping Families Meet Their Needs and Thrive* (Center on Budget and Policy Priorities, February 2025), https://www.cbpp.org/sites/default/files/5-29-24tanf_rev2-26-25_0.pdf

22. States have broad flexibility in how they use TANF funds, and in practice only a small share is spent on basic assistance for families. In 2021, states directed just about one-fifth of TANF and related state spending to monthly cash aid, with much of the rest going to other services or budget areas. See Center on Budget and Policy Priorities, *How States Spend Funds Under the TANF Block Grant* (Washington, DC: CBPP, updated September 2024),
https://www.cbpp.org/research/income-security/state-fact-sheets-how-states-spend-funds-under-the-tanf-block-grant; and U.S. Department of Health and Human Services, Office of Family Assistance, "TANF and MOE Spending and Transfers by Activity, FY 2023," Administration for Children and Families, accessed September 20, 2025,
https://acf.gov/ofa/data/tanf-and-moe-spending-and-transfers-activity-fy-2023

23. See 42 U.S.C. § 601 (a).

24. Center on Budget and Policy Priorities, *Federal Rental Assistance Fact Sheets*, updated January 2025,

https://www.cbpp.org/research/housing/federal-rental-assistance-fact-sheets#US.;

Congressional Budget Office (CBO), *Federal Housing Assistance for Low-Income Households* (CBO, 2015),

https://www.cbo.gov/publication/50782

25. See Chapter 5, "A Mindset Shift in Plain Sight."

26. Annie E. Casey Foundation, "Child Poverty Nearly Triples to 13% Over Three Years," *AECF Blog*, September 12, 2024,

https://www.aecf.org/blog/child-poverty-nearly-triples-to-13-over-three-years

27. P-EBT was established under the Families First Coronavirus Response Act of 2020 as a program separate from SNAP, though administered by state SNAP agencies. See Families First Coronavirus Response Act, Pub. L. No. 116-127, §1101, 134 Stat. 178, 190–92 (2020). Emergency Allotments, by contrast, were authorized under §2302 of the same Act as an expansion of regular SNAP benefits in response to the broader economic crisis; see FNS, "SNAP COVID-19 Waivers and Flexibilities,"

https://www.fns.usda.gov/disaster/pandemic/covid-19/snap-waivers-flexibilities

28. See Elaine Waxman et al., *Documenting Pandemic EBT for the 2020–21 School Year* (Urban Institute, October 26, 2021),

https://www.urban.org/research/publication/documenting-pandemic-ebt-2020-21-school-year;

see also Jim Krieger, Erica Kenney, and Lina Piñero-Walkinshaw, "Pandemic-EBT and Grab-and-Go School Meals: Costs, Reach, and Benefits of Two Approaches to Feeding Children during School Closures—Lessons from COVID-19 Responses," research brief (Healthy Eating Research, August 2022),

https://healthyeatingresearch.org/wp-content/uploads/2022/09/HER-P-EBT-Brief-083122.pdf

29. The federal Child Care and Development Fund (CCDF) subsidizes care for low-income working families, but funding reaches only about one in six eligible children. See Office of Child Care, Administration for Children and Families, *Child Care and Development Fund Report to Congress* (U.S. Department of Health and Human Services, 2023); Nina Chien, *Estimates of Child Care Subsidy Eligibility & Receipt for Fiscal Year 2021* (U.S. Department of Health and Human Services, Office of the Assistant Secretary for Planning and Evaluation, September 11, 2024),

https://aspe.hhs.gov/reports/child-care-eligibility-fy2021;

see also U.S. Department of the Treasury, *The Economics of Child Care Supply in the United States* (U.S. Department of the Treasury, September 2021), 2, https://home.treasury.gov/system/files/136/The-Economics-of-Childcare-Supply-09-14-final.pdf

30. U.S. Treasury, *Economics of Child Care Supply;* see also Todd Hall, Taryn Morrissey, Aaron Sojourner, and Chris Herbst, "Compensation and Staffing Challenges in Child Care: Statewide Evidence from Pandemic Relief Applications," *Education Finance & Policy* 19, no. 3 (Summer 2024): 524–37,

https://direct.mit.edu/edfp/article/19/3/524/116701/Compensation-and-Staffing-Challenges-in-Child-Care

31. A Child Care in America report found that in 41 states and Washington DC, the average annual price of infant center-based care exceeded in-state university tuition. Child Care Aware of America, "Child Care in America: 2024 Price & Supply," May 2025,

https://www.childcareaware.org/price-landscape24

32. Hall et al., "Compensation and Staffing Challenges in Child Care."

33. Rigorous research has shown that investments in early childhood yield large long-term returns in education, health, and economic mobility. For example, a 2023 Urban Institute review found that programs like high-quality preschool and early health supports produce benefits far exceeding their costs, with some interventions returning more than $10 for every $1 invested. Likewise, economist James Heckman and colleagues have demonstrated that high-quality birth-to-five programs for children facing social and economic hardships can deliver annual returns of up to 13% through better education, health, and earnings outcomes. See Elaine Maag et al., *The Return on Investing in Children* (Urban Institute, September 2023),

https://www.urban.org/sites/default/files/2023-09/The%20Return%20on%20Investing%20in%20Children.pdf;

Jorge Luis García, James J. Heckman, Duncan Ermini Leaf, and María José Prados, "Quantifying the Life-Cycle Benefits of an Influential Early Childhood Program," *Journal of Political Economy* 128, no. 7 (July 2020): 2502–41.

34. Kogan et al., *History Shows That Block-Granting.*

35. Valarie Kaur, *See No Stranger: A Memoir and Manifesto of Revolutionary Love,* (One World, 2020), chap. 8.

36. Ben McBride, *Troubling the Water: the Urgent Work of Radical Belonging* (Broadleaf Books, 2023), chap. 6.

37. Barbara McQuade, *Attack from Within: How Disinformation is Sabotaging America* (Seven Stories Press, 2024), chap. 5.

38. Francesca Polletta, *It Was Like a Fever: Storytelling in Protest and Politics* (University of Chicago Press, 2006).

39. Ruth Wilson Gilmore, *Abolition Geography: Essays toward Liberation* (Verso, 2022). See also Mariame Kaba and Tamaa Nopper, *We Do This 'Til We Free Us: Abolitionist Organizing and Transforming Justice* (Haymarket Books, 2021).

40. Beginning in January 1969 at St. Augustine's Episcopal Church in Oakland, California local Black Panthers, driven by volunteers, offered free morning meals to children who arrived at school hungry. In just one year, this program had spread to at least twenty=three cities and fed over 20,000 kids nationwide. See Diane Pien, "Black Panther Party's Free Breakfast Program," February 11, 2010,

https://blackpast.org/african-american-history/black-panther-partys-free-breakfast-program-1969-1980/

41. The Free Breakfast for Children Program, launched in 1969, was one of the Black Panther Party's most visible and impactful "survival programs." By feeding thousands of children daily across dozens of cities, it both met immediate community needs and drew national attention to child hunger. Historians and policy analysts note that the Panthers' program put pressure on federal leaders and helped lay the groundwork for the expansion of the National School Breakfast Program in the 1970s. See Pien, *Black Panther Party's Free Breakfast Program*; Husain Lateef and David Androff, "Children Can't Learn on an Empty Stomach: The Black Panther Party's Free Breakfast Program," *Journal of Sociology & Social Welfare* 44, no. 4 (2017): article 2, https://doi.org/10.15453/0191-5096.3883 ;

Shaun Harrison, Shanteal Lake, and Sam Abbott "How Black Activists Spurred the U.S. Government to Expand School Meal Programs," *Equitable Growth*, February 22, 2022,

https://equitablegrowth.org/how-black-activists-spurred-the-u-s-government-to-expand-school-meal-programs-addressing-child-hunger-and-boosting-future-productivity

42. Ruth Wilson Gilmore, "Where Life Is Precious, Life Is Precious," *On Being with Krista Tippett*, podcast, March 30, 2023, https://onbeing.org/programs/ruth-wilson-gilmore-where-life-is-precious-life-is-precious/

The Forces We Face

1. Thomas L. Friedman, *The World is Flat: A Brief History of the Twenty-First Century* (Farrar, Straus and Giroux, 2005).

2. Board of Governors of the Federal Reserve System, *Economic Well-Being of U.S. Households in 2024* (Federal Reserve, May 2025), https://www.federalreserve.gov/publications/files/2024-report-economic-well-being-us-households-202505.pdf

3. Joanne Goldblum and Colleen Shaddox, *Broke in America: Seeing, Understanding, and Ending US Poverty* (BenBella Books, 2021), chap. 1.

4. Emad Mostaque, *The Last Economy: A Guide to the Age of Intelligent Economics* (Intelligent Internet, 2025).

5. Research on digital currencies underscores their double-edged nature. An International Monetary Fund working paper by Romain Bouis and colleagues finds that central bank digital currencies could improve household welfare by lowering transaction costs and expanding access to finance, but they may also reduce bank deposits and raise funding costs, especially during periods of stress. A study by William Chen and Gregory Phelan from the U.S. Office of Financial Research similarly warns that digital currencies could heighten the risk of bank runs and amplify systemic vulnerabilities. See Romain Bouis, et al., *Central Bank Digital Currencies and Financial Stability: Balance Sheet Analysis and Policy Choices* (IMF Working Paper WP/24/226, October 11, 2024),
https://www.imf.org/-/media/Files/Publications/WP/2024/English/wpiea2024226-print-pdf.ashx; ;
William Chen and Gregory Phelan, *Digital Currency and Banking-Sector Stability* (Office of Financial Research Working Paper 23-01, March 22, 2023),
https://www.financialresearch.gov/working-papers/files/OFRwp-23-01_digital-currency-and-banking-sector-stability.pdf

6. Arindrajit Dube, "A Plan to Reform the Unemployment Insurance System in the United States," The Hamilton Project, Brookings Institution, April 12, 2021,

https://www.brookings.edu/articles/a-plan-to-reform-the-unemployment-insurance-system-in-the-united-states/;

U.S. Government Accountability Office (GAO), *COVID-19: Significant Improvements Are Needed for Overseeing Relief Funds and Leading Responses to Public Health Emergencies*, GAO-21-105291 (GAO, Jan. 27, 2022). During the pandemic, unemployment insurance (UI) systems collapsed under record demand. Antiquated state technology, administrative bottlenecks, and uneven program design delayed payments for months, leaving families without income while bills and rent piled up. Dube emphasizes the need for federal reforms to modernize UI, while GAO documents show how these systemic weaknesses left relief efforts vulnerable to both delays and fraud.

7. See Social Current, "It's Time to Ditch 'Nonprofit': Five & Rising Launches to Unleash the Social Sector's Full Power," September 16, 2025,

https://www.social-current.org/2025/09/its-time-to-ditch-nonprofit-five-rising-launches-to-unleash-the-social-sectors-full-power/;

UnCharitable, directed by Stephen Gyllenhaal (Vision Films, 2023). The Five & Rising campaign, launched by Social Current in 2025 challenges the outdated "nonprofit" label and emphasizes the sector's essential role in delivering social services through community-based organizations. By reframing the narrative and piloting new models of funding and governance, Five & Rising aims to unleash the sector's full power as democratic infrastructure working alongside government. For more, see Chapter 10 of this book and Five & Rising website,

https://www.fiveandrising.org/

8. See Clemens Fuest, Andreas Peichl, and Mathias Dolls, "Automatic Stabilizers and Economic Crisis: US vs. Europe," *VoxEU* (Centre for Economic Policy Research), September 17, 2010,

https://cepr.org/voxeu/columns/automatic-stabilisers-and-economic-crisis-europe-and-us;

Youssouf Kiendrebeogo, Kossi Assimaidou, and Abdoulaye Tall, "Social Protection for Poverty Reduction in Times of Crisis," *Journal of Policy Modeling* 39, no. 6 (2017): 1163–83,

https://www.sciencedirect.com/science/article/abs/pii/S0161893817300947?via%3Dihub. Both studies underscore the comparative strength of European social protections: Fuest et al, ("Automatic Stabilizers and Economic Crisis: US vs. Europe") show that automatic stabilizers—especially unemployment insurance and transfers—are far larger and more responsive in Europe than in the U.S., cushioning household income during downturns. Kiendrebeogo et al. ("Social Protection for Poverty Reductions in Times of Crisis") confirm that countries with stronger social protection systems experience smaller increases in poverty and inequality during crises.

9. Joana Madureira-Lima, Aaron Reeves, Amy Clair, and David Stuckler, "The Great Recession and Inequalities in Access to Health Care: A Study of Unemployment and Unmet Medical Need in Europe in the Economic Crisis," *International Journal of Epidemiology* 47, no. 1 (September 2017): 58–68, https://doi.org/10.1093/ije/dyx193; Organization for Economic Cooperation and Development (OECD), *Universal Health Coverage and Health Outcomes* (OECD Publishing, July 2016), https://www.oecd.org/content/dam/oecd/en/publications/reports/2016/09/universal-health-coverage-and-health-outcomes_446e0f96/932b3cde-en.pdf. Nearly all nations who are part of the Organization for Economic Cooperation and Development (OECD) provide universal health coverage, ensuring that access to care is not tied to employment. This reduces household vulnerability in recessions or pandemics by maintaining continuity of care even when jobs are lost.

10. Shekhar Aiyar and Mai Chi Dao, *The Effectiveness of Job-Retention Schemes: COVID-19 Evidence From the German States*, IMF Working Paper WP/21/242 (International Monetary Fund, 2021), https://www.imf.org/-/media/Files/Publications/WP/2021/English/wpiea2021242-print-pdf.ashx; Institute for Employment Research (IAB), *Short-Time Work in the COVID-19 Crisis: Germany's Safeguard for Jobs and Companies*, Forschungsbericht 05/2023 (Nuremberg: IAB, 2023), https://doku.iab.de/forschungsbericht/2023/fb0523en.pdf. Kurzarbeit prevents mass layoffs and accelerates recovery.

11. Pew Research Center, "Public Trust in Government: 1958-2024," June 24, 2024, https://www.pewresearch.org/politics/2024/06/24/public-trust-in-government-1958-2024/

12. Barbara McQuade, *Attack from Within: How Disinformation is Sabotaging America* (Seven Stories Press, 2024), chap. 5.

13. Jason Stanley, *Erasing History: How Fascists Rewrite the Past to Control the Future* (Simon & Schuster, 2024); see also Timothy Snyder, *On Freedom* (Crown, 2024), chap. on factuality.

14. See, e.g., McQuade, *Attack from Within* and Jason Stanley, *Erasing History*. Both of these works show how disinformation manufactures villains and false certainties that destabilize democratic institutions, distort public health responses, and erode trust in science and elections.

15. Barbara McQuade explains the many ways disinformation is undermining our democracy, including by making people its "unwilling accomplice" by repeating the lies that "they believe to be true." McQuade, *Attack from Within*, chap. 1.

16. See Zachary Parolin et al., *The Initial Effects of the Expanded Child Tax Credit on Material Hardship*, NBER Working Paper 29285 (National Bureau of Economic Research, September 2021), https://www.nber.org/papers/w29285

17. Lilliana Mason, *Uncivil Agreement: How Politics Became Our Identity* (University of Chicago Press, 2018).

18. Nathan P. Kalmoe and Lilliana Mason, *Radical American Partisanship: Mapping Violence, Extremism, and the Psychology of American Politics* (University of Chicago Press, 2022), chap. 4. See also Public Religion Research Institute (PRRI), *Competing Visions of America: An Evolving Identity or a Culture Under Attack? Findings from the 2021 American Values Survey* (PRRI, 2022), https://prri.org/research/competing-visions-of-america-an-evolving-identity-or-a-culture-under-attack.

19. Jamie Susskind writes that "[a]lgorithms are increasingly used to determine our access to the necessities of civilized existence: work, credit, insurance, housing, welfare and much else besides." Jamie Susskind, *The Digital Republic: On Freedom and Democracy in the 21st Century* (Pegasus Books, 2022), chap. 3.

20. Shoshana Zuboff, *The Age of Surveillance Capitalism: The Fight for a Human Future at the New Frontier of Power* (PublicAffairs, 2019).

21. Virginia Eubanks, *Automating Inequality: How High-Tech Tools Profile, Police, and Punish the Poor* (St. Martin's Press, 2018).

22. Kate Crawford, *Atlas of AI: Power, Politics, and the Planetary Costs of Artificial Intelligence* (Yale University Press, 2021).

23. Safiya Umoja Noble, *Algorithms of Oppression: How Search Engines Reinforce Racism* (University Press, 2018) chap. 1 ("Algorithmic oppression is not just a glitch in the system but, rather, is fundamental to the operating system of the web.")

24. Ruha Benjamin, *Viral Justice: How We Grow the World We Want* (Princeton University Press, 2024), chap. 3 ("Technology, in short, can exacerbate inequities if the corresponding social infrastructure is not in place.")

25. Meredith Broussard, *More Than a Glitch: Confronting Race, Gender, and Ability Bias in Tech* (MIT Press, 2023), chap. 1 ("I heard people repeat the same promises about the bright technological future, but I saw the digital world replicate the inequalities of the 'real' world.")

26. Susskind, *The Digital Republic*, Introduction.

27. Scholars and journalists alike have traced how Allegheny County became one of the first jurisdictions to use predictive analytics to support child-welfare screening, an innovation that prompted important questions about bias, transparency, and community trust. Early evaluations documented both the promise and the pitfalls of the Allegheny Family Screening Tool, while later studies examined how the county revised the model over time by shifting from raw scores to "High-Risk" and "Low-Risk" flags, updating variables, and preserving staff discretion. Independent analyses indicate that these changes have strengthened targeting and contributed to reductions in racial disparities in screening and removal decisions. Emily Putnam-Hornstein and Rhema Vaithianathan, "The Allegheny Family Screening Tool: A Predictive Risk Model for Child Welfare Call Screening," *Child Maltreatment* 26, no. 2 (2021): 168–79; Laura Santhanam, "How an Algorithm That Screens for Child Neglect Could Harden Racial Disparities," *PBS NewsHour*, April 29, 2022, https://www.pbs.org/newshour/nation/how-an-algorithm-that-screens-for-child-neglect-could-harden-racial-disparities; Katherine Rittenhouse, María José Prados, Alex Chohlas-Wood, and Dan Ho, *Algorithms, Humans, and Racial Disparities in Child Protection: Evidence from the Allegheny Family Screening Tool* (April 1, 2024), https://krittenh.github.io/katherine-rittenhouse.com/AFST_Disparities.pdf

28. See Code for America, "Benefits Playbook: Designing Human-Centered Applications," November 2024, https://files.codeforamerica.org/2024/10/29152646/benefits-playbook-2024.pdf; Digital Government Hub, "Digital Benefits," https://digitalgovernmenthub.org/benefits/

29. See Intergovernmental Panel on Climate Change (IPCC), *Climate Change 2022: Impacts, Adaptation and Vulnerability. Working Group II Contribution to the Sixth Assessment Report of the IPCC* (Cambridge University Press, 2022); U.S. Government Accountability Office, *Disaster Assistance: Action Needed to Improve Access to Federal Disaster Relief for Underserved Populations* (GAO, 2021).

30. U.S. Government Accountability Office, *Disaster Recovery: Efforts to Identify and Address Barriers to Receiving Federal Recovery Assistance*, GAO-22-105488 (GAO, October 27, 2021), https://www.gao.gov/products/gao-22-105488 ; U.S. Government Accountability Office (GAO), *Small Business Administration: Targeted Outreach about Disaster Assistance Could Benefit Rural Communities*, GAO-24-106755 (GAO, 2024), https://www.gao.gov/assets/gao-24-106755.pdf. These reports document persistent inequities in disaster recovery. For example, GAO found that low-income households, communities of color, older adults, and people with disabilities face barriers accessing federal aid, while rural communities in particular struggle with application complexity and limited awareness of programs.

31. This ProPublica feature investigates how climate change will reshape global migration, using modeling to project where displaced populations may move as rising seas, heat, and drought render parts of the world unlivable. Lustgarten highlights the scale of potential climate-driven displacement and the urgent need for governments to plan for human mobility as a central dimension of climate response. Abrahm Lustgarten, "Where Will Everyone Go?," *ProPublica* and *The New York Times Magazine*, July 23, 2020, https://features.propublica.org/climate-migration/model-how-climate-refugees-move-across-continents/

32. Ruben Juarez et al., *From Crisis to Recovery: Health and Resilience Two Years After the Maui Wildfires* (University of Hawaiʻi Economic Research Organization, June 18, 2025), https://uhero.hawaii.edu/wpcontent/uploads/2025/06UHEROPublicHealthReport_FromCrisisToRecovery.pdf. The report finds that Native Hawaiian communities, renters, and immigrant families experienced disproportionate harm from the fires and continue to face barriers to recovery, underscoring the need for equity-focused approaches in disaster response.

33. University of Texas at Austin Energy Institute, *The Timeline and Events of the February 2021 Texas Electric Grid Blackouts*, July 2021, https://energy.utexas.edu/research/ercot-blackout-2021. This report provides a detailed account of how the Texas power grid failed during a severe February 2021 winter storm, and documents that prolonged outages disproportionately affected communities with lower incomes, underscoring systemic inequities in energy infrastructure and emergency response.

34. The Supplemental Nutrition Assistance Program (SNAP) includes a Disaster-SNAP (D-SNAP) option, which allows states to provide temporary food assistance to households affected by natural disasters. Authorized by the Food and Nutrition Act, D-SNAP can be activated when a presidential disaster declaration includes Individual Assistance. It streamlines eligibility and benefit issuance so families who may not normally qualify for SNAP—or who lost access due to a disaster—can receive support quickly. In recent years, D-SNAP has been deployed after hurricanes, wildfires, floods, and winter storms. See U.S. Department of Agriculture, Food and Nutrition Service, "Disaster Supplemental Nutrition Assistance Program (D-SNAP)," accessed September 2025, https://www.fns.usda.gov/disaster/factsheet.

35. Centers for Medicare & Medicaid Services (CMS), "Section 1135 Waiver Flexibilities," accessed September 20, 2025, https://www.medicaid.gov/resources-for-states/disaster-response-toolkit/section-1135-waiver-flexibilities. Under Section 1135 of the Social Security Act, the secretary of Health and Human Services may authorize temporary waivers that let states adjust Medicaid rules during a declared emergency. These waivers can expand eligibility, streamline enrollment, or cover additional services—flexibilities widely used during the COVID-19 pandemic.

36. William J. Congdon and Wayne Vroman, *Extending Unemployment Insurance Benefits in Recessions: Lessons from the Great Recession* (Urban Institute, prepared for the U.S. Department of Labor, February 2021), https://www.dol.gov/sites/dolgov/files/OASP/evaluation/pdf/ETA_GreatRecession_Extending-Benefits_%20IssueBrief_March2021.pdf. This brief explains how states and the federal government have historically expanded UI durations during economic downturns via Extended Benefits and Emergency Unemployment Compensation to provide additional support when regular UI benefits expire.

37. Jonathan E. Vespa, David M. Armstrong, and Lauren Medina, Demographic Turning Points for the United States: Population Projections for 2020 to 2060 (U.S. Census Bureau, 2020), https://www.census.gov/content/dam/Census/library/publications/2020/demo/p25-1144.pdf By 2034 older adults will outnumber children, by 2045 the U.S. will be "majority-minority," and by 2050 the sixty-five and older share of the population will grow to nearly one in four Americans.

38. Priya Chidambaram, Alice Burns, Tricia Neuman, and Robin Rudowitz, "5 Key Facts About Nursing Facilities and Medicaid," Kaiser Family Foundation, May 28, 2025, https://www.kff.org/medicaid/5-key-facts-about-nursing-facilities-and-medicaid; Susan C. Reinhard, Selena Caldera, Ari Houser, Rita Choula, "Valuing the Invaluable: 2023 Update," AARP, March 2023, https://www.aarp.org/pri/topics/ltss/family-caregiving/valuing-the-invaluable-2015-update/, Together these sources show that Medicaid already finances a large share of nursing facility and long-term care services, while unpaid family caregivers shoulder enormous burdens valued at roughly $600 billion annually.

39. U.S. Department of Health and Human Services (HHS), *Our Epidemic of Loneliness and Isolation: The U.S. Surgeon General's Advisory on the Healing Effects of Social Connection and Community* (HHS, 2023).

40. Cultural competence refers to the capacity of organizations and professionals to work effectively across cultural differences by recognizing, respecting, and adapting to diverse worldviews and practices. Many practitioners now use the term "cultural humility" to stress that this work is never complete but requires ongoing self-reflection, awareness of systemic inequities, and accountability to the communities served. See National Center for Cultural Competence (NCCC), *Conceptual Frameworks/Models, Guiding Values and Principles* (Georgetown University Center for Child and Human Development, 2019), https://nccc.georgetown.edu/foundations/framework.php. The NCCC emphasizes that cultural humility complements competence by framing the work as a continuous process of self-reflection, learning, and accountability to communities rather than as a fixed achievement.

41. Vespa et al., *Demographic Turning Points*.

42. Public Religion Research Institute (PRRI), *Gen Z: America's Diverse and Politically Engaged Generation*, April 2024, https://www.prri.org/wp-content/uploads/2024/04/PRRI-Apr-2024-GenZ-Fact-Sheet-Final.pdf

43. American Psychiatric Association, "New APA Poll: One in Three Americans Feels Lonely Each Week," news release, January 30, 2024, https://www.psychiatry.org/news-room/news-releases/new-apa-poll-one-in-three-americans-feels-lonely-e. See also: HHS, Office of the Surgeon General, *Our Epidemic of Loneliness and Isolation* (HHS, 2023). Both sources highlight elevated rates of loneliness among young and older adults, underscoring why the Surgeon General Dr. Vivek H. Murphy labeled loneliness and isolation a public health crisis with profound consequences for health and well-being.

44. U.S. Census Bureau, *S1601: Language Spoken at Home: 2022 American Community Survey 1-Year Estimates,* https://data.census.gov/table/ACSST1Y2022.S1601?g=040XX00US01

45. U.S. Bureau of Labor Statistics, "Occupational Outlook Handbook: Healthcare Occupations," last modified August 28, 2025, https://www.bls.gov/ooh/healthcare/home.htm; see also U.S. Bureau of Labor Statistics, "Occupational Outlook Handbook: Social Workers," last modified August 2025, https://www.bls.gov/ooh/community-and-social-service/social-workers.htm ; U.S. Bureau of Labor Statistics, "Occupational Employment and Wage Statistics: Eligibility Interviewers, Government Programs," July 23, 2025, https://www.bls.gov/oes/tables.htm.

46. Timothy Snyder, *On Tyranny: Twenty Lessons from the Twentieth Century,* (Tim Duggan Books, 2017), prologue. See also Tracy Wareing Evans and Karen Heller Key, "It's All One History," *Our Dream Deferred,* podcast, APHSA, November 9, 2021, Libsyn, https://aphsa.libsyn.com/its-all-one-history

47. adrienne maree brown, *Emergent Strategy: Shaping Change, Changing Worlds* (AK Press, 2017).

48. Rebecca Solnit, *Hope in the Dark: Untold Histories, Wild Possibilities* (Haymarket Books, 2016); Heather McGhee, *The Sum of Us: What Racism Costs Everyone and How We Can Prosper Together* (One World, 2021).

The Architecture of U.S.

1. The human services workforce—public agencies and their nonprofit community-based partners—is itself a substantial employer and purchaser across U.S. localities. At the public level, local governments collectively employ over 14.7 million people (including county governments employing some 3.6 million), making public service a major source of local employment. National Association of Counties, *County Economies 2024: Under the Hood of National Economic Trends* (NACo, 2024),

https://www.naco.org/resource/county-economies-2024-under-hood-national-economic-trends.

Meanwhile, the public sector's reach extends beyond direct government jobs. The Urban Institute research shows that in the largest U.S. cities, publicly driven employment (that is, government as well as education, social services, and health care funded by government) comprises on average 31% of total jobs. Brett Theodos and Brady Meixell, *Public Sector Employment and Its Role in Local Economic Development* (Urban Institute, April 2024),

https://www.urban.org/sites/default/files/2024-04/Public_Sector_Employment_and_Its_Role_in_Local_Economic_Development.pdf .

On the social services side, nonprofits employed some 12.8 million people in 2022 (roughly 9.9 % of nongovernment employment), making the public–nonprofit workforce ecosystem a cornerstone of local economies. Chelsea L. Newhouse, *2024 Nonprofit Employment Report*, Nonprofit Employment Data Project (George Mason University, December 2024),

https://nonprofitcenter.schar.gmu.edu/wp-content/uploads/2024/12/Nonprofit-Employment-Report-12.24-Full-Text-2.pdf

2. Unlike targeted programs like public assistance, Social Security is often described as a universal benefit. It is more accurately *universal in principle*, as it aims to cover people in the workforce, regardless of income so long as they contribute to the program through payroll taxes (via FICA or self-employment taxes). Most people who earn sufficient work credits (typically forty credits, or about ten years of work) become eligible for retirement benefits. Its universality is limited by these work requirements, and some groups are covered by other government pension programs. See Social Security Administration, "Social Security Credits and Benefit Eligibility: Number of Credits Needed for Retirement Benefits," accessed September 12, 2025,

https://www.ssa.gov/benefits/retirement/planner/credits.html

3. The Earned Income Tax Credit (EITC) is a refundable tax credit for low- to moderate-income working individuals and families. Eligibility is based on income and family size, with benefits increasing as earnings rise, then phasing out at higher income levels. Because it is refundable, workers can receive the credit as a cash refund even if their tax liability is zero. In 2022, the EITC lifted an estimated 5.4 million people out of poverty, including nearly 3 million children. See Internal Revenue Service, "Earned Income Tax Credit (EITC)," accessed September 25, 2025, https://www.irs.gov/credits-deductions/individuals/earned-income-tax-credit-eitc;

and Center on Budget and Policy Priorities, "Policy Basics: The Earned Income Tax Credit," updated April 2023,

https://www.cbpp.org/sites/default/files/atoms/files/policybasics-eitc.pdf

4. The U.S. Department of Agriculture estimates that each dollar of SNAP benefits generates about $1.50 in economic activity, as benefits are spent quickly in local grocery stores and retail outlets. See Patrick Canning and Rosanna Mentzer Morrison, "Quantifying the Impact of SNAP Benefits on the U.S. Economy and Jobs," *Amber Waves* (USDA Economic Research Service), July 18, 2019,
https://www.ers.usda.gov/amber-waves/2019/july/quantifying-the-impact-of-snap-benefits-on-the-u-s-economy-and-jobs

5. Child care assistance likewise sustains a vital sector that produced more than $152 billion in economic activity and supported 2.2 million jobs in 2022. See The Conference Board, *Child Care in State Economies: The Regional and National Economic Impacts of the Child Care Sector*, December 10, 2014,
https://www.conference-board.org/press/child-care-in-state-economies-part-3

6. Local housing subsidies and capital spending on affordable housing also stimulate demand for contractors, materials, and maintenance services, producing ripple effects through regional supply chains. A 2019 Pennsylvania analysis found that every $10 million invested in affordable housing construction generated $19.6 million in economic output and supported 110 jobs. See Housing Alliance of Pennsylvania, *Pennsylvania Needs a State Housing Tax Credit* (Harrisburg: Housing Alliance of Pennsylvania, October 2019),
https://housingalliancepa.org/economic-impact

7. Disability-service organizations demonstrate similar multiplier effects. A recent study of New Jersey providers found that member organizations generated significant economic benefits across regional economies. See Brian Backstrom and Patrick Schumacher, *The Economic Impact of ACCSES NJ's Member Organizations* (Rockefeller Institute of Government, June 2024),
https://rockinst.org/wp-content/uploads/2024/07/Economic-Impact-of-ACCSES-NJs-Member-Organizations.pdf

8. RxKids, "Cash for Pregnant Moms and Babies," https://rxkids.org. See also Mona Hanna and H. Luke Shaefer, *Rx Kids: Results from the Rx Kids Participant Survey & Maternal Wellbeing Research Study* (Rx Kids, University of Michigan, September 2024),
https://rxkids.org/wp-content/uploads/2024/09/RxKids_Research_Brief.pdf.

9. Darrick Hamilton, "The Moral Agenda for Economic Rights," Bellagio Breakthrough Essay, Rockefeller Foundation, February 27, 2023,

https://www.rockefellerfoundation.org/bellagio-breakthroughs/darrick-hamilton-on-the-moral-agenda-for-economic-rights .

See also Darrick Hamilton with Grieve Chelwa and Avi Green, "Identity Group Stratification, Political Economy & Inclusive Economic Rights," in *Creating a New Moral Political Economy*, *Dædalus* 152 (1), Winter 2023, 154-67, https://doi.org/10.1162/daed_a_01973

10. See Chapter 2 "The New Deal: Promise and Boundaries."

11. See Chapter 3 Sidebar: "Nixon's Failed Reform."

12. U.S. Congress, House Committee on Ways and Means, *Hearings on the Family Assistance Act of 1970*, 91st Cong., 2nd sess. (Government Printing Office, 1970).

13. See Mayors for a Guaranteed Income, *Mayors for a Guaranteed Income*, accessed September 30, 2025, https://www.mayorsforagi.org/.

14. Stockton's guaranteed income pilot is documented in "Preliminary Analysis: SEED's First Year," Stockton Economic Empowerment Demonstration, March 2021, https://www.stocktondemonstration.org/.

See also the book by former Stockton Mayor Michael Tubbs, *The Deeper the Roots: A Memoir of Hope and Home* (Flatiron Books, 2021).

15. Springboard to Opportunities, *Holistic Prosperity: An Abundance-Based Framework to Develop Programs and Systems that are Grounded in Trust, Equity, and a Belief that All People Deserve a Life of Dignity* (Springboard, September 2024), 12, https://springboardto.org/wp-content/uploads/2024/09/Holistic-Prosperity-Full-White-Paper-1.pdf. This white paper notes that the Magnolia Mothers Trust (MMT) program has supported 435 mothers across five cohorts. Contemporary third-party evaluations confirm positive outcomes. See Social Insights, *Magnolia Mother's Trust 2023–2024 Evaluation & Case Study Report* (Springboard to Opportunities, 2024), https://springboardto.org/wp-content/uploads/2024/10/MMT-2023-2024-Eval-Case-Study-Report.pdf; Eyitayo Onifade, Kwanele Shishane, Fele Elonge, and Lakeithia Glover, "Guaranteed income: Experiences of African American Mothers in the Magnolia Mother's Trust Project," *Journal of Community Practice* 31, no. 3 (2023), https://www.researchgate.net/publication/369274403_Guaranteed_income_experiences_of_African_American_mothers_in_the_Magnolia_Mother%27s_Trust_Project

16. Lucius Couloute et al., *The American Guaranteed Income Studies: Durham, North Carolina—Excel Pilot Program Evaluation Report* (Center for Guaranteed Income Research, University of Pennsylvania, 2023). Available for download at the University of Pennsylvania School of Social Policy & Practice, https://sp2.upenn.edu/groundbreaking-experiments-with-guaranteed-income-for-formerly-incarcerated-individuals-show-promising-results. See also Trinity College, "New Study: Guaranteed Income for Formerly Incarcerated Shows Promise," February 14, 2025, https://www.trincoll.edu/news/new-study-guaranteed-income-for-formerly-incarcerated-shows-promise

17. See Mayors for a Guaranteed Income, *About*, accessed September 30, 2025, https://www.mayorsforagi.org/.

18. S. Balakrishnan et al., "Household Responses to Guaranteed Income," *NBER Working Paper* no. 33209 (National Bureau of Economic Research, 2024),
https://www.nber.org/papers/w33209

19. Denver Basic Income Project, *One-Year Impact Evaluation: Denver Basic Income Project* (Denver Basic Income Project, 2023),
https://denverbasicincomeproject.org/research

20. The "cliff effect" describes what happens when a small increase in income leads to a sudden loss of public benefits, leaving families worse off financially than before the increase. For example, a parent may accept a modest raise only to lose child care assistance or Medicaid coverage, making the new job unsustainable. See Federal Reserve Bank of Atlanta. "What Are Benefits Cliffs?," accessed September 10, 2025,
https://www.atlantafed.org/economic-mobility-and-resilience/advancing-careers-for-low-income-families/what-are-benefits-cliffs

21. Federal Reserve Bank of Atlanta, "What Are Benefits Cliffs?"

22. Federal Reserve Bank of Atlanta, "Career Ladder Identifier and Financial Forecaster (CLIFF)," accessed September 25, 2025,
https://www.atlantafed.org/economic-mobility-and-resilience/advancing-careers-for-low-income-families/cliff-tool

23. Elias Ilin, Alex Ruder, and Alvaro Sanchez, "Mitigating Benefits Cliffs: The Career MAP Program in Washington, DC," *Partners Update*, Federal Reserve Bank of Atlanta, October 4, 2023,

https://www.atlantafed.org/community-development/publications/partners-update/2023/10/04/mitigating-benefits-cliffs-the-career-map-program-in-washington-dc. See also Elias Ilin and Alvaro Sanchez, "Mitigating Benefits Cliffs for Low-Income Families: District of Columbia Career Mobility Action Plan as a Case Study" (Atlanta Fed CED Discussion Paper No. 01-23, September 2023),

http://dx.doi.org/10.29338/dp2023-01

24. States across the country are experimenting with ways to soften or eliminate the "benefits cliff," where a small increase in earnings triggers a sharp loss of support. The American Public Human Services Association (APHSA) maintains a national *Benefit Cliff Resource Hub* that catalogs state strategies—from transitional benefits and tapered phase-outs to cross-program alignment—and highlights how even small policy changes can reduce financial volatility for working families. See APHSA, *Benefit Cliff Resource Hub*,

https://aphsa.org/benefit-cliff-dashboard/#about.

The National Conference of State Legislatures (NCSL) provides additional analysis of the cliff problem and documents the range of legislative and administrative solutions emerging across states. For an overview, see NCSL, "Introduction to Benefits Cliffs and Public Assistance Programs," updated December 17, 2024,

https://www.ncsl.org/human-services/introduction-to-benefits-cliffs-and-public-assistance-programs.

For recent policy snapshots, see Walker Stevens, "Snapshot: Mitigating TANF Benefits Cliffs," NCSL, March 1, 2024,

https://www.ncsl.org/human-services/mitigating-tanf-benefits-cliffs;

and Walker Stevens, "Snapshot: Mitigating SNAP Benefits Cliffs," NCSL, January 17, 2024,

https://www.ncsl.org/human-services/mitigating-snap-benefits-cliffs.

For a foundational cross-program review, see NCSL, *Moving on Up: Helping Families Climb the Economic Ladder by Addressing Benefits Cliffs* (Washington, DC: NCSL/ACF, July 2019),

https://documents.ncsl.org/wwwncsl/Human-Services/Benefits-Cliffs_v03_web.pdf

25. Theresa Anderson et al., *Balancing at the Edge of the Cliff: Experiences and Calculations of Benefit Cliffs, Plateaus, and Trade-offs* (Urban Institute, 2022),

https://www.urban.org/sites/default/files/publication/105321/balancing-at-the-edge-of-the-cliff_0.pdf.

26. The principle of "money follows the person" emerged from disability rights law and the Supreme Court's *Olmstead v. L.C.* (1999) decision, which affirmed that under the Americans with Disabilities Act, people with disabilities have the right to receive services in the most integrated setting appropriate. In practice, this principle meant that funding should support individuals in their preferred community settings rather than being locked into institutional care. Building on this, Congress established the Money Follows the Person demonstration in the Deficit Reduction Act of 2005, providing states with enhanced federal Medicaid funding to help beneficiaries transition out of nursing facilities and other institutions. Since 2007, more than 100,000 people have made such transitions through MFP. See Medicaid and CHIP Payment and Access Commission (MACPAC), *Report to Congress on Medicaid and CHIP*, March 2022, 1–2,

https://www.macpac.gov/wp-content/uploads/2022/03/March-2022-Report-to-Congress-on-Medicaid-and-CHIP.pdf;

Centers for Medicare & Medicaid Services, "Money Follows the Person (MFP)," accessed September 10, 2025,

https://www.medicaid.gov/medicaid/long-term-services-supports/money-follows-person

27. Annie E. Casey Foundation, *Opportunity Passport®: Financial Capacity for Young People Who Experience Foster Care*, February 10, 2025,

https://assets.aecf.org/m/resourcedoc/aecf-opportunitypassport-2025.pdf

28. Matthew H. Morton et al., *Developing a Direct Cash Transfer Program for Youth Experiencing Homelessness: Results of a Mixed Methods, Multistakeholder Design Process* (Chapin Hall at the University of Chicago, October 2020),

https://www.chapinhall.org/wp-content/uploads/Developing-a-Direct-Cash-Transfer-Program-for-Youth.pdf

; Ann Oliva and Sonya Acosta, *Direct Cash Transfers and Federal Rental Assistance: The Impact of Direct Cash Transfers and Federal Rental Assistance: Implications Among Young Adults at Risk of or Experiencing Homelessness* (Chapin Hall at the University of Chicago, November 2022),

https://www.chapinhall.org/wp-content/uploads/5-Cash-Transfers-Policy-Toolkit_Housing-Vouchers.pdf

29. Former foster youth participating in the cohort "reported a decrease in experiences of homelessness and increased full-time enrollment in school and employment." County of Santa Clara, *Guaranteed Basic Income Pilot Programs*,

https://guaranteedincomesv.org/; Santa Clara County, *Transition Age Youth Annual Report FY 2020-2021* (County of Santa Clara, 2021), 3, https://files.santaclaracounty.gov/migrated/Transition-Age-Youth-FY-2021-Annual-Report.pdf

30. Casey Family Programs, *How Do Economic Supports Benefit Families and Communities*, January 2025, https://www.casey.org/media/25.07-QFF-TS_Economic-Supports.pdf . See also, APHSA and Chapin Hall, *Evidence to Impact: State Policy Options to Increase Access to Economic & Concrete Supports as a Child Welfare Prevention Strategy*, June 2023, https://www.chapinhall.org/wp-content/uploads/Chapin-Hall_APHSA_Evidence-to-Impact_June-2023.pdf ; Meg Dygert, "Transforming Child Welfare: The Collaborative Efforts of APHSA and Chapin Hall," *APHSA Catalyst Blog*, April 21, 2025, https://aphsa.org/resources/transforming-child-welfare-thecatalyst/

31. Amelie A. Hecht, Keshia M. Pollack Porter, and Lindsey Turner, "Impact of the Community Eligibility Provision of the Healthy, Hunger-Free Kids Act on Student Nutrition, Behavior, and Academic Outcomes: 2011–2019," *American Journal of Public Health* 110, no. 8 (2020), https://ajph.aphapublications.org/doi/pdf/10.2105/AJPH.2020.305743; Maureen K. Spill et al., "Universal Free School Meals and School and Student Outcomes," *JAMA Network Open* 7, no. 8 (2024), https://pmc.ncbi.nlm.nih.gov/articles/PMC11316229/

32. School-Based Health Alliance, *Findings from the 2022 National Census of School-Based Health Centers* (2023), https://sbh4all.org/wp-content/uploads/2023/10/FINDINGS-FROM-THE-2022-NATIONAL-CENSUS-OF-SCHOOL-BASED-HEALTH-CENTERS-09.20.23.pdf. Michael Arenson, Phillip J. Hudson, Naehyung Lee, and Betty Lai, "The Evidence on School-Based Health Centers: A Review," *Global Pediatric Health* 6 (2019), https://pmc.ncbi.nlm.nih.gov/articles/PMC6381423/pdf/10.1177_2333794X19828745.pdf

33. Ruth Curran Neild, Wendy McClanahan, and Sandra Jo Wilson, *Afterschool Programs: A Review of Evidence Under the Every Student Succeeds Act* (The Wallace Foundation / Research for Action, 2019), https://wallacefoundation.org/sites/default/files/2024-10/afterschool-programs-a-review-of-evidence-under-the-essa.doi_.10.59656%252FYD-OS2963.001.pdf; Afterschool Alliance, *The Latest Research on the Impact of Afterschool and Summer Programs* (September 2024), https://afterschoolalliance.org/documents/The-Latest-Research-on-the-Impact-of-Afterschool-and-Summer-Programs-2024.pdf

34. William R. Johnston et al., *Illustrating the Promise of Community Schools: An Assessment of the Impact of the New York City Community Schools Initiative* (RAND Corporation, 2020), https://www.rand.org/pubs/research_reports/RR3245

35. Sharon O'Malley, "Libraries Hire Social Workers as Mental Health Issues Soar," *Route Fifty* (March 10, 2022), https://www.route-fifty.com/management/2022/03/libraries-hire-social-workers-mental-health-and-homelessness-soars/363021;

Annie Qing, "Library Program Offers Path to Employment, Stability," *NACo County News* (October 2, 2024),

https://www.naco.org/news/library-program-offers-path-employment-stability;

Tony Rehagen, "How Denver Public Library Is Improving Services for Its Most Disadvantaged Patrons: And Reimagining What a Library Can Be in the Process," *5280 Magazine* (January 15, 2020),

https://5280.com/how-denver-public-library-is-improving-services-for-its-most-disadvantaged-patrons

36. Matt Enis, "Delaware to Expand Statewide Telehealth Program," *Library Journal*, July 1, 2022, https://www.libraryjournal.com/story/delaware-to-expand-statewide-telehealth-program-ala-annual-2022

37. In cities such as Seattle and Los Angeles—which have received climate or emergency funding to convert libraries into heat refuges—libraries are being officially recognized as community resilience hubs. In Seattle, five branches are being upgraded to serve as "extreme-heat refuges," and in Los Angeles, selected libraries are now being pilot-tested as augmented cooling centers with extended hours and dedicated space for respite. Amy Merck, "U.S. Public Libraries Serve as Cooling Centers in Extreme Weather," *Library Journal*, August 9, 2019,

https://www.libraryjournal.com/story/US-Public-Libraries-Serve-as-Cooling-Centers-in-Extreme-Weather;

John Ryan, "Five More Seattle Libraries to Become Extreme-Heat Refuges," KUOW News, August 21, 2024, https://www.kuow.org/stories/five-more-seattle-libraries-to-become-extreme-heat-refuges; Erin Stone, "Read A Book. Escape The Heat. LA Launching Cooling Center Pilot Program At Libraries," *LAist*, June 17, 2024, https://laist.com/news/climate-environment/read-a-book-escape-the-heat-la-launching-cooling-center-pilot-program-at-libraries; Alison Stone, "What Do Public Libraries Have to Do with Climate Justice?" *Nonprofit Quarterly*, November 9, 2023, https://nonprofitquarterly.org/what-do-public-libraries-have-to-do-with-climate-justice/

38. Maya Rossin-Slater, Christopher J. Ruhm, and Jane Waldfogel, "The Effects of California's Paid Family Leave Program on Mothers' Leave-Taking and Subsequent Labor Market Outcomes," NBER Working Paper 17715 (2011),

https://www.nber.org/system/files/working_papers/w17715/w17715.pdf;

Courtney Coile, Maya Rossin-Slater, and Amanda Su, "The Impact of Paid Family Leave on Families with Health Shocks," NBER Working Paper 30739 (2022; revised 2025), https://www.nber.org/system/files/working_papers/w30739/w30739.pdf;

Hannah K. Davison, "The Case for Offering Paid Leave: Benefits to the Employer and Employee," *Community, Work & Family* 26, no. 6 (2023).

39. International Center for Research on Women and European Bank for Reconstruction and Development, *Workplace Flexibility at Patagonia Delivers Over 90% Return on Investment: Case Study* (2019),

https://www.icrw.org/wp-content/uploads/2019/07/EBRD-Patagonia-Case-Study-Web-version.pdf

40. Ben Theodos et al., *An Evaluation of the Impacts and Implementation Approaches of Financial Coaching Programs* (Urban Institute, October 2015),

https://www.urban.org/sites/default/files/2022-04/2000448-an-evaluation-of-the-impacts-and-implementation-approaches-of-financial-coaching-programs.pdf

41. Mecklenburg County, North Carolina. *Community Resource Centers*, accessed September 10, 2025,

https://dcr.mecknc.gov/crc

42. See Perry County Job and Family Services, "Transportation," accessed September 15, 2025, https://www.perryjfs.org/JFS-Children-Families-Transportation.html;

Perry County Ohio, "Perry County Transit," accessed September 15, 2025,

https://perrycountyohio.gov/services/perry-county-ohio-transit

43. See Perry County Job and Family Services, "OhioMeansJobs," accessed September 15, 2025, https://www.perryjfs.org/JFS-Employment-Training-Ohio-Means-Jobs.html

Belonging By Design

1. Timothy Snyder, *On Freedom* (Crown, 2024).

2. john a. powell, *The Power of Bridging: How to Build a World Where We All Belong* (Sounds True, 2024), chap. 7.

3. Brené Brown, *Atlas of the Heart: Mapping Meaningful Connection and the Language of Human Experience* (Random House, 2021), 58-59 (awe and wonder); 63-65 (curiosity and interest).

4. Dacher Keltner, *Awe: The New Science of Everyday Wonder and How it Can Transform Your Life* (Penguin Press, 2023), chap. 1.

5. Francesca Gino, "The Business Case for Curiosity," *Harvard Business Review* (September–October 2018), https://hbr.org/2018/09/the-business-case-for-curiosity

6. Sendhil Mullainathan and Eldar Shafir, *Scarcity: Why Having Too Little Means So Much* (Times Books, 2013).

7. Mariana Mazzucato, "The Role of a Mission-Oriented Framework for a Progressive Economy," *Roosevelt Institute Blog*, April 29, 2025,
https://rooseveltinstitute.org/blog/mission-oriented-framework-for-economy/.
Mazzucato is a leading economist and professor at University College London (UCL), where she founded and directs UCL's Institute for Innovation and Public Purpose. Her research focuses on the economics of innovation and the role of the state in driving growth. Her influential books include *The Entrepreneurial State* (Anthem Press, 2013), *The Value of Everything* (Allen Lane, 2018), and *Mission Economy : A Moonshot Guide to Changing Capitalism* (Allen Lane, 2021).

8. The Global Flourishing Study is a multiyear collaboration between Gallup and researchers at Harvard University designed to measure well-being across cultures and over time. Drawing on nationally representative surveys in more than twenty countries, the study examines key dimensions of flourishing—including belonging, hope for the future, meaning, and close social relationships—and finds strong links between social connection, optimism, and overall life evaluation. See Global Flourishing Study, "A Collaborative Inquiry into Human Well-Being." https://globalflourishingstudy.com/

9. Heather McGhee, *The Sum of Us: What Racism Costs Everyone and How We Can Prosper Together* (One World, 2021)

10. Jonathan Haidt and Dacher Keltner, "Moral Elevation and the Prosocial Contagion of Virtue," *Journal of Personality and Social Psychology* 84, no. 4 (2003): 703–14; see also Jill Suttie, "How Seeing the Good in People Can Help Bridge Our Differences" *Greater Good Magazine*, August 7, 2018,

https://greatergood.berkeley.edu/article/item/how_seeing_the_good_in_people_can_help_bridge_our_differences

11. powell, *The Power of Bridging*, chap. 7.

12. powell, *The Power of Bridging*, chap. 7.

13. Future Caucus is a cross-partisan network of Gen Z and millennial legislators that emphasizes bridging polarization through collaborative governance. The State Future Caucus Network includes chapters in nearly every state, with programming designed to help young lawmakers develop leadership skills, build trust across party lines, and advance bipartisan policy agendas. Future Caucus, "State Future Caucus Network," accessed October 5, 2025,

https://futurecaucus.org/future-caucus/state-future-caucus-network.

Its "Legislative Victories" web page showcases bipartisan bills in the areas of criminal justice reform, housing, health, and democracy that were authored by young legislators acting across ideological divides. Future Caucus, "Legislative Victories," accessed October 5, 2025,

https://futurecaucus.org/legislative-victories

14. Deep Canvassing is a relational organizing method used by groups like People's Action. Instead of traditional door-to-door persuasion campaigns, trained volunteers engage residents in longer, empathetic conversations. The goal is not to win an argument but to listen, share personal stories, and ask open-ended questions that help people reflect on their own values and experiences. By doing so, canvassers create space for connection—even across partisan divides. This practice has been shown to reduce polarization and build empathy, making it a powerful tool for bridging differences and cultivating belonging. People's Action's Deep Canvassing Program:

https://peoplesaction.org/programs/deep-canvassing/

15. Braver Angels is a national nonprofit working to reduce political polarization by bringing together self-identified conservatives ("Reds") and progressives ("Blues") in structured dialogues. Their most recognized model—the Red/Blue Workshop—uses guided exercises such as assumption-surfacing, listening circles, and paired sharing to help participants move past stereotypes, listen more deeply, and find areas of common concern. Over time, Braver Angels has expanded its programming to include issue-focused Common Ground Workshops, one-on-one conversations, and citizen debates designed less to persuade than to model respectful engagement. Like deep canvassing and story circles, Braver Angels shows that there are many ways everyday people can practice bridge-building, choosing the format that resonates most with them. See Braver Angels, accessed October 2, 2025,

https://braverangels.org/

16. Story Circles are a structured form of dialogue in which small groups gather to share personal stories in response to one or two guiding questions. Each participant is given equal time to speak, while others listen without interruption or debate. The format—used by local nonprofits, civic groups, and organizations such as Everyday Democracy—quickly builds trust, especially among people who might not otherwise meet. By grounding conversation in lived experience rather than argument, Story Circles help surface common values and strengthen relationships across lines of difference. See Ben Fink, "How-and-Why to Facilitate a Story Circle," *Arts Midwest*, October 1, 2025,

https://artsmidwest.org/resources/ideas/how-and-why-to-facilitate-a-story-circle

17. Research shows that community gardens strengthen social cohesion and civic engagement. One study found that gardeners were more likely to know their neighbors, trust them, and participate in community life compared to residents not involved in gardening. Katherine Alaimo, Thomas M. Reischl, and Julie Ober Allen, "Community Gardening, Neighborhood Meetings, and Social Capital," *Journal of Community Psychology* 38, no. 4 (May 2010): 497-514,

https://doi.org/10.1002/jcop.20378

18. See chapter 8 "Policy in the Places We Live."

19. Tracy Wareing Evans, "Shifting Structural Power to Advance Race Equity," *Policy & Practice*, American Public Human Services Association (April 2022).

20. Full Frame Initiative. "Centering Community Self-Assessment." *Wellbeing Resource Library*, accessed September 11, 2025,

https://fullframeinitiative.org/resources/centering-community-self-assessment-tool/

21. Barbara Lipietz, Savvas Verdis, and Catarina Heeckt, *Public Innovation: Building Capacity in Europe's City Governments* (LSE Cities, London School of Economics and Political Science, November 2024),
https://www.lse.ac.uk/Cities/Assets/Documents/Research-Reports/Public-Innovation-building-capacity-in-Europes-city-governments.pdf

22. UK Policy Lab, *Public Design in the UK Government: A Review of the Landscape and Its Future Development* (London: Cabinet Office, 2024; updated August 2025),
https://www.gov.uk/government/publications/the-public-design-evidence-review/public-design-in-the-uk-government-a-review-of-the-landscape-and-its-future-development-html

23. The Children's Bureau's Capacity Building Collaborative highlights multiple jurisdictions—such as Minnesota, Nevada, Florida, and the Kenaitze Tribe—in which youth, parents, and caregivers with lived experience are embedded as paid consultants and core team members in service redesign. These partners hold equal decision-making authority in shaping independent living services, extended foster care, kinship supports, Continuous Quality Improvement processes, and court improvement work. D. Crystal Coles and Julie Murphy, *Incorporating Lived Experience Into Child Welfare Capacity Building: Highlights From the Children's Bureau's Child Welfare Capacity Building Collaborative* (James Bell Associates, 2023),
https://acf.gov/sites/default/files/documents/cb/Incorporating%20Lived%20Experience%20Into%20Child%20Welfare%20Capacity%20Building.pdf.
Complementing this, iFoster's *Lived Experience Guide to Fixing Foster Care* gathers over 6,000 voices calling for person-centered, family-driven redesign—from reunification supports to stepdown care after exit—demonstrating how co-design is reshaping the system's most foundational practices. iFoster, *Lived Experience Guide to Fixing Foster Care* (iFoster, 2023),
https://voiceoffostercare.org/wp-content/uploads/2023/05/Lived-Experience-Guide-to-Fixing-Foster-Care.pdf

24. "L.A. REPAIR Participatory Budgeting," City of Los Angeles, accessed October 2, 2025,
https://repair.lacity.gov/

25. LA County, *Community Budget Guidelines*, May 2024,
https://mitchell.lacounty.gov/wp-content/uploads/2024/05/Community_Budget_Guidelines-1.pdf

26. The *PA Care Partnership Toolkit* outlines Pennsylvania's statewide *System of Care* framework, which requires counties to expand the role of youth and families as decision-makers at every level—individual, county, and state. The model calls for shared decision making in policy, funding, and accountability, going beyond traditional advisory or consumer councils to embed community authority in system governance. While implementation varies by county, the framework represents a structural evolution toward *power with*—a codified expectation that people most affected by policy should have real authority in shaping it. This stands in contrast to many state-level models where advisory groups provide feedback but hold limited influence over decision making. By formalizing co-governance as part of county practice, Pennsylvania offers a roadmap for other states and localities seeking to operationalize shared power in human services. PA Care Partnership.*System of Care: A Comprehensive Toolkit for County Implementation—Enhancing Your Strengths to Build a System of Care* (PA Care Partnership, August 2020), https://www.pacarepartnership.org/uploads/PA_Care_Partnership_Toolkit_-_ELECTRONIC_VERSION_FINAL.pdf

27. "Narrative Initiative," accessed September 17, 2025, https://narrativeinitiative.org/

Democracy by Design

1. Timothy Snyder, *On Freedom* (Crown, 2024).

2. New York City Department of Education, "NYC Community Schools–Our Results," accessed October 10, 2025, https://infohub.nyced.org/in-our-schools/working-with-nycps/community-schools/nyc-community-schools-our-results;
Brendon McConnell, Parunjodhi Munisamy, and Mariyana Zapryanova, "Community Schools and Student Behavioral Outcomes: Evidence From New York City," August 22, 2025, https://brendonmcconnell.github.io/pdf/NYC-CS.pdf

3. Partnership for the Future of Learning, "Cincinnati's Community Learning Centers: On the Rise," accessed October 10, 2025,
https://futureforlearning.org/media/cincinnati-film-series.
See also Reuben Jacobson, "Greater Cincinnati's Community Learning Centers Lead Place-Based Learning and Holistic Neighborhood Development," Brookings, November 22, 2022,

https://www.brookings.edu/articles/greater-cincinnatis-community-learning-centers-lead-place-based-learning-and-holistic-neighborhood-development

4. Beeck Center for Social Impact + Innovation, "Digital Benefits Network, "Implementing Benefits Eligibility + Enrollment Systems: A Review of State Practices" (Georgetown University, 2025), accessed September 20, 2025,

https://digitalgovernmenthub.org/get-involved/implementing-benefits-eligibility-enrollment-systems-a-review-of-state-practices

5. Beeck Center for Social Impact + Innovation and Massive Data Institute, "AI-Powered Rules as Code: Experiments with Public Benefits Policy," Georgetown University, 2025,

https://digitalgovernmenthub.org/publications/ai-powered-rules-as-code-experiments-with-public-benefits-policy;

Beeck Center for Social Impact + Innovation, "The Digital Benefits Network Showcases Twelve Generative AI Experiments for Benefits Policy at Policy2Code Demo Day," Georgetown University, November 25, 2024,

https://beeckcenter.georgetown.edu/the-digital-benefits-network-showcases-twelve-generative-ai-experiments-for-benefits-policy-at-policy2code-demo-day

6. American Public Human Services Association, *AI-Powered SNAP Modernization: Analysis of Policy Issues Impacting the Use of Artificial Intelligence in SNAP Case Processing*, November 2024,

https://aphsa.org/wp-content/uploads/2024/11/11_14_2024-APHSA-AI-Powered-SNAP-Modernization-part-2.pdf

7. Efforts to build public-sector capacity for responsible AI are emerging across the country. The Center for Civic Futures provides research, tools, and partnerships to help states and localities govern new technologies in ways that advance equity and democratic participation. The Rockefeller Foundation, in partnership with the Center for Civic Futures, has launched the AI Readiness Project, which is focused on strengthening state capacity to deploy AI responsibly in public systems. See Center for Civic Futures, "Home," accessed November 2025,

https://www.centerforcivicfutures.org;

The Rockefeller Foundation, "Rockefeller Foundation and Center for Civic Futures Launch AI Readiness Project to Build State Capacity for Responsible AI," November 4, 2025,

https://www.rockefellerfoundation.org/news/rockefeller-foundation-and-center-for-civic-futures-launch-ai-readiness-project-to-build-state-capacity-for-responsible-ai/

8. Marissa Sheldon, "States that Have Passed Universal Free School Meals (So Far)," Hunter College, New York City Food Policy Center, April 9, 2024,

https://www.nycfoodpolicy.org/states-with-universal-free-school-meals-so-far-update/

9. In 2022, New Mexico voters approved Constitutional Amendment 1, increasing distributions from the Land Grant Permanent Fund—a sovereign wealth fund sustained by oil, gas, and mineral revenues—to expand early childhood education and child care programs. The amendment, together with the state's Early Childhood Trust Fund established in 2020, creates an endowment model for sustained funding. Implementation of universal child care began November 2025, making New Mexico the first U.S. state to embed early childhood care as a constitutionally protected public investment. Office of Governor Michelle Lujan Grisham, "New Mexico Is First State in Nation to Offer Universal Child Care," *Governor of New Mexico Press Office*, September 8, 2025,

https://www.governor.state.nm.us/2025/09/08/new-mexico-is-first-state-in-nation-to-offer-universal-child-care/; see also Lena Bilik, "New Mexico Offers Free Childcare for All. The Federal Government Should Follow Suit," *Roosevelt Institute Blog*, September 10 2025,

https://rooseveltinstitute.org/blog/new-mexico-offers-free-childcare-for-all/

10. Sarah Klein, Martha Hostetter, Roosa Tikkanen, and Douglas McCarthy, *How New Mexico's Community Health Workers Help Meet Patients' Nonmedical Needs* (Commonwealth Fund, February 2020),

https://www.commonwealthfund.org/publications/case-study/2020/feb/new-mexico-community-health-workers; New Mexico Human Services Department, "New Mexico Medicaid Expands Services with Community Health Workers," June 6, 2024,

https://www.hca.nm.gov/2024/06/06/new-mexico-medicaid-expands-services-with-community-health-workers

11. North Carolina Integrated Care for Kids (NC InCK), "Information for Family Navigators – NC InCK," accessed November 23, 2025,

https://ncinck.org/family-navigators

12. Chloe Green, Colleen Psomas, Matt Stagner, and Alex Bauer, "Human Services' Unique Position," *Policy & Practice*, APHSA, Spring 2023,

https://trayinc.cld.bz/Policy-Practice-Spring-2023

13. See Mayors for Guaranteed Income, "Counties for Guaranteed Income, and Legislators for Guaranteed Income,"
https://www.mayorsforagi.org/

14. See Chapter 5 "A Mindset Shift in Plain Sight."

15. Mona Hanna-Attisha and H. Luke Shaefer, *Rx Kids: Results from the Rx Kids Participant Survey & Maternal Wellbeing Research Study* (Rx Kids, University of Michigan, September 2024),
https://rxkids.org/wp-content/uploads/2024/09/RxKids_Research_Brief.pdf.
See also, Cecilia Nowell, "The US Town That Pays Every Pregnant Woman $1500: We're Not Ok With Our Babies Being Born Into Poverty." *The Guardian*, September 15, 2025,
https://www.theguardian.com/us-news/2025/sep/15/rx-kids-flint-michigan-pregnancy

16. Sixto Cancel, *A Foster Care System Where Every Child Has a Loving Home*, TED, filmed April 2022 in Vancouver, BC, TED2022, video, 10:33,

https://www.ted.com/talks/sixto_cancel_a_foster_care_system_where_every_child_has_a_loving_home. See also https://www.thinkofus.org/

17. Michael Becketts, interview by J. B. Wogan, *On the Evidence*, podcast, Fairfax County Community Corner, January 2023,
https://www.fairfaxcounty.gov/familyservices/community-corner/2023-01-michael-becketts-joins-mathematicas-on-the-evidence-podcast

18. See Chapter 5 "A Mindset Shift In Plain Sight."

19. For more on this idea, see the Roosevelt Institute's overview of Mariana Mazzucato's mission-oriented approach: *A Mission-Oriented Framework for the Economy*, October 13, 2022,
https://rooseveltinstitute.org/blog/mission-oriented-framework-for-economy/

20. Code for America, "Social Safety Net Program," accessed September 13, 2025,
https://codeforamerica.org/programs/social-safety-net/

21. Main Street Alliance, "Time's Up Launches Care Economy Business Council" May 20, 2021,

https://mainstreetalliance.org/press-releases/times-up-launches-care-economy-business-council-including-main-street-alliance-small-business-members-to-reimagine-nations-caregiving-infrastructure

22. See Care Can't Wait Coalition, *Building a Durable and Equitable Care Infrastructure*, March 2021,
https://nwlc.org/wp-content/uploads/2021/04/PolicyAgenda_CareCantWait_20210330a.pdf

23. "How a $50 Million Philanthropic Investment Is Bolstering Coalitions of Care Workers and Advocates," *Philanthropy*, September 12, 2024.

24. Five & Rising. accessed September 20, 2025. https://www.fiveandrising.org/; Jody Levison-Johnson, "Stop Calling Us 'Nonprofit': It's Time for a New Name for the $1.4 Trillion Engine of Progress," *Inside Philanthropy*, October 30, 2025,

https://www.insidephilanthropy.com/home/stop-calling-us-nonprofit-its-time-for-a-new-name-for-the-1-4-trillion-engine-of-progress

25. *UnCharitable*, a documentary film directed by Stephen Gyllenhaall, challenges long-standing misconceptions about the nonprofit sector, arguing that outdated funding norms and cultural expectations severely limit its ability to drive social change. Through interviews, storytelling, and sector analysis, the film calls for bold reforms that would allow community-based organizations to operate with the flexibility, capital, and ambition their missions demand. To see the film, visit this site:
https://uncharitablemovie.com/

26. Richmond's Office of Community Wealth Building was established in 2014 and remains a national model for advancing economic mobility, neighborhood resilience, and cross-sector collaboration. See City of Richmond, *Office of Community Wealth Building*,
https://www.rva.gov/community-wealth-building/wealth-building

27. Antonio M. Oftelie, *Leadership for a Networked World*, Technology and Entrepreneurship Center at Harvard, "The Human Services Value Curve," accessed October 5, 2025,
https://lnwprogram.org.

Created by Dr. Oftelie and advanced through a more than decade long partnership between Leadership for a Networked World and the American Public Human Services Association, the Value Curve framework has guided annual forums of agency leaders focused on advancing public value and outcomes for children and families. See e.g., Leadership for a Networked World, *2019 Health and Human Services Summit: Purpose, Passion and Impact for the Future* (Harvard University, 2019). That work continues today with a renewed focus on what it takes for communities to flourish.

28. Rebecca Solnit, *Hope in the Dark: Untold Histories, Wild Possibilities*, 3rd ed. (Haymarket Books, 2016).

SELECTIVE BIBLIOGRAPHY

This bibliography highlights the works—past and present—that most shaped the ideas in this book. It mirrors the journey of the chapters: from the roots we inherited, to the systems we live within, to the possibilities we can claim next.

SECTION I—Excavating the Roots
Historical Foundations, Reformers, and the Cultural Inheritance

- Addams, Jane. *Democracy and Social Ethics.* Macmillan, 1902.
  —Addams argues that democracy is lived through everyday relationships and collective responsibility, challenging the limits of individualism and moral judgment.
- Addams, Jane. *Twenty Years at Hull-House.* Macmillan, 1910.
  —A vivid account of the settlement house movement, illuminating how proximity, community, and shared purpose can transform both neighborhoods and civic life.
- Baldwin, James. *Collected Essays.* Edited by Toni Morrison. Library of America, 1998.
  —Baldwin's uncompromising reflections on race, identity, and the American Dream reveal how national narratives shape belonging—and how honesty makes repair possible.
- Douglass, Frederick. *Narrative of the Life of Frederick Douglass, an American Slave.* Edited by William L. Andrews

and William S. McFeely. W.W. Norton, 1997.

—A foundational testimony of American injustice and a fierce argument for human dignity, freedom, and the nation's unfinished moral reckoning.

- Du Bois, W.E.B. *The Souls of Black Folk*. A.C. McClurg, 1903.

  —Du Bois names the "Veil," double consciousness, and the psychological architecture of racial caste, exposing the roots of inequality embedded in early American life.

- Harrington, Michael. *The Other America: Poverty in the United States*. Scribner, 1962. Reprint, Simon & Schuster, 2012.

  —The book that awakened a nation to the depth of hidden poverty and helped spur the War on Poverty, challenging the myth that prosperity was shared.

- King, Martin Luther Jr. *Where Do We Go from Here: Chaos or Community?* Beacon Press, 1967.

  —King's work calls for economic justice, structural reform, and a reimagining of the social contract—ideas as urgent today as in 1967.

SECTION II—Systems in Plain Sight

Policy, Structural Inequality, and the Design of Public Institutions

- Edin, Kathryn J., H. Luke Shaefer, and Timothy J. Nelson. *The Injustice of Place*. Mariner Books, 2023.

  —A powerful examination of regional poverty, showing how place-based disadvantage is rooted in policy choices—not personal shortcomings.

- Goldblum, Joanne, and Colleen Shaddox. *Broke in America*. BenBella Books, 2021.

- —A clear, accessible overview of how scarcity is built into our systems and what it would take to ensure that basic needs are reliably met across the country.
- Quadagno, Jill. *The Color of Welfare: How Racism Undermined the War on Poverty.* Oxford University Press, 1994.
  —A seminal analysis of how racial politics undermined the War on Poverty and shaped the U.S. welfare system—critical for understanding today's policy divides.
- Rank, Mark, Lawrence M. Eppard, and Heather E. Bullock. *Poorly Understood: What America Gets Wrong About Poverty.* Oxford University Press, 2021.
  —A myth-busting synthesis of research on poverty, mobility, and structural barriers, offering evidence that pushes back on deeply held misconceptions.
- Rothstein, Richard. *The Color of Law.* Liveright Publishing, 2017.
  —A definitive account of how federal, state, and local governments engineered segregation and the racial wealth gap—policy design that continues to reverberate across America today.

SECTION III — Democracy by Design
Narrative Change, Belonging, Bridging, and Future Possibility

- Barber II, William. *White Poverty.* Liveright Publishing, 2024.
  —Barber reframes poverty as a moral and democratic crisis affecting people of all races, offering a movement-based vision for a more just economy and society.

- Benjamin, Ruha. *Viral Justice: How We Grow the World We Want.* Princeton University Press, 2024.
  —Benjamin shows how small acts of care and imagination can scale into systemic change, arguing for justice as something we grow in community.
- brown, adrienne maree. *Emergent Strategy.* AK Press, 2017.
  —A guide to adaptive, relational, movement-building practices inspired by nature and complexity—tools for designing systems that heal rather than harm.
- Desmond, Matthew. *Poverty, by America.* Crown, 2023.
  —Desmond reveals how poverty persists because it benefits the powerful, urging readers to rethink their assumptions about entitlement, responsibility, and national priorities.
- Kaba, Mariame, and Tamaa Nopper. *We Do This 'Til We Free Us.* Haymarket Books, 2021.
  —A compelling vision for community-led safety and abolitionist practice, rooted in collective imagination and everyday acts of courage.
- Kaur, Valarie. *See No Stranger.* One World, 2020.
  —Kaur blends memoir and moral philosophy to introduce "Revolutionary Love" as a framework for building a society anchored in wonder, belonging, and reciprocity.
- McGhee, Heather. *The Sum of Us.* One World, 2021.
  —A deeply researched explanation of how racism costs everyone—and how multiracial solidarity can unlock a new era of shared prosperity.
- powell, john a. *The Power of Bridging.* Sounds True, 2024.
  —An exploration of belonging and "bridging" as essential democratic practices that strengthen communities and expand who is included in the circle of human concern.

- Solnit, Rebecca. *Hope in the Dark*. Haymarket Books, 2004.
  —A meditation on how hope grows from struggle, reminding us that social change is nonlinear and built through consistent, collective action.
- Snyder, Timothy. *On Tyranny*. Tim Duggan Books, 2017.
  —A concise, urgent set of lessons for resisting authoritarian drift and protecting democratic norms in everyday life.
- Snyder, Timothy. *On Freedom*. Crown, 2024.
  —A companion volume that examines how freedom is misused and misunderstood—and how reclaiming it requires shared responsibility and civic imagination.
- Markovits, Daniel. *The Meritocracy Trap*. Penguin Press, 2019.
  —A sharp critique of how meritocracy harms not just the poor but the middle and upper classes, revealing a deeper structural flaw in the American Dream.
- Wilkerson, Isabel. *Caste: The Origins of Our Discontents*. Random House, 2020.
  —A sweeping argument that America's racial hierarchy functions as a caste system, illuminating the hidden rules that shape opportunity and belonging.
- Zaki, Jamil. *Hope for Cynics*. Grand Central Publishing, 2024.
  —A science-driven exploration of human goodness, showing how empathy, cooperation, and connection can be strengthened even in polarized times.

APPENDICES

Appendix A

Definitions of Poverty in the United States

In the United States, there is no single way to measure poverty. Multiple definitions exist, each created for a different purpose and each capturing only part of the reality of economic hardship. These measures shape who is counted, who qualifies for assistance, and how the nation understands insecurity and need.

This appendix offers a brief reference guide to the most common poverty definitions used in policy, research, and public conversation. No single definition fully reflects the lived experience of poverty. Taken together, however, these measures provide important context for the arguments in this book and for understanding how economic precarity is assessed and addressed.

Official Poverty Measure (OPM)

What it is: The federal government's traditional definition of poverty.

How it works: Based on a 1960s formula: three times the cost of a "minimum food diet." Adjusted for inflation and family size.

What it misses: Modern costs of child care, housing, health care, and transportation. Differences in cost of living across the country. Taxes, benefits, or debt burdens.

Supplemental Poverty Measure (SPM)

What it is: An updated measure that reflects actual household expenses.

How it works: Counts cash income, taxes, and benefits like SNAP and housing subsidies. Subtracts out-of-pocket medical and work expenses (including child care). Adjusts for local cost of living.

What it misses: Does not fully capture the cost of stability in high-cost regions. Does not measure asset insecurity.

Deep Poverty

What it is: Extreme income deprivation.

How it works: Income below 50 percent of the official poverty line.

What it misses: Conditions of homelessness, instability, or chronic hardship. Family debt or unmeasured expenses.

Persistent or Generational Poverty

What it is: Poverty that spans time or generations.

How it works: Persistent poverty refers to individuals or families experiencing poverty for multiple years. Generational poverty refers to two or more generations living in poverty.

What it misses: Structural causes and community-level barriers. Variations in local opportunity or discrimination.

Near Poverty/Low Income

What it is: People above the poverty line who still struggle to meet basic needs.

How it works: Often defined as living below 200 percent of the federal poverty line. Many program eligibility rules are based on this threshold.

What it misses: The significant gap between income and the real cost of living. Stress and insecurity among families who are technically "not poor."

Asset Poverty

What it is: A measure of financial fragility.

How it works: A household is "asset poor" when it lacks the savings or assets to cover basic expenses for three months.

What it misses: Income-based measures may look stable even when savings are near zero. Does not account for credit access or debt loads.

Material Hardship

What it is: A direct measure of unmet needs.

How it works: Surveys track whether people can afford rent, utilities, food, medical care, transportation, or child care.

What it misses: Does not directly track income or long-term financial mobility.

Subjective or Lived Poverty

What it is: People's own perceptions of their ability to meet needs and feel secure.

How it works: Draws on self-reported experiences of stress, instability, and difficulty responding to everyday challenges or emergencies.

What it misses: Lacks standardization and cannot fully convey the daily trade-offs, constraints, and cumulative pressures that shape lived experience.

Each definition draws a different boundary around who is considered "poor." When poverty is defined narrowly by income alone, it obscures the daily trade-offs that shape people's lives: choosing between rent and food, delaying medical care, juggling unstable work, or living with constant uncertainty about what the next month will bring. Even broader measures struggle to capture the cumulative stress, constrained choices, and emotional toll of economic precarity.

Taken together, these definitions offer useful tools for policy and research. But none fully capture what it means to live under conditions of scarcity and instability. Throughout this book, poverty is understood in its broadest sense: not only as a lack of income, but as the lived experience of navigating systems that too often make stability fragile and well-being harder to reach.

APPENDIX B

Narrative Resources You Can Use

Changing the welfare story isn't abstract—it's work we can do. These organizations offer tools, language, and frameworks for anyone in human services (or alongside it) who wants to practice new narratives.

Reframing human services (start here)

- *National Reframing Human Services Initiative (with FrameWorks):* Field-tested framing that builds public will for human services—core story, well-being values, and sample language.
- *FrameWorks Institute—Building a New Narrative on Human Services:* Research-based toolkit with do/don't guidance for op-eds, testimony, and public messaging.
- *American Public Human Services Association—Productive Narrative Tools:* Practical tools and tips for framing human services.

Family-centered approaches

- *Ascend + FrameWorks—Framing Two-Generation Approaches:* Evidence-based playbook for supporting approaches that center parents and children together without triggering blame or zero-sum thinking.

Narrative change on poverty/social and economic mobility

- *ideas42—Shifting Harmful Narratives about Poverty in the U.S.:* Lessons from working with communities to replace harmful narratives with constructive ones.
- *NextGen Human Services—Narrative Change: Helping Us Make Sense of the World:*Tips for flipping the script so the stories of people most impacted by poverty are heard.

Additional perspectives

- *Narrative Initiative—Toward New Gravity:*An accessible overview of how narratives shape culture and politics, with tools for advancing equitable stories.
- *Narrative Initiative—Narrative Guide for Immigrant Futures:*Insights and tools on designing narratives that disrupt fear-based mindsets and advance pro-immigrant solutions.

ACKNOWLEDGMENTS

This book grew out of many conversations across leadership retreats, long calls, and countless texts, and the quiet moments in between where ideas take shape. It is impossible to capture the full constellation of people who have influenced its pages, but I want to honor as many as I can.

First and foremost, my deepest thanks to Karen Heller Key, my dear friend, co-host, thinking partner, and guide. Karen walked with me from the very first spark of this idea through outlines, rewrites, detours, and late-stage edits. She pushed my thinking when it needed stretching, encouraged me when the vision grew cloudy, and brought joy and possibility to every conversation. This book would not exist without her steady presence and brave imagination.

I am profoundly grateful to the colleagues who read a full draft of the manuscript, challenged ideas, and sharpened arguments—Raquel Hatter, Jody Levison-Johnson, Matt Lyons, and Natalie Williams. Your thoughtful comments helped build a clearer, stronger, more generous book. Thank you for your honesty, wisdom, and time.

I am also grateful to my copy editor, Lila Stromer, whose careful eye strengthened this book in ways both visible and unseen. Her technical precision and thoughtful questions helped bring clarity and consistency to my writing.

To my colleagues across the nation who lead state and local human services agencies: You shaped so much of what I have learned about courageous leadership and public purpose. The current and former APHSA team, along with the many thousands of members who make up that extraordinary network, taught me what it means to serve with integrity, humility, and heart. There are far too many of you to name here individually (I wish I could!), but please know that your work and your example run through every chapter.

I am equally indebted to the dozens of partner organizations that have informed and inspired my journey in the human and social services sector. A special acknowledgment to my peers at Social Current, the FrameWorks Institute, The Kresge Foundation, Ascend at the Aspen Institute, and Leadership for a Networked World at Harvard University. Your research, partnerships, insights, and steadfast commitment to building thriving communities helped this book find its grounding.

I also want to honor the mentors who shaped my leadership and strengthened my belief in public service as a force for good. Among them, I am grateful to my former boss, Janet Napolitano, whose example of principled, pragmatic leadership continues to influence how I think about governance, responsibility, and the role of public institutions in people's lives. I carry forward lessons from her—and from many other teachers and guides—throughout this work.

To guests on the *Our Dream Deferred* podcast: Your voices helped spark the direction of this book. Historian Timothy Snyder, social psychologist Betsy Levy Paluck, Nate Kendall-Taylor, Derrick Anderson, and so many others—your willingness to explore the deeper currents shaping our society opened doors I did not know existed.

I also want to acknowledge the writers, scholars, and journalists whose work accompanied me throughout my research. Many of them appear in the selective bibliography; each offered a lens that helped me to understand our American story more fully. I was especially grateful to encounter Jill Quadagno's *The Color of Welfare*, published thirty years before this book and thirty years after the War on Poverty. Her rigorous account of how racism undermined antipoverty efforts illuminated history with a clarity and courage that continue to resonate for me and the human services sector. This book builds on her insights and seeks to carry them forward.

This book is dedicated to the human services workforce—and to my family—because both shaped the heart of this project. Human services professionals are among the most unsung builders of well-being in our democracy. Every day, you carry hope into people's lives through acts of care that often go unseen. I wrote this book to honor you and reveal why your work matters and how much possibility it creates.

Personal Thanks

To my friends, near and far, old and new, who offered encouragement, love, and steady reminders to keep going, including my closest friend and confidant, Angie Rodgers, and the remarkable women of the NPS sisterhood. Thank you for the laughter, reality checks, and pep talks.

To my late-mother, whose love and patience still anchor me. She gave me the tools to ask questions, listen deeply, and search for the full story. I carry her voice with me in every chapter.

To my father, who instilled in me a love for public and community service. His example shaped my belief in what strong, caring people and institutions can do.

To my sister, Tamlin Lorenz, who has always been there with steady support and fierce loyalty.

And **to my husband, Tim, and my son, Sean**, thank you for listening to countless ideas, enduring long stretches of research and writing, and reminding me to rest when I forgot to do so. Your love is my greatest source of joy and my constant reminder of what well-being looks like in practice.

ABOUT THE AUTHOR

Tracy Evans (professionally known for many years as Tracy Wareing) has spent more than twenty-five years working at both the frontlines and highest levels of the nation's human services system. As president and CEO of the American Public Human Services Association for more than a decade, she became a leading national voice, working with Republican and Democratic leaders alike, on how public benefit programs shape—and are shaped by—our culture, politics, and policy. She has testified before Congress, advised federal agencies, and worked with governors and community leaders across the country to redesign systems that touch millions of lives each day.

Her career has spanned state and federal service, including leadership of Arizona's Department of Economic Security and senior advisory roles to U.S. Department of Homeland Security Secretary Janet Napolitano during the Obama administration. She began her public service career as an attorney in child welfare, advocating for the safety and well-being of children and families.

Tracy's writing and commentary have appeared in national magazines, scholarly journals, and online forums, and she co-hosted the widely distributed podcast *Our Dream Deferred*, which brought together unexpected voices to examine the forces that shape American society. She currently serves as chair of the board of Social Current, a national network of community-based social service organizations, and she is a fellow of the National Academy of Public Administration.

Her work is guided by a lifelong commitment to the common good, inspired by her parents' dedication to public service and education. In *American Welfare: Reclaiming the Dream for All of U.S.*, she draws on her deep experience, her curiosity about human behavior, and insights from history, sociology, and neuroscience to reveal how cultural narratives about poverty and government have distorted our democracy, and how we can reimagine them for a more just and prosperous future.

Although she spent much of her life in Arizona, Tracy now lives in Arlington, Virginia, with her husband, their teenage son, and three very spoiled dogs—Triumph, Trinity, and Nitra.

www.ingramcontent.com/pod-product-compliance
Lightning Source LLC
LaVergne TN
LVHW061531070526
838199LV00010B/448